Florida's Best Native Landscape Plants

Florida A&M University, Tallahassee
Florida Atlantic University, Boca Raton
Florida Gulf Coast University, Ft. Myers
Florida International University, Miami
Florida State University, Tallahassee
New College of Florida
University of Central Florida, Orlando
University of Florida, Gainesville
University of North Florida, Jacksonville
University of South Florida, Tampa
University of West Florida, Pensacola

University Press of Florida

Gainesville · Tallahassee · Tampa · Boca Raton

Pensacola · Orlando · Miami · Jacksonville · Ft. Myers · Sarasota

Florida's Best Native Landscape Plants

200 Readily Available Species
for Homeowners and Professionals

Gil Nelson

Copyright 2003 by Association of Florida Native Nurseries
Printed in China on acid-free paper

15 14 13 12 11 10   8 7 6 5 4 3

Library of Congress Cataloging-in-Publication Data
Nelson, Gil, 1949-
Florida's best native landscape plants: 200 readily available species for
homeowners and professionals / Gil Nelson.
p. cm.
Includes bibliographical references (p.).
ISBN 978-0-8130-2644-2 (pbk.: alk. paper)
1. Native plants for cultivation—Florida. 2. Landscape plants—Florida. I. Title.
SB439.26.F6N46 2003
716'.09759—dc21   2003047338

The University Press of Florida is the scholarly publishing agency for the State
University System of Florida, comprising Florida A&M University, Florida Atlantic
University, Florida Gulf Coast University, Florida International University, Florida
State University, New College of Florida, University of Central Florida, University
of Florida, University of North Florida, University of South Florida, and University
of West Florida.

University Press of Florida
15 Northwest 15th Street
Gainesville, FL 32611-2079
www.upf.com

To David Chiappini in recognition of his tireless efforts
in bringing this book into being

Contents

Species by Category

TREES, LARGE AND SMALL

Acacia farnesiana
Acer rubrum
Acer saccharum subsp. *floridanum*
Acoelorrhaphe wrightii
Aesculus pavia
Agarista populifolia
Annona glabra
Ardisia escallonioides
Avicennia germinans
Baccharis halimifolia
Betula nigra
Bursera simaruba
Calyptranthes pallens
Capparis cynophallophora
Carpinus caroliniana
Carya aquatica
Carya glabra
Castanea pumila
Celtis laevigata
Cephalanthus occidentalis
Cercis canadensis
Chamaecyparis thyoides
Chionanthus virginicus
Chrysobalanus icaco
Chrysophyllum oliviforme
Citharexylum spinosum

Coccoloba diversifolia
Coccoloba uvifera
Coccothrinax argentata
Conocarpus erectus
Cordia sebestena
Cornus florida
Cornus foemina
Crataegus flava
Cyrilla racemiflora
Diospyros virginiana
Erythrina herbacea
Eugenia spp.
Euonymus americanus
Ficus aurea
Forestiera segregata
Fraxinus caroliniana
Fraxinus pennsylvanica
Gordonia lasianthus
Hamamelis virginiana
Ilex cassine
Ilex opaca
Ilex x attenuata 'East Palatka'
Illicium spp.
Juniperus virginiana
Krugiodendron ferreum
Laguncularia racemosa
Liquidambar styraciflua
Liriodendron tulipifera

Lyonia ferruginea
Lysiloma latisiliquum
Magnolia grandiflora
Magnolia virginiana
Malus angustifolia
Morus rubra
Myrica cerifera
Nyssa spp.
Nyssa sylvatica
Ostrya virginiana
Persea spp.
Pinus clausa
Pinus elliottii
Pinus palustris
Pinus taeda
Platanus occidentalis
Prunus angustifolia
Prunus caroliniana
Quercus alba
Quercus hemisphaerica
Quercus laevis
Quercus laurifolia
Quercus myrtifolia
Quercus nigra
Quercus shumardii
Quercus virginiana
Rhizophora mangle
Roystonea regia
Sabal palmetto
Salix spp.
Sassafras albidum
Sideroxylon foetidissimum
Sideroxylon salicifolium
Sideroxylon tenax
Styrax americanus
Swietenia mahagoni
Taxodium distichum
Thrinax morrisii
Thrinax radiata
Ulmus alata
Ulmus americana
Ulmus crassifolia
Vaccinium arboreum
Viburnum obovatum
Zanthoxylum fagara

SHRUBS AND SHRUB SUBSTITUTES

Acacia farnesiana
Acrostichum danaeifolium
Aesculus pavia
Agarista populifolia
Annona glabra
Ardisia escallonioides
Asimina spp.
Baccharis halimifolia
Borrichia spp.
Callicarpa americana
Calycanthus floridus
Calyptranthes pallens
Capparis cynophallophora
Castanea pumila
Cephalanthus occidentalis
Chrysobalanus icaco
Clethra alnifolia
Coccoloba uvifera
Coccothrinax argentata
Conradina spp.
Cornus foemina
Cyrilla racemiflora
Ernodea littoralis
Erythrina herbacea
Eugenia spp.
Euonymus americanus
Forestiera segregata
Garberia heterophylla
Hamelia patens
Hibiscus coccineus
Hydrangea quercifolia
Hypericum spp.
Ilex glabra
Ilex vomitoria
Illicium spp.
Itea virginica
Iva spp.
Laguncularia racemosa
Lantana involucrata
Lycium carolinianum
Lyonia ferruginea
Lyonia lucida
Myrcianthes fragrans
Myrica cerifera

Persea spp.
Prunus angustifolia
Prunus caroliniana
Psychotria nervosa
Quercus myrtifolia
Randia aculeata
Rapanea punctata
Rhapidophyllum hystrix
Rhizophora mangle
Rhododendron austrinum
Rhododendron canescens
Rhus copallinum
Sabal etonia
Sabal minor
Serenoa repens
Sideroxylon tenax
Sophora tomentosa
Spartina bakeri
Styrax americanus
Suriana maritima
Symphyotrichum carolinianum
Thalia geniculata
Tripsacum dactyloides
Uniola paniculata
Vaccinium arboreum
Vaccinium spp.
Viburnum dentatum
Viburnum obovatum
Yucca aloifolia
Yucca filamentosa
Zamia pumila
Zanthoxylum fagara

PALMS

Acoelorrhaphe wrightii
Coccothrinax argentata
Rhapidophyllum hystrix
Roystonea regia
Sabal etonia
Sabal minor
Sabal palmetto
Serenoa repens
Thrinax morrisii
Thrinax radiata

GRASSES

Andropogon spp.
Aristida stricta var. *beyrichiana*
Distichlis spicata
Eragrostis spp.
Muhlenbergia capillaris
Panicum spp.
Sorghastrum secundum
Spartina alterniflora
Spartina bakeri
Spartina patens
Sporobolus virginicus
Tripsacum dactyloides
Uniola paniculata
Zizaniopsis miliacea

WILDFLOWERS

Asclepias spp.
Borrichia spp.
Coreopsis spp.
Crinum americanum
Echinacea purpurea
Eryngium spp.
Gaillardia pulchella
Helianthus spp.
Hibiscus coccineus
Hymenocallis latifolia
Ipomoea imperati
Ipomoea pes-caprae
Iris spp.
Lachnanthes caroliana
Liatris spp.
Lobelia cardinalis
Lonicera sempervirens
Mimosa strigillosa
Nymphaea odorata
Piloblephis rigida
Pontederia cordata
Rudbeckia hirta
Ruellia caroliniensis
Sagittaria spp.
Salvia coccinea
Saururus cernuus
Sesuvium portulacastrum

Solidago spp.
Stokesia laevis
Zephyranthes atamasco

VINES

Bignonia capreolata
Gelsemium sempervirens
Ipomoea imperati
Ipomoea pes-caprae
Lonicera sempervirens
Passiflora incarnata

FERNS

Acrostichum danaeifolium
Blechnum serrulatum
Nephrolepis spp.
Osmunda cinnamomea
Osmunda regalis
Woodwardia spp.

GROUND COVER

Andropogon spp.
Aristida stricta var. *beyrichiana*
Bacopa spp.
Blechnum serrulatum
Cladium jamaicense
Crinum americanum
Distichlis spicata
Eragrostis spp.
Ernodea littoralis
Juncus effusus
Licania michauxii
Mimosa strigillosa
Muhlenbergia capillaris
Panicum spp.
Paspalum spp.
Piloblephis rigida
Polygonum spp.
Sesuvium portulacastrum
Sorghastrum secundum
Spartina bakeri
Spartina patens

Sporobolus virginicus
Yucca filamentosa

WETLAND AND AQUATIC PLANTS

Acer rubrum
Acrostichum danaeifolium
Annona glabra
Bacopa spp.
Betula nigra
Blechnum serrulatum
Canna flaccida
Carya aquatica
Cephalanthus occidentalis
Chamaecyparis thyoides
Cladium jamaicense
Cornus foemina
Crinum americanum
Cyrilla racemiflora
Eleocharis spp.
Equisetum hyemale
Fraxinus caroliniana
Fraxinus pennsylvanica
Gordonia lasianthus
Helianthus spp.
Hymenocallis latifolia
Ilex cassine
Ilex glabra
Iris spp.
Itea virginica
Juncus effusus
Lachnanthes caroliana
Lobelia cardinalis
Magnolia virginiana
Nephrolepis spp.
Nymphaea odorata
Nyssa aquatica
Nyssa sylvatica
Osmunda cinnamomea
Osmunda regalis
Panicum spp.
Platanus occidentalis
Polygonum spp.
Pontederia cordata
Quercus laurifolia

Quercus nigra
Rhizophora mangle
Sagittaria spp.
Saururus cernuus
Scirpus spp.
Styrax americanus
Symphyotrichum carolinianum
Taxodium distichum
Thalia geniculata
Ulmus americana
Viburnum dentatum
Viburnum obovatum
Woodwardia spp.
Zizaniopsis miliacea

DROUGHT TOLERANT PLANTS

Acacia farnesiana
Capparis cynophallophora
Citharexylum spinosum
Coccothrinax argentata
Crataegus flava
Ernodea littoralis
Gaillardia pulchella
Garberia heterophylla
Helianthus spp.
Ipomoea imperati
Ipomoea pes-caprae
Iva spp.
Juniperus virginiana
Lantana involucrata
Licania michauxii
Mimosa strigillosa
Paspalum spp.
Quercus laevis
Quercus myrtifolia
Randia aculeata
Sabal etonia
Sideroxylon tenax
Sophora tomentosa
Thrinax morrisii
Thrinax radiata
Uniola paniculata
Zamia pumila

SALT TOLERANT PLANTS

Acacia farnesiana
Acrostichum danaeifolium
Ardisia escallonioides
Avicennia germinans
Baccharis halimifolia
Borrichia spp.
Capparis cynophallophora
Citharexylum spinosum
Coccoloba diversifolia
Coccoloba uvifera
Conocarpus erectus
Cordia sebestena
Distichlis spicata
Ernodea littoralis
Eugenia spp.
Gaillardia pulchella
Hymenocallis latifolia
Ilex vomitoria
Ipomoea imperati
Ipomoea pes-caprae
Iva spp.
Laguncularia racemosa
Lycium carolinianum
Panicum spp.
Paspalum spp.
Rapanea punctata
Rhizophora mangle
Sesuvium portulacastrum
Sideroxylon foetidissimum
Sideroxylon tenax
Sophora tomentosa
Spartina alterniflora
Spartina bakeri
Spartina patens
Sporobolus virginicus
Suriana maritima
Thrinax morrisii
Thrinax radiata
Uniola paniculata
Zamia pumila

Species by Common Name

Acknowledgments

Numerous individuals and organizations have provided a wide range of assistance and support in the writing, development, and publication of this book.

Foremost, I would like to thank the Association of Florida Native Nurseries (AFNN), and especially David Chiappini, AFNN copresident and owner of Chiappini Farms Native Nursery. David provided the spark, spirit, and leadership that brought this book into being. It was David's idea that a book such as this be made available, and it was his persistence that raised both the funds and support that ensured the book's completion. He was involved in every step of the process, including reading and commenting on the manuscript and helping to locate photographs for the book's illustrations. His diligence, drive, and friendship are all appreciated. AFNN members David Drylie (Green Images/Native Landscape Plants), David Pais (Agrosystems), Brightman Logan (Central Florida Native Flora), and Jane Thompson (Indian Trails Native Nursery) were initial and important supporters of the project, and their encouragement, assistance, and support are much appreciated.

I also owe a great debt to Gary Henry and Jeff Caster, both of the Florida Department of Transportation (FDOT), for their significant assistance with ensuring that this book became a reality. One of the last actions by Gary Henry before he retired after thirty years with FDOT was to secure the funding for this project. His service and foresight are much appreciated. I also thank Jeff for passing the manuscript on to FDOT staff, especially William Moriaty, who reviewed it and made valuable corrections and additions. Other important supporters include Jay Allen (RSS Field Services), Jerry Fritz (SUNCO), Dr. Mark V. and Mary B. Barrow, and Cammie Donaldson, editor of the AFNN Plant and Services Directory.

I owe a special thanks to Jean Hancock and Susan Trammell, the book's artists, for the outstanding illustrations that grace the following pages. Jean's willingness to take on the first half of this project quelled significant worries and is sincerely appreciated. Her penchant for quality and accuracy, knowledge of scientific illustration, and delightful demeanor made for an enjoyable and memorable experience. I also much appreciate Susan's willingness to take on the second half of the book and her dedication to quality as well as her impressive talent. In many ways, Jean's and Susan's art constitutes one of the best aspects of the book.

The other color images that accompany each account were contributed by a number of photographers. These photographs bring the plants to life in ways that could never be accomplished with mere text. I am grateful to Henry Aldrich, Loran Anderson, Bill Boothe, Kathy Burks, Debbie Chayet, Shirley Denton, Eleanor Dietrich, Phil Flood, Chris Griffiths, Roger Hammer, Walter Judd, Mike Kenton, Sharon LaPlante, Claudia Larsen, Heidi Moore, Jeff Norcini, David Pais, Susan Trammell, Betty Wargo, and Ann Williams for their contributions. Thanks, also, to June Cussen at Pineapple Press for gracious permission to use photos from my previous books *Trees of Florida, Shrubs and Woody Vines of Florida,* and *Ferns of Florida.*

The phonetic pronunciations of Latin names were provided by Mark Garland. I especially appreciate Mark's efficiency and meticulous attention to detail.

Several people reviewed and commented on the manuscript during its development. I particularly appreciate the candid and extremely helpful input from both Dr. Steve Christman and David Chiappini. Dr. David Hall, well-known Florida botanist and botanical educator, provided numerous helpful resources as well as support. His earlier work for the Institute for Food and Agricultural Sciences was most helpful.

I also thank Ken Scott, director of the University Press of Florida (UPF). Ken's interest in the project encouraged our efforts, and he and the staff at UPF provided excellent technical assistance during the development and final production of the book.

Introduction

This book is a guide to the two hundred best native landscape plants for Florida. The species included have been selected for their ready availability from a number of the state's native plant nurseries, as well as for their general hardiness, popularity, and ease of use in both commercial and residential landscapes. As a result, the book will be useful to gardeners, homeowners, commercial developers, professional landscape architects and designers, and road builders. Though not designed as a guide to restoration of native ecosystems, a process that depends on detailed analyses and levels of specificity beyond the scope of what is presented here, the book will nevertheless be useful to those charged with selecting easy-to-obtain native species for use in state and local park plantings.

Why Use Native Plants?

Florida's flora includes one of the largest assortments of spontaneously occurring species in North America. More than 4,100 kinds of plants have been cataloged within its boundaries. Of these, about 2,800 are considered native, meaning that they were present when the first European explorers arrived nearly five hundred years ago. The other 1,300 are non-native species that found their way into the state through agricultural, horticultural, or land management practices, or by inadvertent transport by ships, cars, planes, boats, and people. These numbers do not include approximately 25,000 garden species, some of which themselves may someday become naturalized in the state.

Florida's battle with non-native plants is legendary. Controlling and eradicating such species as Brazilian pepper, melaleuca, Australian pine, popcorn tree, tropical soda apple, skunk vine, and the Old World and Japanese climbing ferns are seemingly unending struggles that annually consume large amounts of state and local tax revenues. Moreover, these species constitute only a handful of the more than 125 species that are currently listed by the Florida Exotic Pest Plant Council as invasive or having a strong potential to invade, destroy, or irreparably alter Florida's most precious natural areas.

It is little wonder, then, that native plant landscaping has become a popular—and in many respects necessary—approach to gardening. An increasing number of amateurs and professionals alike are turning to the use of native species.

Conservation and Sustainability

Using native rather than alien plants enhances conservation of our natural resources and usually ensures a low maintenance and sustainable garden. Traditionally, the value of a planted landscape has been measured by how well it serves humans. Effective designs were judged on such factors as appearance, or how well they provided for shade, screening, or other human needs. More recently, landscapers and gardeners have also begun to measure their creations by how well they satisfy the need for water and energy efficiency, provide for wildlife habitat and the conservation of biological diversity, contribute to the preservation of endangered species, and sustain themselves without human intervention.

Soil and Water Conservation. Conservation of soil and water is the guiding principle behind native plant landscaping. Modern landscape design has evolved to the point where local ecology and water requirements dictate plant selection and placement. "Xeric land-scaping," which originated in dry western states to address chronic water shortages, was one of the first attempts at this. Florida, although not as arid as the western states, experiences seasonal droughts, water shortages, and a variety of other environmental stresses. Here, the concept of xeric landscaping has been expanded to include the development of naturalistic landscapes in which native plants are matched to appropriate environments. Natural systems provide the models for this type of landscape and include every site condition from desert to swamp. Properly sited native plants satisfy the need for water and soil efficiency, while tolerating Florida's environmental extremes.

Sustainability. Traditional practices, like modern farming or the maintenance of mani-cured lawns, have relied heavily upon the continual control of the stresses, or limiting factors, that affect the growth, survival, reproductive capacity, and general health of plants. These stresses, which include the shortage of water and energy, fluctuating temperature, pests and diseases, and the limited availability of the chemical elements that provide the building blocks for growth, are present in every environment. Under natural systems and over many centuries, plants become biologically adapted to environmental circumstances and evolve methods for dealing with the stresses imposed by the habitats in which they live. For gardeners, this means that plants adapted to the stresses of a particular site may have specific initial needs upon planting but once established will thrive with a minimum of care.

Consider a site that is cultivated, fertilized, enriched with humus, adjusted for pH, and cleared of trees for maximum light exposure. With the addition of plants not matched to local conditions, the stage is set for perpetual maintenance, depletion of soil fertility, and the potential for invasive weeds to spread into and disrupt nearby and not-so-nearby natural areas. Having to constantly control stresses violates the notion of sustainability. The most successful and sustainable landscape matches the plants with the prevalent stresses.

Properly grouping native plants in their natural associations provides options not available with non-native species. There is a subtle beauty and cohesiveness within a natural system, a beauty that arises out of symmetry, harmony, and interdependence. With planning and forethought, this same sense and beauty can be replicated in managed landscapes. Whether left untrimmed or manicured to fit into the aesthetic of a formal garden, such naturalistic settings will furnish shelter and food for local wildlife, as well as provide for conservation and sustainability.

About the Species Accounts

The following species accounts describe the most commonly available native landscape plants in Florida. Each account follows the same format and includes succinct synopses of the featured species' appearance, best features, culture, and uses.

Perhaps the best aspects of the accounts are the watercolor illustrations commissioned especially for this book. These splendid original paintings by artists Jean C. Putnam-Hancock and Susan Trammell capture the essence as well as the details of each species, at the same time highlighting their beauty and grace. Accompanying the watercolor art are color photographs, by an assortment of photographers, that capture the plants in natural or landscape settings.

Each account begins with the plant's common and scientific names as well as the botanical family to which it is assigned. Though common names are important appellations that often capture our imagination and impart important information about a plant's habits or characteristics, it is the scientific name that should guide our purchases. Scientific names are governed by a set of international rules that attempt to ensure that each plant has only one valid and unique name. Since scientific names are sometimes difficult to pronounce, a phonetic spelling of each name is also included, followed by notes on each plant's size, height, and spread.

The body of each account includes a section on landscape use, which highlights both the popular and unique uses of the plant in the landscape. This section also emphasizes the plant's particular value for difficult situations, such as along road shoulders or highway mediums, for providing ornamentation in parking lots, or for beautifying canals and retention ponds. Each species' growth form is described, and notes are provided on the native range and distribution in Florida and the United States. The section on each plant's characteristics includes descriptions of flowers, leaves, fruit, and bark, with particular attention given to those characters that are showy, unique, or particularly valued in the garden.

The section on culture details each species' preferences for soil conditions, exposure, and supplemental irrigation, as well as the generally accepted USDA Cold Hardiness Zones. Where possible, a longevity estimation is given. It should be noted that little empirical data is available about the life spans of plants. What is known is gleaned primarily from anecdotal information provided by gardeners, foresters, field botanists, and professional landscape designers.

A statement about each species' best features outlines its more important horticultural characteristics and is followed by a listing of companion plants. These companion species are those known to occur together in natural areas, and in association with the plant featured in the account. They have also been selected because they are, for the most part, readily available from native nurseries and make excellent additions to the garden. An accounting of known cultivars and closely related species is also included, where appropriate. Also noted are any known toxic and allergenic properties, pests, diseases, and other disadvantages, to assist the reader in appropriately using the species in the landscape.

Florida's Best Native Landscape Plants

Acacia farnesiana

uh-KAY-shuh far-nee-see-AY-nuh

Sweet Acacia

Family: Fabaceae or Leguminosae
Small tree or shrub
Height: 8 to 20 feet
Spread: 6 to 10 feet

LANDSCAPE USE

An excellent barrier shrub that can also be used as a specimen tree. An excellent choice for road and powerline rights-of-way and highway medians.

FORM

An upright, thorny, multistemmed, densely branched shrub or small tree with zigzag branches. Oval in outline with a rounded to sometimes flattened top, the flat-topped form more frequently seen in coastal specimens.

NATIVE RANGE

Pinelands, shell middens, coastal hammocks. Most common in southernmost Florida and southern California, but also occurring in Texas, Louisiana, Arizona, New Mexico, Mexico, Central and South America, Puerto Rico, and the Bahamas. May be used in landscaping where temperatures do not drop below 20 degrees F.

CHARACTERISTICS

Flowers: Bright yellow, fragrant, borne in globular, ½-inch-diameter clusters. Year-round.

Leaves: Alternate, about 4 inches long, and finely divided into many small, soft, medium-green leaflets.

Fruit: A 2- to 3-inch-long, cylindrical, oblong, thick, "woody," reddish brown to purplish pod with shiny brown seeds. Often borne in 3- to 5-pod clusters.

Bark: Reddish brown.

CULTURE

Soil: Prefers well-drained, loose, alkaline soils. Salt tolerant.

Exposure: Full sun.

Water: Drought tolerant, but will not tolerate wet soils.

Hardiness Zones: 9 to 11.

Life Span: Relatively short-lived; probably less than 30 years.

BEST FEATURES

Bright yellow flowers. Finely divided, fernlike foliage. Drought and salt tolerance. Rapid growth.

COMPANION PLANTS

Beautyberry (*Callicarpa americana*), Florida privet (*Forestiera segregata*), white indigoberry (*Randia aculeata*), tough buckthorn (*Sideroxylon tenax*).

DISADVANTAGES

Short life span. May develop root rot in wet soil. Thorny branches may limit use in some situations.

SIMILAR AND RELATED SPECIES

Cinnecord (*Acacia choriophylla*), a rare species of the Florida Keys, is often planted in southernmost Florida and the Keys. It, too, has ball-like clusters of bright yellow flowers, but its leaflets are much larger than those of sweet acacia, and it has few to no spines at maturity.

Acer rubrum

AY-ser ROO-brum

Red Maple

Family: Sapindaceae
Medium to large tree
Height: 30 to 70 feet
Spread: 20 to 40 feet

LANDSCAPE USE

Excellent specimen tree, especially for moist sites. Beautiful in lawns and parks. Particularly useful along moist highway and road shoulders and for providing cover around retention ponds, drainage swales, canal banks, and parking lots. Allow plenty of room for growth. Excellent fall color.

FORM

An erect, typically single-trunked tree, with a relatively narrow crown and ascending branches.

NATIVE RANGE

Swamps and floodplains. Southern Newfoundland, across southern Canada, southward throughout the eastern United States and Florida, west to Minnesota, Oklahoma, and Texas. Locally adapted stock performs better; plants from distant origins will likely give poor results.

CHARACTERISTICS

Flowers: Tiny, red, very showy, borne in profuse clusters before new leaf growth; male and female flowers produced on separate trees. Late winter to very early spring.

Leaves: Opposite, simple, palmately 3- to 5-lobed, medium green above, coated below with a dense covering of whitish hairs, variable in size, 2–6 inches long, 2–4 inches wide (individual trees may have leaves tending toward either of these extremes), margins toothed, and the leaf stalk and central leaf veins red. Exceptionally beautiful in fall with color ranging from soft yellow to reddish.

Fruit: Red, 2-winged, V-shaped, 1½–2½ inches long. Very showy. Spring.

Bark: Silvery gray; smooth when young, becoming roughened with age.

CULTURE

Soil: Prefers low, wet soils but will tolerate moist upland locations.

Exposure: Does best in dappled shade but will tolerate full sun. Young trees, especially, should be protected from strong sun.

Water: Prefers wet to moist conditions. Trees planted on drier sites will require supplemental irrigation.

Hardiness Zones: 3 to 10.

Life Span: Relatively short-lived; 50 to 80 years under cultivation.

BEST FEATURES

Grows fairly quickly and provides excellent color in winter, spring, and fall. Tiny red flowers appear in profusion as early as January, prior to emergence of new leaves, followed by conspicuous, bright red, winged samaras, or keys, which remain on the tree for several weeks and serve as an indicator of spring. Foliage sometimes turns red to yellowish in late fall, especially in the northern and north-central parts of the state. Can grow in either wet or moist upland soils. The smooth, silvery gray bark and handsome green leaves with red stalks and veins make it attractive year-round.

COMPANION PLANTS

River birch (*Betula nigra*), bald cypress (*Taxodium distichum*), pipestem (*Agarista populifolia*), loblolly bay (*Gordonia lasianthus*), dahoon (*Ilex cassine*), swamp dogwood (*Cornus foemina*), buttonbush (*Cephalanthus occidentalis*), leather fern (*Acrostichum danaeifolium*), Virginia willow (*Itea virginica*), wax myrtle (*Myrica cerifera*), climbing aster (*Symphyotrichum carolinianum*).

DISADVANTAGES

Somewhat short-lived, subject to decay and disease if the bark or trunk is injured, intolerant of long periods of drought (especially if situated in well-drained uplands). Foliage and twigs may be damaged by leafhoppers and borers.

CULTIVARS

Red maple has given rise to at least 57 cultivars that exhibit a variety of leaf sizes and fall color. None are regularly used in Florida landscaping. For best results, plants should be selected from Florida-grown stock, especially from the region in which the plant is to be used.

SIMILAR OR RELATED SPECIES

Four other maples occur in Florida: box elder (*A. negundo*), silver maple (*A. saccharinum*), Florida sugar maple (*A. saccharum* subsp. *floridanum*), and chalk maple (*A. saccharum* subsp. *leucoderme*). All four occur in Florida only in the northern half of the peninsula or in the central panhandle.

9

Acer saccharum subsp. *floridanum*

AY-ser SA-kuh-rum flo-ri-DAY-num

Florida Sugar Maple

Family: Sapindaceae
Small to medium-sized tree
Height: Typically 25 to 50 feet, potentially to 85 feet
Spread: 25 to 45 feet

LANDSCAPE USE
Does well as a specimen tree in rich soils, or as an understory tree in mesic hammocks and slopes.

FORM
An erect, straight-trunked tree with a spreading crown.

NATIVE RANGE
Mesic hammocks and slope forests. Central peninsular Florida, northward to southern Virginia, and west to Arkansas, Oklahoma, east Texas, and southern Missouri.

CHARACTERISTICS
Flowers: Inconspicuous, bell-shaped, greenish, borne in clusters in early spring prior to or with the growth of the new leaves.

Leaves: Opposite, simple, 3–6 inches long and wide, with 3 to 5 squared lobes. Soft green in summer, turning yellow to salmon in fall.

Fruit: A pair of 1-inch-long, brownish samaras; maturing in midsummer.

Bark: Gray; smooth on young trunks, becoming furrowed and ridged with age.

CULTURE
Soil: Prefers acid, rich to sandy soils, but often occurs over limestone as well as on ravine slopes and in sandy upland woods.

Exposure: Full sun to shade. Prefers a northern exposure.

Water: Prefers moist but not wet conditions.

Hardiness Zones: 8 to 9.

Life Span: 50 to 100 years.

BEST FEATURES
Attractive form; fall color.

COMPANION PLANTS
Red buckeye (*Aesculus pavia*), pignut hickory (*Carya glabra*), loblolly pine (*Pinus taeda*), Shumard oak (*Quercus shumardii*), basswood (*Tilia americana*), American hophornbeam (*Ostrya virginiana*), yaupon (*Ilex vomitoria*), needle palm (*Rhapidophyllum hystrix*), Carolina jessamine (*Gelsemium sempervirens*), cross vine (*Bignonia capreolata*).

CULTIVARS
None; however, the present species is seen listed under a variety of botanical names, including *A. barbatum* and *A. floridanum*.

SIMILAR AND RELATED SPECIES
Four other maples occur in Florida, two of which bear a resemblance to the present species. The most similar in appearance is chalk maple (*A. saccharum* subsp. *leucoderme*). The undersides of its leaves are green, whereas those of Florida sugar maple are grayish. Silver maple (*A. saccharinum*) is also somewhat similar, but the lobes of its leaves are pointed and the terminal lobe narrows toward its base. Both of these species occur in Florida only in the central panhandle.

Acoelorrhaphe wrightii

ay-see-lo-RAY-fee RY-tee-eye

Paurotis Palm

Family: Arecaceae or Palmae
Fan palm
Height: 20 to 30 feet
Spread: 15 to 25 feet

LANDSCAPE USE

Used in clumps to soften the corners of houses and other buildings, or at the corners of suburban lots. Excellent along retention ponds and canal banks, and for providing a tropical effect in moist to wet highway medians and rights-of-way. May form large clumps and should be planted in locations that allow for expansion.

FORM

An attractive, clump-forming, multistemmed palm, with a leaning stature, slender, matted trunk, and stiff, fan-shaped leaves. Sometimes so densely foliated as to hide the trunk.

NATIVE RANGE

Swamps and hammocks. Florida Everglades, parts of the West Indies, Mexico, Central America.

CHARACTERISTICS

Flowers: Whitish to greenish, individually inconspicuous but borne in showy, 3-foot-long, branching and arching clusters above the leaves.

Leaves: Green on both sides, stiff, to about 3 feet wide, and fan shaped.

Fruit: Rounded, shiny black, about ½ inch in diameter.

Bark: Brown; often covered with a thick, fibrous matting.

CULTURE

Soil: Occurs naturally in wet places, but will adapt to drier sites.

Exposure: Full sun. Tolerant of salt air. Not cold hardy.

Water: Prefers moist conditions. Will tolerate slightly brackish water.

Hardiness Zones: 10 to 11.

Life Span: Over 50 years; will continue to sprout from roots.

BEST FEATURES

Clump-forming habit. Leaning trunk. Salt tolerance. Tendency to produce dense foliage from the ground up.

COMPANION PLANTS

Buttonwood (*Conocarpus erectus*), dahoon (*Ilex cassine*), Simpson's stopper (*Myrcianthes fragrans*), red maple (*Acer rubrum*), Florida thatch palm (*Thrinax radiata*).

DISADVANTAGES

Scales and beetles can be minor pests.

SIMILAR AND RELATED SPECIES

Silver palm (*Coccothrinax argentata*) also has fan-shaped leaves that are silvery on one side and green on the other. It occurs on coastal dunes and rocky pinelands from about Palm Beach County southward, including the Keys. The brittle thatch palm (*Thrinax morrisii*) and the Florida thatch palm (*T. radiata*), which also occur in southernmost Florida and the Keys, also have fan-shaped leaves.

Acrostichum danaeifolium

uh-KRAH-sti-kum da-nay-ee-FO-lee-um

Leather Fern

Family: Pteridaceae
Large, shrublike fern
Height: 6 to 8 feet
Spread: 5 to 10 feet

LANDSCAPE USE

Ideal for pond edges and low, wet, or swampy sites with ample room for its large vertical size as well as its tendency to form dense thickets. This large fern is shrublike in habit and can also be used along moist to wet roadsides.

FORM

An erect to arching or leaning, very showy evergreen fern with large, dark green, stiff, pinnately divided fronds that are up to 10 feet tall and 2 feet wide.

NATIVE RANGE

Brackish and freshwater marshes. From about Dixie and St. Johns Counties south throughout the peninsula. More common in the southern part of the state.

CHARACTERISTICS

Leaves: Large, pinnately divided, erect to arching, to about 10 feet tall. Dark green above, paler below. Lower surfaces of fertile fronds conspicuously and densely coated with attractive reddish to golden brown spore cases.

CULTURE

Soil: Typically found in wet soils of fresh or brackish marshes.
Exposure: Does best in dappled shade, but will tolerate moderate sun. Intolerant of freezing temperatures.
Water: Requires wet soils for best development.
Hardiness Zones: 9 to 11.
Life Span: Individual fronds die back with age, but plants are long-lived.

BEST FEATURES

Rugged, hardy, adaptable, with few problems. Its primeval aspect lends an interesting vertical accent to the landscape.

COMPANION PLANTS

The much smaller swamp fern (*Blechnum serrulatum*) makes an excellent companion, as do cordgrasses (*Spartina* spp.), saltgrass (*Distichlis spicata*), salt bush (*Baccharis halimifolia*), Christmasberry (*Lycium carolinianum*), sea oxeye (*Borrichia frutescens*), saltwort (*Batis maritima*), marsh elder (*Iva frutescens*), buttonwood (*Conocarpus erectus*), black mangrove (*Avicennia germinans*), white mangrove (*Laguncularia racemosa*), and red mangrove (*Rhizophora mangle*).

DISADVANTAGES

Leather fern grows to be quite large and can exceed its bounds in very small ponds or pools.

SIMILAR AND RELATED SPECIES

The rare golden leather fern (*A. aureum*) is found sparingly in brackish coastal waters of the state's southern tip.

Aesculus pavia

ES-kew-lus PAY-vee-uh

Red Buckeye

Family: Sapindaceae
Small tree or large shrub
Height: 6 to 35 feet
Spread: 6 to 20 feet

J. C. Putnam H.

LANDSCAPE USE

Excellent small tree or understory shrub with interesting 5-parted, palmately compound leaves and very showy red, tubular flowers that are attractive to hummingbirds and butterflies. Begins blooming early in its life cycle, sometimes when only a few feet tall.

FORM

A small, clump-forming shrub or small tree with single or multiple trunks and spreading to rounded crown.

NATIVE RANGE

Calcareous hammocks, stream banks, moist woodlands. Virginia, southward to central Florida, and west to east Texas.

CHARACTERISTICS

Flowers: Red, tubular, very showy, about 1½ inches long, borne in showy, open, 8- to 10-inch-long panicles at the tips of branches. February to April.

Leaves: Opposite, palmately 5-parted, to about 6 inches long on a long leaf stalk; margins of leaflets toothed.

Fruit: A rounded, golden brown capsule that splits in autumn to expose one to several shiny, dull red to reddish brown seeds ranging in size from ¾ inch to 1½ inches in diameter.

Bark: Grayish brown and warty.

CULTURE

Soil: Does well in a variety of soil types from moist to dry.

Exposure: Occurs naturally in rich, shaded beech-magnolia woods, but tolerates and becomes more densely branched in full sun.

Water: Plants grown in full sun should be irrigated. Performs best as an understory plant.

Hardiness Zones: 4 to 9.

Life Span: Relatively short-lived; probably less than 50 years.

BEST FEATURES

Essentially pest free and will grow in relatively poor, dry soil. Its red flowers can be magnificent in early spring, especially on plants grown in full sun, and are excellent for attracting butterflies and hummingbirds. Its coarse texture, coppery new growth, interesting leaves, and large, golden brown fruit make it an enticing, three-season landscape plant.

COMPANION PLANTS

Longleaf pine (*Pinus palustris*), pignut hickory (*Carya glabra*), Shumard oak (*Quercus shumardii*), sugarberry (*Celtis laevigata*), sweetgum (*Liquidambar styraciflua*), basswood (*Tilia americana*), winged elm (*Ulmus alata*), blue beech (*Carpinus caroliniana*), fringetree (*Chionanthus virginicus*), American holly (*Ilex opaca*), American hophornbeam (*Ostrya virginiana*), beautyberry (*Callicarpa americana*), Cherokee bean (*Erythrina herbacea*), yaupon (*Ilex vomitoria*), needle palm (*Rhapidophyllum hystrix*), blue-stem palmetto (*Sabal minor*), oakleaf hydrangea (*Hydrangea quercifolia*).

DISADVANTAGES

Leaves and fruit are poisonous, a consideration when planning for landscapes that might be occupied by children. Sometimes defoliates early in the fall and begins new growth in fall, though it may remain bare of leaves until midspring.

CULTIVARS

Cultivars are not commonly available in the trade, but naturally occurring forms are known, as is a yellow-flowered variety (*A. pavia* var. *flavescens*) that does not occur in Florida.

ALLERGENIC AND TOXIC PROPERTIES

Seeds and leaves are poisonous to both people and pets and if eaten may cause nausea, vomiting, and abdominal pain.

SIMILAR AND RELATED SPECIES

Bottlebrush buckeye (*A. parviflora*) occurs in southern Georgia along the Chattahoochee River, not far north of the state line, and west to southern Alabama but is not known to occur naturally in Florida. Though not native to Florida, this latter species does well in northwest Florida as evidenced by some beautiful specimens in the Tallahassee area.

Agarista populifolia

a-guh-RIS-tuh pah-pew-li-FO-lee-uh

Pipestem, Fetterbush

Family: Ericaceae
Shrub to small tree
Height: 6 to 14 feet
Spread: 5 to 8 feet

J. C. Putnam H

LANDSCAPE USE

Serves equally well as a specimen plant, to screen patios or yard borders, or to soften the corners of homes, outbuildings, or other structures. Can be pruned and used as a foundation plant or hedge, or to maintain a smaller form, but is at its best in dappled shade along riverbanks, pond edges, or the banks of freshwater springs and spring runs.

FORM

A tall, evergreen, typically multistemmed, somewhat arborescent shrub with arching to leaning branches and simple, bright green leaves.

NATIVE RANGE

Swamps, mesic and wetland hammocks. Southeastern South Carolina, southward to north-central peninsular Florida.

CHARACTERISTICS

Flowers: White, urn-shaped, ⅜ inch long, borne in many-flowered racemes at the leaf axils; very showy. Spring.
Leaves: Alternate, simple, lance shaped, shiny green, 2–4 inches long.
Fruit: A rounded, brown capsule.
Bark: Trunk brown, fissured, often flaking off in showy strips. Young twigs light brown.

CULTURE

Soil: Moist to dry, acid soils, with pH 5.0–6.0.
Exposure: Does best in dappled shade, but tolerates deep shade. Does not perform very well in full sun.
Water: Plants grown in well-drained, sandy soils may require periodic irrigation.
Hardiness Zones: 7 to 9.
Life Span: Relatively short-lived; probably not much more than 50 years under cultivation.

BEST FEATURES

An easy-to-grow evergreen that is very showy during its spring flowering period. An excellent addition to naturalistic landscapes, especially in shady areas along streams. The evergreen habit and profuse clusters of showy white flowers add to its appeal.

COMPANION PLANTS

Dog-hobbles (*Leucothoe axillaris* and *L. racemosa*), red maple (*Acer rubrum*), wax myrtle (*Myrica cerifera*), pinxter azalea (*Rhododendron canescens*), loblolly bay (*Gordonia lasianthus*), titi (*Cyrilla racemiflora*), Virginia willow (*Itea virginica*), highbush blueberries (*Vaccinium* spp.), summersweet (*Clethra alnifolia*), cinnamon fern (*Osmunda cinnamomea*).

DISADVANTAGES

Old stems require pruning.

SIMILAR AND RELATED SPECIES

Pipestem is a member of the heath family. Many members of this family, among them the blueberries (*Vaccinium* spp.), mountain laurel (*Kalmia latifolia*), native azaleas (*Rhododendron* spp.), and dog-hobbles (*Leucothoe* spp.), make excellent landscape plants.

Andropogon spp.

an-dro-PO-gahn

Bluestems and Broomsedges

Family: Poaceae or Gramineae
Tall ground cover, specimen
Grass
Height: 1 to 6 feet, depending upon species
Spread: Spreads by self-sown seeds as allowed

J. C. Putnam 44

LANDSCAPE USE

As a group, the bluestems and broomsedges are attractive, often shrublike, ground covers that may be used in flower gardens, as part of grass and wildflower meadows, massed in single-species or mixed clumps at corners or in beds, or as a major component of highway rights-of-way plantings. Bushy bluestem (*A. glomeratus*) is a relatively tall, clump-forming plant with a bushy, pinkish inflorescence and narrow leaves. Broomsedge (*A. virginicus*) is one of the most popular and widely used members of this group. Several varieties of broomsedge are available, including one (*A. virginicus* var. *glaucus*) that features silvery-bluish leaves much of the year. As a group, the broomsedges and bluestems should be cut to within a few inches of the ground in mid- to late winter. Broomsedge is more vigorous when regularly burned.

FORM

A clump-forming grass with erect to arching culms and conspicuous inflorescences.

NATIVE RANGE

Flatwoods, sandhills, ditches, old fields, and disturbed sites. Several species range widely across eastern North America and throughout Florida.

CHARACTERISTICS

Flowers: Typically borne near the top of the culm; very showy, ranging in color from silvery or whitish to somewhat pinkish, depending upon species. Fall.

Leaves: Narrow; copper colored to bluish green.

Fruit: A tiny grain. Fall to winter.

CULTURE

Soil: Acid to very acid or sandy soils, depending upon species.

Exposure: Full sun.

Water: Moderate. Bushy bluestem prefers moist soil; broomsedge tolerates dry to moist soil.

Hardiness Zones: 6 to 10.

Life Span: Perennial.

BEST FEATURES

Valued for their green to bluish green summer leaves, showy fall flowering and fruiting period, and winter leaves, which last well into the season and, in some species, turn an attractive coppery color.

COMPANION PLANTS

A variety of wildflowers, including tickseeds (*Coreopsis* spp.) and black-eyed Susan (*Rudbeckia hirta*) make good companion plants, as well as muhly grass (*Muhlenbergia capillaris*), other species of *Andropogon*, lopsided Indiangrass (*Sorghastrum secundum*), coontie (*Zamia pumila*), saw palmetto (*Serenoa repens*), wiregrass (*Aristida stricta* var. *beyrichiana*), wax myrtle (*Myrica cerifera*), eastern gamagrass (*Tripsacum dactyloides*), and slash pine (*Pinus elliottii*).

DISADVANTAGES

Must be cut back annually. Leaves of some species become unattractive in midwinter.

SIMILAR AND RELATED SPECIES

Eleven species of *Andropogon* occur in Florida, three of which have several varieties. At least five species are available in the nursery trade. These include, in addition to those considered above, *A. brachystachyus*, *A. gerardii*, and *A. ternarius*.

Annona glabra

a-NO-nuh GLAY-bruh

Pond Apple

Family: Annonaceae
Large shrub to small tree
Height: 15 to 35 feet
Spread: 10 to 20 feet

LANDSCAPE USE

Most at home in wet sites such as stream banks or in the edges of ponds or pools. May also serve as a specimen plant in drier sites.

FORM

A relatively short, somewhat spreading small tree or large shrub, often with twisted, gnarly trunk and branches. Trunk sometimes swollen or buttressed at base (the latter character most often true for plants situated in very wet sites).

NATIVE RANGE

Swamps and stream banks. Southernmost Florida, tropical America, and the Caribbean.

CHARACTERISTICS

Flowers: Pale yellow to cream colored, with 6 petals that are ½–1 inch long, the outer 3 of which are red-spotted at base.

Leaves: Alternate, oval, pointed at the tip, about 6 inches long, deep green, and often reflexed upward along the midrib.

Fruit: Large, oblong, fleshy, turning from green to pale yellow with brown spots as it matures; edible but not particularly tasty.

Bark: Reddish brown; scaly and fissured.

CULTURE

Soil: Occurs naturally in wet to saturated soils but is adaptable to drier sites.

Exposure: Full sun, but tolerates moderate to quite deep shade; produces flowers and fruits more abundantly in open sun.

Water: Watering is not required in wet sites but may be required in drier sites, especially during periods of drought or low rainfall.

Hardiness Zones: 10 to 11.

Life Span: Moderately long-lived; some individuals may become old.

BEST FEATURES

The attractive, pale yellow flowers, shiny deep green leaves, and often picturesque form make this an interesting specimen in urban landscapes.

COMPANION PLANTS

Buttonbush (*Cephalanthus occidentalis*), Virginia willow (*Itea virginica*), cypresses (*Taxodium* spp.), pop ash (*Fraxinus caroliniana*), swamp dogwood (*Cornus foemina*), scarlet hibiscus (*Hibiscus coccineus*), swamp fern (*Blechnum serrulatum*), red maple (*Acer rubrum*), dahoon (*Ilex cassine*), royal fern (*Osmunda regalis*), leather fern (*Acrostichum danaeifolium*).

DISADVANTAGES

Large fruits are seldom eaten by mammals and often litter the ground under the tree, making for an untidy scene.

ALLERGENIC AND TOXIC PROPERTIES

Seeds are said to be toxic.

SIMILAR AND RELATED SPECIES

Though the two plants are not related, the leaves of pond apple bear a resemblance to those of both the strangler and shortleaf figs (*Ficus aurea* and *F. citrifolia*).

Ardisia escallonioides

ar-DEE-zee-uh es-ka-lo-nee-OY-deez

Marlberry

Family: Myrsinaceae
Large shrub to small tree
Height: Potentially to 21 feet; more often a shrub not exceeding about 10 feet
Spread: 3 to 8 feet

LANDSCAPE USE
May be used as a hedge or foundation plant, or as a background or shrub component in shady gardens.

FORM
Typically grows as an erect, moderately compact evergreen shrub. May also become a slender tree.

NATIVE RANGE
Tropical and hardwood hammocks. South-central to southern Florida, the Keys, and the West Indies.

CHARACTERISTICS
Flowers: Small, fragrant, white, borne in dense, showy, branching clusters near the tips of branches. Nearly year-round.
Leaves: Alternate, dark, lustrous green, often reflexed upward from the midrib, to about 6 inches long.
Fruit: Shiny, black, $\frac{5}{16}$-inch-diameter drupes borne in conspicuous clusters.
Bark: Thin and grayish.

CULTURE
Soil: Prefers the thin, fertile soils of hammocks; is somewhat tolerant of alkaline soils.
Exposure: Occurs naturally as an understory shrub in hammocks, but performs well in a variety of light conditions; salt tolerant.
Water: Supplemental irrigation is usually not required.
Hardiness Zones: 9 to 11.
Life Span: Moderate.

BEST FEATURES
Valued for its conspicuous clusters of white, highly fragrant flowers that provide color in at least three seasons; its attractive, shiny black berries, which attract birds; and its evergreen habit. Excellent shrub for shaded landscapes. Relatively pest free.

COMPANION PLANTS
Stoppers (*Eugenia* spp. and *Myrcianthes fragrans*), pigeon plum (*Coccoloba diversifolia*), myrsine (*Rapanea punctata*), wild lime (*Zanthoxylum fagara*), white indigoberry (*Randia aculeata*), royal palm (*Roystonea regia*), Jamaica caper (*Capparis cynophallophora*), sparkleberry (*Vaccinium arboreum*), firebush (*Hamelia patens*), wild coffees (*Psychotria* spp.), sugarberry (*Celtis laevigata*), spicewood (*Calyptranthes pallens*), satinleaf (*Chrysophyllum oliviforme*).

DISADVANTAGES
Brittle.

SIMILAR AND RELATED SPECIES
Marlberry is similar to and sometimes confused with myrsine (*Rapanea punctata*) when not in flower or fruit. Two non-native species of *Ardisia*, including coral ardisia (*A. crenata*) and shoebutton ardisia (*A. elliptica*), both of which are listed as Category I invasive pest plants by the Florida Exotic Pest Plant Council, are extremely aggressive and should be avoided.

Aristida stricta var. *beyrichiana*

uh-RIS-ti-duh STRIK-tuh bay-ri-kee-AY-nuh

Wiregrass

Family: Poaceae or Gramineae
Ground cover, grass
Height: 2 to 4 feet
Spread: 2 to 3 feet

J.C. Putnam H

LANDSCAPE USE

An essential ingredient in the restoration of longleaf pinelands and wiregrass savannas. Individual clumps may be used in flower beds, along driveways, or to conceal foundations. Should be used more often in highway roadside plantings in the difficult upper reaches of highway rights-of-way.

FORM

A bunchgrass that produces dense clumps of narrow, in-rolled, wiry leaves. Leaves erect when young, tending to relax and become arched with age.

NATIVE RANGE

A. stricta var. *beyrichiana* is one of two recently recognized varieties of wiregrass. The reported range of variety *beyrichiana* extends from South Carolina, south throughout Florida, and west to Mississippi, and the reported range of variety *stricta* is to the north of this region. An essential ground cover component in sandhill and flatwoods communities.

CHARACTERISTICS

Flowers: Borne on an elongated stem above the leaves. May be produced any time of year.

Leaves: Very narrow and in-rolled so as to appear wiry; typically green when fresh, turning brown with age.

Fruit: A tiny yellow grain. Produced only after fire.

CULTURE

Soil: Occurs in poor, acid, sandy soils with little to no organic matter. Tolerates both moist and dry sites.

Exposure: Full sun to part shade.

Water: Supplemental irrigation is usually not required.

Hardiness Zones: 7 to 11.

Life Span: Long-lived.

BEST FEATURES

Clumps planted in flower beds tend to maintain their size. Excellent for the restoration of native pinelands.

COMPANION PLANTS

As many as 200 species of herbaceous and woody plants occur in the same habitat with wiregrass, including gopher apple (*Licania michauxii*), beargrass (*Nolina brittoniana*), broomsedge (*Andropogon virginicus*), redroot (*Lachnanthes caroliana*), several species of lowbush blueberries (*Vaccinium* spp.), lopsided Indiangrass (*Sorghastrum secundum*), summer haw (*Crataegus flava*), slash and longleaf pines (*Pinus elliottii* and *P. palustris*), beautyberry (*Callicarpa americana*), Chickasaw plum (*Prunus angustifolia*), saw palmetto (*Serenoa repens*), and coral honeysuckle (*Lonicera sempervirens*).

DISADVANTAGES

Clumps may become less dense with age. Retains dead foliage, which may be unattractive.

SIMILAR AND RELATED SPECIES

A. stricta var. *stricta* is quite similar; see comments for native range, above.

Asclepias spp.

us-KLEE-pee-us

Milkweeds

Family: Asclepiadaceae
Perennial wildflowers
Height: 1 to 3 feet
Spread: 1 to 2 feet

LANDSCAPE USE

As a group, the milkweeds are very showy plants with interesting flowers, and are exceptional butterfly plants. Most species are excellent for mixed wildflower and butterfly gardens, roadsides, and other hot, dry situations.

FORM

Two species are regularly available in the nursery trade. Butterfly weed (*A. tuberosa*) is a 2- to 3-foot tall, taprooted, clump-forming species that produces many reddish orange to orange flowers. Swamp milkweed (*A. perennis*) is erect, grows 2 feet tall, and has white to pinkish flowers.

NATIVE RANGE

Butterfly weed occurs in sandy uplands, woodland edges, roadsides, and other such sunny places from Canada southward throughout Florida, and westward to Texas. Swamp milkweed grows in shady floodplain forests, swamps, and wet woodlands from South Carolina, south to central peninsular Florida, and west to Texas.

CHARACTERISTICS

Flowers: Those of butterfly weed are bright reddish orange to orange and are produced in large, profusely flowered and very showy clusters; spring to fall. Those of swamp milkweed are white to pinkish and are also borne profusely in large, showy clusters; spring to fall.

Leaves: Opposite, narrowly lance shaped to grasslike.

Fruit: A 3- to 5-inch-long pod that splits open to release cottony seed clusters.

CULTURE

Soil: Butterfly weed prefers dry to slightly moist soils but is intolerant of wet conditions. Swamp milkweed prefers wet soils and can tolerate occasional inundation.

Exposure: Full sun for butterfly weed; shade to part shade for swamp milkweed.

Water: Dry conditions are best for butterfly weed; moist to wet conditions are best for swamp milkweed.

Hardiness Zones: 4 to 10 for butterfly weed; 8 to 9 for swamp milkweed.

Life Span: Long-lived perennials that will reseed and spread.

BEST FEATURES

Excellent butterfly plants. Showy flowers. Unique and intricate flower morphology with downturned petals and sepals and upright hoods and horns.

COMPANION PLANTS

For swamp milkweed: buttonbush (*Cephalanthus occidentalis*), Virginia willow (*Itea virginica*), swamp fern (*Blechnum serrulatum*), scarlet hibiscus (*Hibiscus coccineus*), swamp tupelo (*Nyssa sylvatica* var. *biflora*), water tupelo (*N. aquatica*). For butterfly weed: Carolina jessamine (*Gelsemium sempervirens*), coral honeysuckle (*Lonicera sempervirens*), Florida paintbrush (*Carphephorus corymbosus*), blazing stars (*Liatris* spp.).

DISADVANTAGES

Plants in northern Florida lose their leaves and go dormant in winter.

ALLERGENIC AND TOXIC PROPERTIES

All milkweed species should be suspected of toxicity. The latex (sap) may irritate the skin. The roots of *A. tuberosa*, though used medicinally, may cause diarrhea and vomiting.

SIMILAR AND RELATED SPECIES

More than 20 species of milkweeds are native to Florida, none of which are easily confused with the two described here. Care should be taken to avoid the several non-native species that are available at many outlets.

Asimina spp.

uh-SI-mi-nuh

Pawpaws

Family: Annonaceae
Shrubs to very small trees
Height: 5 to 30 feet, depending on species
Spread: 1½ to 10 feet, depending on species

LANDSCAPE USE

With the exception of common pawpaw (*A. triloba*), which grows into a small tree, most pawpaws are used as free-standing shrubs, in butterfly gardens, or in naturalistic landscapes. At least three species are generally available in Florida, including *A. obovata, A. parviflora,* and *A. triloba.*

FORM

Medium-sized to large deciduous shrubs or small trees, depending upon species.

NATIVE RANGE

Various habitats—from scrub, coastal dunes, and sandhills to mesic woodlands—depending upon species. Individual species range from the south-central peninsula to the panhandle.

CHARACTERISTICS

Flowers: Those of *A. triloba* and *A. parviflora* are small, dull red, inconspicuous, and hang below the leaves. Those of *A. obovata* are large, bright white, borne in profusion, and very showy.

Leaves: Alternate, medium to dark green, 6–12 inches long, mostly widest above the middle.

Fruit: A rounded, fleshy, yellow-green berry, 1–6 inches long.

Bark: Light to dark brown; often roughened on old plants.

CULTURE

Soil: *A. obovata* prefers well-drained, sandy soils; *A. triloba* and *A. parviflora* perform best on well-drained, moist sites.

Exposure: Full sun for *A. obovata;* part sun to shade for *A. triloba* and *A. parviflora.*

Water: Dry sites are best for *A. obovata;* moist, well-drained conditions are best for *A. triloba* and *A. parviflora.*

Hardiness Zones: 8 to 10 for *A. obovata;* 5 to 9 for *A. triloba;* 7 to 9 for *A. parviflora.*

Life Span: Moderately long-lived; probably in excess of 50 years.

BEST FEATURES

A. obovata has showy white flowers. All three species described here, as well as others, are the larval food of the zebra swallowtail butterfly. All three species are essentially pest free.

COMPANION PLANTS

Tarflower (*Bejaria racemosa*), fetterbush (*Lyonia lucida*), scrub hickory (*Carya floridana*), sand pine (*Pinus clausa*), Chapman and myrtle oaks (*Quercus chapmanii* and *Q. myrtifolia*), wax myrtle (*Myrica cerifera*), shiny blueberry (*Vaccinium myrsinites*), gopher apple (*Licania michauxii*), butterfly weed (*Asclepias tuberosa*).

DISADVANTAGES

Flowers of *A. triloba* and *A. parviflora* are inconspicuous and not very showy.

CULTIVARS

Cultivars of *A. triloba* are reported but are generally not available in Florida.

ALLERGENIC AND TOXIC PROPERTIES

Certain species may cause vomiting, stomach pain, and headache, if ingested.

SIMILAR AND RELATED SPECIES

Eight species of pawpaws occur in Florida, at least three of which, including *A. obovata,* are endemic to the state. Besides those described here, polecat bush (*A. incana*) and netted pawpaw (*A. reticulata*) are also sometimes used in landscaping and gardening.

Avicennia germinans

a-vi-SE-nee-uh JER-mi-nanz

Black Mangrove

Family: Avicenniaceae
Medium-sized tree
Height: 10 to 40 feet
Spread: 10 to 30 feet

LANDSCAPE USE

Used for screening and to reduce erosion along low-energy brackish shores and inlets.

FORM

A medium-sized, densely foliated tree with oval, dark green leaves. Produces numerous "breathing roots" (pneumatophores), which protrude from muddy bottoms around the tree.

NATIVE RANGE

Essentially a coastal species of low-energy saltwater shores. Southernmost Florida and the West Indies. Extends up the east coast of Florida to near Jacksonville and up the west coast to just north of Tampa.

CHARACTERISTICS

Flowers: Small, white with a yellow base, individually inconspicuous but produced in short, branched spikes that terminate the branches. Very fragrant. Year-round.

Leaves: Opposite, oval to elliptic, green above, grayish below, 2–5 inches long, surfaces often vested with visible salt crystals which have been secreted through special salt glands in the leaves.

Fruit: Green, fleshy, laterally flattened, containing one large seed that often germinates while still on the tree and splits open to expose the seed.

Bark: Grayish and smooth when young, becoming dark brown and fissured with age.

CULTURE

Soil: Prefers moist, salty soil.

Exposure: Full sun. Somewhat cold tolerant, but will not grow to a large size north of its normal range.

Water: Prefers moist conditions. Will tolerate daily dousings of salty water.

Hardiness Zones: 10 to 11.

Life Span: 50 to 100 years.

BEST FEATURES

Excellent for salty shorelines in full sun. Flowers are attractive to bees, which produce a fine honey from its nectar.

COMPANION PLANTS

Buttonwood (*Conocarpus erectus*), red mangrove (*Rhizophora mangle*), white mangrove (*Laguncularia racemosa*).

ALLERGENIC AND TOXIC PROPERTIES

Sprouting seeds are reported to be poisonous but are also reported to be edible when cooked.

SIMILAR AND RELATED SPECIES

Four mangrove species occur along Florida's southern coastline. Black mangrove, along with the three companion plants listed above, are somewhat similar but are easily distinguished by leaf shape and color, and fruit.

Baccharis halimifolia

BA-kuh-ris ha-li-mi-FO-lee-uh

Salt Bush, Groundsel Tree, Sea Myrtle

Family: Asteraceae or Compositae
Shrub to very small tree
Height: 5 to 20 feet
Spread: 5 to 12 feet

LANDSCAPE USE

Useful as a large shrub, filler, or massed in difficult soil situations, especially in coastal settings. Excellent for naturalistic settings and roadsides.

FORM

An oval to rounded, freely branched, multistemmed, hardy, semievergreen to deciduous, cold-tolerant shrub usually not exceeding about 12 feet in height.

NATIVE RANGE

Occurs in a variety of situations from coastal to inland, often on very poor soil. Throughout Florida, north to Massachusetts, and west to Texas.

CHARACTERISTICS

Flowers: Tiny, white to greenish white, borne profusely in conspicuous, short-stalked, showy heads. Male and female flowers borne on separate plants. Fall.

Leaves: 1–3 inches long, to about 1½ inches wide, often deeply toothed near and at the apex, shiny to grayish green.

Fruit: Tiny seeds (achenes) attached to showy, cottony masses of fine bristles (pappus) that carry the seeds in the wind and make the plant very showy during fruiting.

Bark: Smooth and grayish brown.

CULTURE

Soil: Does best in moist soil, but will adapt to very dry acid or alkaline conditions.

Exposure: Full sun to part shade. Can withstand temperatures as low as -20 degrees F.

Water: Prefers moist conditions but requires no watering, even on dry sites, once established.

Hardiness Zones: 5 to 9.

Life Span: Probably somewhat short-lived, but perhaps to 50 years.

BEST FEATURES

Very hardy and tolerant of a wide array of soil types. Grows well in poor soils, including along the coast near salt marshes (hence the common names). Responds well to pruning. Flowers visited by monarch butterflies.

COMPANION PLANTS

Leather fern (*Acrostichum danaeifolium*), buttonbush (*Cephalanthus occidentalis*), scarlet and swamp hibiscus (*Hibiscus coccineus* and *H. grandiflorus*), water hyssop (*Bacopa monnieri*), yellow canna (*Canna*

flaccida), Christmasberry (*Lycium carolinianum*), sea oxeyes (*Borrichia* spp.), marsh elder (*Iva frutescens*).

DISADVANTAGES

Will readily reseed and spread beyond its planting site.

CULTIVARS

At least one cultivar is known but is not readily available in Florida.

ALLERGENIC AND TOXIC PROPERTIES

Some people report being highly allergic to the pollen. Also reported to be harmful to livestock.

SIMILAR AND RELATED SPECIES

Two other species are native to Florida. Silverling (*B. glomeruliflora*), which is similar, occurs mostly in floodplains and has stalkless flower clusters. Saltwater false willow (*B. angustifolia*) has very narrow leaves and occurs mostly in brackish marshes, coastal swales, and along beaches.

Bacopa spp.

buh-KO-puh

Water Hyssop and Lemon Bacopa

Family: Veronicaceae
Ground cover
Height: To about 6 inches
Spread: Potentially forming extensive mats

1mm

Two species are used in landscaping, lemon bacopa (*B. caroliniana*), with blue flowers, and water hyssop (*B. monnieri*), with mostly white to sometimes pinkish flowers. Both are used as ground covers along saturated edges, wet swales, and the mowed edges of retention ponds.

FORM
Low-growing, mat-forming, succulent, perennial herbs with small but numerous and obvious blue or whitish flowers.

NATIVE RANGE
Ponds, streams, marshes, brackish edges, and margins of cypress ponds. Throughout Florida, north to southeastern Virginia, west to Texas.

CHARACTERISTICS
Flowers: Tubular, 5-lobed, spreading, borne singly in leaf axils; those of lemon bacopa are blue, and those of water hyssop are white to light purple or pale pink. Summer.
Leaves: Opposite, succulent; those of lemon bacopa clasping, aromatic, and lemon-scented, and those of water hyssop nonclasping, mostly widest at the tip, and nonaromatic.
Fruit: A small, inconspicuous capsule.

CULTURE
Soil: Wet, saturated soils, pH 5.0–7.0.
Exposure: Sun to part shade.
Water: An aquatic plant; often shallowly inundated.
Hardiness Zones: 8 to 10.
Life Span: Perennial.

BEST FEATURES
B. monnieri is a host plant for the white peacock butterfly. *B. caroliniana* has lemon-scented leaves. Both are excellent ground covers in wet to saturated situations.

COMPANION PLANTS
Buttonbush (*Cephalanthus occidentalis*), rose mallow and scarlet and swamp hibiscus (*Hibiscus moscheutos, H. coccineus,* and *H. grandiflorus*), sand cordgrass (*Spartina bakeri*), giant cutgrass (*Zizaniopsis miliacea*), climbing aster (*Symphyotrichum carolinianum*), sea oxeyes (*Borrichia* spp.), salt bush (*Baccharis halimifolia*).

SIMILAR AND RELATED SPECIES
A third species, *B. innominata,* also occurs in central and northern Florida but is not often used in landscaping.

Betula nigra

BE-tew-luh NY-gruh

River Birch

Family: Betulaceae
Medium to large tree
Height: 40 to 80 feet
Spread: 20 to 60 feet

LANDSCAPE USE

Best used as a specimen or accent tree in lawns, parks, and golf courses. Does best in moist to seasonally wet areas. Often planted in attractive multistemmed clumps. Excellent as an accent tree around retention ponds and along moist roadsides.

FORM

A tall, erect, deciduous, single- or multistemmed tree with peeling outer bark that exposes a layer of coppery-tan to salmon or peach-colored inner bark that is especially showy in winter.

NATIVE RANGE

Wet sites along rivers and floodplains. Massachusetts, south to northern peninsular Florida, and west to Kansas.

CHARACTERISTICS

Flowers: Tiny, borne in drooping catkins.
Leaves: Alternate, doubly toothed, 2–5 inches long, turning pale yellow in fall.
Fruit: Tiny, borne in catkins.
Bark: Outer bark silvery, cream, salmon, orange-brown, to dark reddish brown; peels in large, irregular plates to expose coppery-tan inner bark.

CULTURE

Soil: Prefers acid soils, with pH below 6.5; tolerates moderately compacted soil and overwatering.
Exposure: Full sun, but tolerates part shade.
Water: Prefers wet sites and may be inundated for several months at a time, but also adapts well to drier sites and may not need supplemental watering once deep roots are established.
Hardiness Zones: 4 to 9.
Life Span: Fast growing and moderately long-lived; 50–100 years.

BEST FEATURES

Grows quickly. Its shaggy, multicolored bark makes an attractive addition to the landscape.

COMPANION PLANTS

Hazel alder (*Alnus serrulata*), sycamore (*Platanus occidentalis*), sweetgum (*Liquidambar styraciflua*), Coastal Plain willow (*Salix caroliniana*), blue beech (*Carpinus caroliniana*), American hophornbeam (*Ostrya virginiana*), red maple and box elder (*Acer rubrum* and *A. negundo*), sugarberry (*Celtis laevigata*), magnolia and sweetbay (*Magnolia grandiflora* and *M. virginica*), pipestem (*Agarista populifolia*), sweetshrub (*Calycanthus floridus*).

DISADVANTAGES

Drops its leaves in winter and its catkins in summer and early fall. Sometimes attacked by leaf miners and twig girdlers. Mostly pest free but may develop leaf spots in moist years.

CULTIVARS

At least two cultivars are known for this species, but neither is used in Florida.

ALLERGENIC AND TOXIC PROPERTIES

The pollen is known to be an airborne allergen.

SIMILAR AND RELATED SPECIES

River birch is the only birch that grows easily in the southeast. Blue beech (*Carpinus caroliniana*) and American hophornbeam (*Ostrya virginiana*), of the same family, also make good landscape trees.

Bignonia capreolata

big-NO-nee-uh ka-pree-o-LAY-tuh

Cross Vine

Family: Bignoniaceae
High-climbing woody vine
Height: Climbing to 50 feet
Spread: Clasping to tree trunks with tendrils; may spread over a large area

LANDSCAPE USE

Used in naturalistic landscapes, especially on larger trees, as a wall covering, or pruned to large trellises. Excellent for covering fences.

FORM

A high-climbing, semievergreen, woody vine with opposite, compound leaves and showy, trumpet-shaped, reddish orange flowers.

NATIVE RANGE

Floodplain forest, wet hammocks, and rich woods. Central peninsular Florida, north to Virginia and Illinois, and west to eastern Texas, but cultivated in Florida south of its native range.

CHARACTERISTICS

Flowers: Tubular, 2–3 inches long, reddish orange outside, yellowish inside, often borne in showy clusters. Spring and early summer. Visited by hummingbirds.

Leaves: Opposite, compound, dark green, with 2 opposite leaflets on stalks about half the length of the petiole.

Fruit: A narrow, 4- to 8-inch-long, dry, light brown capsule, splitting to expose 4 rows of winged seeds.

Bark: Smooth, brown to purplish brown, woody, to about 1 inch in diameter. The common name comes from the characteristic cross that is visible when larger stems are transversely sectioned.

CULTURE

Soil: Prefers rich, moist, well-drained soils, but will grow in a wide range of soils.

Exposure: Sun to shade; flowers best in full sun.

Water: Irrigation not required once established.

Hardiness Zones: 6 to 9.

Life Span: To at least 50 years.

BEST FEATURES

Fast growing and hardy. Attractive foliage. Showy spring flowers. May be trained as a ground cover if mowed and pruned and sited away from trees or other support. Holdfasts are not destructive to brick and wood walls.

COMPANION PLANTS

Carolina jessamine (*Gelsemium sempervirens*), coral honeysuckle (*Lonicera sempervirens*), coontie (*Zamia pumila*), pinxter azalea (*Rhododendron canescens*), yaupon (*Ilex vomitoria*), needle palm (*Rhapidophyllum hystrix*), beautyberry (*Callicarpa americana*), American hophornbeam (*Ostrya virginiana*), redbud (*Cercis canadensis*).

DISADVANTAGES

Its fast-growing habit may make this species difficult to control in small gardens.

SIMILAR AND RELATED SPECIES

The flowers of cross vine are similar to those of trumpet creeper (*Campsis radicans*), which are also tubular and reddish orange but lack the yellow center.

Blechnum serrulatum

BLEK-num se-roo-LAY-tum

Swamp Fern

Family: Blechnaceae
Ground cover
Height: 1 to 5 feet
Spread: Spreading by underground
runners and forming large patches

LANDSCAPE USE

An excellent ground cover for relatively large, moist sites at the edges of ponds, swamps, and marshes.

FORM

An erect, shiny green fern rapidly spreading by underground stems.

NATIVE RANGE

Swamps, cypress-dominated wetlands, wet prairies, and hammocks. One of the most common ferns from the central peninsula southward. A large, robust population at St. Andrews State Park, near Panama City, suggests that it might be successfully grown well north of its normal range.

CHARACTERISTICS

Leaves: 1–4 feet tall, erect, stiff, shiny green, pinnately divided into numerous leaflets. Produces sori (clusters of spore cases) in distinctive lines paralleling the central veins on the lower surface of the leaflets.

CULTURE

Soil: Moist, acid soil.
Exposure: Part shade to full or nearly full sun (if in moist situation).
Water: Prefers moist to wet sites.
Hardiness Zones: 8 to 10.
Life Span: Reproducing by spores and underground stems; will persist for many years.

BEST FEATURES

Coppery, bronze, to pinkish color of new leaves is very attractive. Hardy, forming dense fernery in moist soil. Shiny green foliage.

COMPANION PLANTS

Climbing aster (*Symphyotrichum carolinianum*), string lily (*Crinum americanum*), royal fern (*Osmunda regalis*), pond apple (*Annona glabra*), buttonbush (*Cephalanthus occidentalis*), Virginia willow (*Itea virginica*), scarlet hibiscus (*Hibiscus coccineus*), swamp bay (*Persea palustris*), Coastal Plain willow (*Salix caroliniana*), cypresses (*Taxodium* spp.), red maple (*Acer rubrum*), strangler fig (*Ficus aurea*), dahoon (*Ilex cassine*).

DISADVANTAGES

Somewhat aggressive and may spread, sometimes rapidly, beyond the original planting.

SIMILAR AND RELATED SPECIES

Swamp fern may be confused with several members of the maiden ferns (*Thelypteris* spp.) but lacks lobed or deeply cut leaflets. Hammock fern (*Blechnum occidentale*) occurs rarely in Florida but is not used horticulturally.

Borrichia spp.

bo-RI-kee-uh

Sea Oxeyes

Family: Asteraceae or Compositae
Low shrub
Height: 5 feet
Spread: 1 foot individually, but forming colonies

LANDSCAPE USE

Excellent for wet coastal saline environments, especially along the edges of retention ponds, coastal swales, and canal banks. Two species occur in Florida. *B. frutescens,* the more common species, will form large colonies.

FORM

Low, erect, perennial shrubs with leafy stems, succulent, grayish to dull green leaves, with an irregular, cylindrical form and yellow, daisylike flowers.

NATIVE RANGE

Salt marshes, mangrove swamps, and beaches. *B. arborescens* is limited in Florida to Miami-Dade and Monroe Counties but also occurs in the West Indies. *B. frutescens* occurs throughout the state and north along the coast to Virginia.

CHARACTERISTICS

Flowers: A tough, knotty, 1-inch-wide head of yellow disk and ray flowers. Showy. Spring and summer, potentially year-round in south Florida.

Leaves: Fleshy to succulent, elliptic to oblanceolate, 1–3 inches long; grayish green in *Borrichia frutescens,* and light green in *B. arborescens.*

Fruit: Tiny, dry, hard achenes formed within the drying head of disk flowers.

Bark: Grayish brown.

CULTURE

Soil: Prefers wet, saline soils.

Exposure: Full sun.

Water: Both species are obligate wetland plants and can tolerate regular dousings of salt water.

Hardiness Zones: 8 to 10 for *B. frutescens;* 10 to 11 for *B. arborescens.*

Life Span: Perennial; colonies can persist for many years.

BEST FEATURES

Tolerant of salty environments. Showy yellow flowers.

COMPANION PLANTS

Saltgrass (*Distichlis spicata*), black mangrove (*Avicennia germinans*), white mangrove (*Laguncularia racemosa*), red mangrove (*Rhizophora mangle*), salt bush (*Baccharis halimifolia*), cordgrasses (*Spartina* spp.), goldenrod (*Solidago sempervirens*), marsh elder (*Iva frutescens*).

SIMILAR AND RELATED SPECIES

A hybrid between these two species has been reported. No other Florida shrub of coastal saline environments resembles these species, with the possible exception of camphor daisy (*Rayjacksonia phyllocephala*), which occurs on dunes of the western central and southern peninsula.

Bursera simaruba

BIR-suh-ruh si-muh-ROO-buh

Gumbo Limbo

Family: Burseraceae
Medium-sized tree
Height: 20 to 60 feet
Spread: 20 to 50 feet

J. C. Putnam H.

LANDSCAPE USE

A popular specimen, shade, and street tree in southern Florida.

FORM

A large-trunked, spreading, relatively low-branched tree with shiny, peeling bark.

NATIVE RANGE

A canopy tree of West Indian hardwood hammocks and tropical woodlands from south-central Florida southward. Also in the West Indies, Central America, and Mexico.

CHARACTERISTICS

Flowers: Greenish, small, borne in 2- to 5-inch-long spikes. Winter and spring.

Leaves: Alternate, deciduous, 6–8 inches long, divided into opposite, 3-inch-long leaflets with sharp-pointed tips and unequal bases.

Fruit: A red, $5/16$-inch-long capsule containing 1–2 triangular, bony seeds.

Bark: Thick, smooth, lustrous, bronze to reddish, sometimes separating into thin, papery scales.

CULTURE

Soil: Occurs naturally in thin, well-drained soils of tropical and coastal hammocks, but is adaptable to many well-drained soil types from acid to basic.

Exposure: Sun to part shade; both drought and salt tolerant.

Water: Supplemental irrigation is not required.

Hardiness Zones: 10 to 11.

Life Span: Moderately long-lived.

BEST FEATURES

Fast-growing. Beautiful, shaggy, bronze-colored bark. Delicate, glossy green compound foliage. Interesting, often contorted shape. An excellent shade or specimen tree.

COMPANION PLANTS

Pigeon plum and seagrape (*Coccoloba diversifolia* and *C. uvifera*), myrtle-of-the-river (*Calyptranthes zuzygium*), crabwood (*Gymnanthes lucida*), marlberry (*Ardisia escallonioides*), Jamaica caper (*Capparis cynophallophora*).

DISADVANTAGES

Sheds its leaves during winter.

CULTIVARS

Gumbo limbo varies in bark color and should be selected carefully for forms that offer the most picturesque bark.

SIMILAR AND RELATED SPECIES

No other tree of tropical Florida has the appearance of gumbo limbo.

Callicarpa americana

ka-li-KAR-puh uh-me-ri-KAY-nuh

Beautyberry

Family: Lamiaceae or Labiatae
Small shrub
Height: 4 to 8 feet
Spread: 3 to 6 feet

J.C. Putnam H.

LANDSCAPE USE

Commonly used as a specimen shrub for its prolific, attractive, purple fruit. Also often massed in shrub beds, situated in naturalistic landscape settings, or along woodland edges. A very showy plant for roadside plantings, especially in such difficult situations as highway medians and the edges of road and powerline rights-of-way. May be mowed yearly to make a much fuller plant.

FORM

A loosely branched, irregularly spreading, graceful shrub with arching branches.

NATIVE RANGE

Occurs in a wide variety of woodlands across much of eastern North America and throughout Florida.

CHARACTERISTICS

Flowers: Small, sometimes inconspicuous, pink to lavender, borne on new growth. Late spring and summer.

Leaves: Opposite, deciduous, simple, aromatic, 3–6 inches long, with long stalks and prominent veins.

Fruit: Conspicuous, showy, purplish drupes borne in dense clusters along the branches. Late summer, fall, and into early winter.

Bark: Brownish gray.

CULTURE

Soil: Prefers rich soils but is tolerant of a variety of slightly acid, well-drained conditions, including poor and sandy soils.

Exposure: Full sun to part shade. Produces more flowers and fruit in full sun.

Water: Watering may be required to establish nursery-grown stock. Once established, supplemental irrigation is usually not required except in poor soils.

Hardiness Zones: 6 to 11.

Life Span: Relatively short-lived; usually under 10 years, but is easily and often naturally propagated for a continuing presence in the landscape.

BEST FEATURES

Graceful form. Showy purple fruit is attractive to birds and lasts into the winter if not eaten. Can be severely pruned to maintain a more compact form.

COMPANION PLANTS

Sparkleberry (*Vaccinium arboreum*), flowering dogwood (*Cornus florida*), sweetshrub (*Calycanthus floridus*), witch hazel (*Hamamelis virginiana*), needle palm (*Rhapidophyllum hystrix*), scrub palmetto and cabbage palm (*Sabal etonia* and *S. palmetto*), Chickasaw plum (*Prunus angustifolia*), gopher apple (*Licania michauxii*), lopsided Indiangrass (*Sorghastrum secundum*), summer haw (*Crataegus flava*), slash and longleaf pines (*Pinus elliottii* and *P. palustris*).

DISADVANTAGES

Drops its leaves early in the season, though it may be evergreen to nearly evergreen in southern Florida.

SIMILAR AND RELATED SPECIES

A white-fruited form, *C. americana* forma *lactea*, is also available. Both the white- and purple-fruited varieties may be used together to create a very interesting combination.

Calycanthus floridus

ka-li-KAN-thus FLO-ri-dus

Sweetshrub

Family: Calycanthaceae
Large shrub
Height: 6 to 10 feet
Spread: 4 to 8 feet

J.C. Putnam H.

LANDSCAPE USE
Serves well in a shrub border along a shaded patio or deck where the flower aroma can be enjoyed, or in shady, mixed shrub beds or naturalistic landscapes. An old and cherished southern landscape plant.

FORM
An upright, multistemmed, clump-forming deciduous shrub that readily spreads from underground stems.

NATIVE RANGE
Rich woods and the edges of floodplains. Pennsylvania, southward to northern Florida, and west to Mississippi.

CHARACTERISTICS
Flowers: Deep red, reddish brown, or maroon, sweetly fragrant (on most plants), and 2 inches wide. March and April.
Leaves: Opposite, deciduous, elliptical in outline, 3–5 inches long, dark green above, gray-green below, aromatic when bruised.
Fruit: A 3-inch-long, greenish to brownish, typically fragrant capsule bearing red seeds. Summer and fall.
Bark: Brownish gray; aromatic when crushed.

CULTURE
Soil: Occurs naturally in rich, moist earth, but will adapt to a variety of soils from alkaline to acid as long as they are moist.
Exposure: Prefers shade, but tolerates part sun.
Water: Ground should be kept moist, but not wet.
Hardiness Zones: 5 to 9.
Life Span: Long-lived for a shrub; in excess of 50 years.

BEST FEATURES
Long-lived and relatively pest free. Most prized for its deep red to nearly maroon flowers, which produce a distinctive fruity, almost strawberrylike fragrance, and its yellow autumn leaves.

COMPANION PLANTS
Pipestem (*Agarista populifolia*), strawberry bush (*Euonymus americanus*), Florida anise (*Illicium floridanum*), red buckeye (*Aesculus pavia*), winged elm (*Ulmus alata*), flowering dogwood (*Cornus florida*), hickories (*Carya* spp.), witch hazel (*Hamamelis virginiana*), mountain laurel (*Kalmia latifolia*), highbush blueberry (*Vaccinium corymbosum*), sourwood (*Oxydendrum arboreum*), redbud (*Cercis canadensis*).

DISADVANTAGES
Sheds its leaves in winter. Otherwise, trouble free and resistant to insects and diseases.

CULTIVARS
As many as 10 cultivars are known, but none of them are widely used in Florida.

ALLERGENIC AND TOXIC PROPERTIES
Suspected of causing symptoms similar to those of strychnine poisoning in livestock.

SIMILAR AND RELATED SPECIES
C. floridus var. *glaucus* occurs in hammocks and along stream banks in the central panhandle. Otherwise, sweetshrub is the only member of its family that occurs in Florida.

Calyptranthes pallens

ka-lip-TRAN-theez PA-lenz

Spicewood

Family: Myrtaceae
Shrub to small tree
Height: 20 feet
Spread: 5 to 10 feet

Typically used in naturalistic landscapes but also quite useful as a screen or hedge, a small, freestanding tree, or a dense shrub.

FORM
A large, often multitrunked shrub or small tree with a dense, rounded crown and aromatic foliage.

NATIVE RANGE
Tropical hardwood hammocks and hammock edges. Miami-Dade and Monroe Counties, the West Indies, and Mexico.

CHARACTERISTICS
Flowers: Tiny, inconspicuous, green to whitish, and borne in clusters; fragrant. March to September.
Leaves: Opposite, oval, shiny, to about 3 inches long. Foliage on some plants is very fragrant.
Fruit: A purplish black or reddish, ¼-inch-diameter berry.
Bark: Grayish to whitish; thin.

CULTURE
Soil: Prefers rich, somewhat moist soil. Intolerant of wet soils but is adaptable to dry situations.
Exposure: Shade to full sun.
Water: Prefers moist, well-drained to moderately dry situations.
Hardiness Zones: 10 to 11.
Life Span: Over 50 years.

BEST FEATURES
Dense crown, fragrant foliage, lustrous leaves, and upright form are major assets. Fruit is attractive to birds.

COMPANION PLANTS
Gumbo limbo (*Bursera simaruba*), satinleaf (*Chrysophyllum oliviforme*), marlberry (*Ardisia escallonioides*), stoppers (*Eugenia* spp.), mahogany (*Swietenia mahagoni*), myrsine (*Rapanea punctata*), strangler fig (*Ficus aurea*), white indigoberry (*Randia aculeata*), Florida gamagrass (*Tripsacum floridanum*), wild coffee (*Psychotria nervosa*).

SIMILAR AND RELATED SPECIES
Several of the stoppers (*Eugenia* spp.) have similar leaves. Myrtle-of-the-river (*Calyptranthes zuzygium*) is closely related and quite similar. It is rare in the wild but is also a useful landscape plant that is available from a few native plant nurseries.

Canna flaccida

KA-nuh FLAK-si duh (or FLA-si-duh)

Yellow Canna

Family: Cannaceae
Aquatic
Height: 2 to 4 feet
Spread: Will spread by underground stems as allowed

J. C. Putnam H.

LANDSCAPE USE

Appropriate for shallow ponds, pools, wet ditches, and marshes, where standing water is present. An important component in marsh restoration efforts. Should be more often used to beautify roadside ditches, drainage swales, canal banks, and retention ponds.

FORM

An erect, herbaceous perennial from an underground stem.

NATIVE RANGE

Swamps and marshes. North Carolina southward, throughout the Florida peninsula, and west to about Santa Rosa County.

CHARACTERISTICS

Flowers: Showy, about 3 inches long, consisting of 3 greenish sepals, 3 yellow petals, and 3 highly modified, bright yellow stamens with curly margins that are easily misconstrued as petals. Spring and summer.
Leaves: Alternate and spiraling the stem, oval, lance shaped, or oblong-elliptic in outline, deep green, about 6 inches wide, to about 2 feet long.
Fruit: A 3-parted, roughened capsule, about 2 inches wide and containing dark brown to blackish seeds.

CULTURE

Soil: Saturated to very moist soil. Adapts well to disturbed sites.
Exposure: Full sun to part shade.
Water: Requires standing water.
Hardiness Zones: 8 to 10.
Life Span: A perennial that reproduces vegetatively by underground stems.

BEST FEATURES

The bright yellow, highly modified flowers are beautiful, interesting, and showy. The large green leaves add lushness to wetland gardens.

COMPANION PLANTS

String lily (*Crinum americanum*), blue flags (*Iris virginica* and *I. hexagona*), climbing aster (*Symphyotrichum carolinianum*), buttonbush (*Cephalanthus occidentalis*), sand cordgrass (*Spartina bakeri*), leather fern (*Acrostichum danaeifolium*), salt bush (*Baccharis halimifolia*), scarlet hibiscus (*Hibiscus coccineus*).

DISADVANTAGES

Leaf roller caterpillars can be a major problem.

SIMILAR AND RELATED SPECIES

A number of non-native cannas are available in the horticultural trade but should be avoided in favor of this attractive and readily available native.

Capparis cynophallophora

KA-puh-ris sy-no-fa-LAH-fo-ruh

Jamaica Caper

Family: Brassicaceae
Large shrub to small tree
Height: 15 to 18 feet; sometimes more shrublike
Spread: 6 to 10 feet

LANDSCAPE USE

May be used as an accent or specimen plant as well as to screen patios and outdoor sitting areas. Excellent for difficult areas such as parking lots.

FORM

An erect, evergreen shrub or small tree with a dense, compact, rounded crown and typically pyramidal shape.

NATIVE RANGE

Typically occurring on the edges of tropical hardwood and upland coastal hammocks in southern Florida, the West Indies, and tropical America.

CHARACTERISTICS

Flowers: White when new, purplish with age, fragrant, with 4 petals and numerous purple stamens with yellow anthers. Spring to summer.
Leaves: Alternate, simple, leathery, shiny dark green above, densely brown-spotted below, 2–4 inches long and variable in size.
Fruit: A conspicuous, 12-inch-long, long-stalked, brown pod that opens to reveal a line of seeds held together by striking red tissue. Spring to fall.
Bark: Reddish brown, becoming fissured with age.

CULTURE

Soil: Neutral to somewhat alkaline, well-drained soil. Salt and drought tolerant.
Exposure: Sun to part shade.
Water: Supplemental irrigation not required.
Hardiness Zones: 10 to 11.
Life Span: Moderate.

BEST FEATURES

Its attractive flowers, stiff, shiny green leaves, and natural pyramidal or rounded shape that reduces the need for pruning make this an exceptional plant in south Florida landscapes.

COMPANION PLANTS

Spicewood (*Calyptranthes pallens*), marlberry (*Ardisia escallonioides*), cocoplum (*Chrysobalanus icaco*), gumbo limbo (*Bursera simaruba*), coontie (*Zamia pumila*), fiddlewood (*Citharexylum spinosum*), sugarberry (*Celtis laevigata*), satinleaf (*Chrysophyllum oliviforme*), seagrape and pigeon plum (*Coccoloba uvifera* and *C. diversifolia*), lancewood (*Ocotea coriacea*), Cherokee bean (*Erythrina herbacea*).

SIMILAR AND RELATED SPECIES

The more sprawling limber caper (*C. flexuosa*), a closely related and somewhat similar tropical shrub, is a larval food plant for butterflies and is an excellent companion to the Jamaica caper.

Carpinus caroliniana

kar-PY-nus ka-ro-li-nee-AY-nuh

Blue Beech, Hornbeam, Musclewood

Family: Betulaceae
Medium-sized tree
Height: To about 30 feet
Spread: 15 to 25 feet

LANDSCAPE USE

Excellent for rich, shaded woodlands or as a specimen in areas free of root disturbance.

FORM

A small to medium-sized, erect, straight-trunked, deciduous tree with tight, grayish, fluted bark and a rounded to irregular crown of shiny green, doubly toothed leaves.

NATIVE RANGE

Calcareous hammocks and floodplains. Nova Scotia and Minnesota, southward to central peninsular Florida, and west to Texas.

CHARACTERISTICS

Flowers: Greenish, small, with male and female flowers borne in separate catkins. Male flowers borne in cylindrical catkins. Female flowers subtended by attractive, 3-lobed bracts. Early spring.
Leaves: Alternate, simple, 2–5 inches long, to about 2 inches wide, shiny above, margins sharply and doubly toothed, veins paired and parallel.
Fruit: A tiny nutlet borne at the base of a 3-lobed bract.
Bark: Bluish gray, smooth, sinewy, and fluted, having a muscular appearance, hence one of the common names.

CULTURE

Soil: Prefers rich, moist, acid to neutral soil.
Exposure: Shade to part shade.
Water: Occurs naturally in moist to wet situations. Will tolerate periodic flooding.
Hardiness Zones: 2 to 9.
Life Span: Long-lived; 150 years or more.

BEST FEATURES

Slow growing and long-lived. Interesting bark. Shade tolerant. Fall color. Larval food plant for tiger swallowtail and red-spotted purple butterflies. Wildlife food.

COMPANION PLANTS

Live oak and laurel oak (*Quercus virginiana* and *Q. laurifolia*), sweetgum (*Liquidambar styraciflua*), loblolly and shortleaf pines (*Pinus taeda* and *P. echinata*), beautyberry (*Callicarpa americana*), highbush blueberries (*Vaccinium* spp.), Virginia creeper (*Parthenocissus quinquefolia*), Carolina jessamine (*Gelsemium sempervirens*), flowering dogwood (*Cornus florida*), hickories (*Carya* spp.), magnolia (*Magnolia grandiflora*).

DISADVANTAGES

Does not tolerate root disturbance. Difficult to transplant.

CULTIVARS

At least two cultivars are reported but are not generally available in Florida.

ALLERGENIC AND TOXIC PROPERTIES

Pollen may be an airborne allergen.

SIMILAR AND RELATED SPECIES

The American hophornbeam (*Ostrya virginiana*), also of the birch family, is closely related and somewhat similar. It has shaggy bark and occurs on better-drained sites.

Carya aquatica

KA-ree-uh uh-KWAH-ti-kuh

Water Hickory

Family: Juglandaceae
Large tree
Height: To 100 feet or more
Spread: To 50 feet

LANDSCAPE USE

Moist to wet naturalistic settings. Excellent for retention ponds, swales, canal banks, and riverbank stabilization.

FORM

A large, erect, shaggy-barked, deciduous tree with an irregular, spreading crown, compound leaves, and large, hard fruit typical of the hickories. Trunks on old trees may exceed 3 feet in diameter.

NATIVE RANGE

Levees, riverbanks, and floodplain forests. Southeastern Virginia, southward to south-central Florida, west to Texas.

CHARACTERISTICS

Flowers: Male and female flowers small, borne in separate, 3-inch-long catkins on the same tree. Spring.

Leaves: Alternate, compound, with 7–17 narrow, 4- to 5-inch-long, lance-shaped, toothed leaflets.

Fruit: A relatively thin-husked, 1- to 2-inch-wide capsule with 4 winged sutures and a hard, bitter kernel. Often borne in clusters.

Bark: Grayish to brown, splitting and stripping off in thin plates with maturity, similar to the bark of the non-native pecan tree (*C. illinoinensis*).

CULTURE

Soil: Wet, rich, acid soils.

Exposure: Full sun to part shade.

Water: Prefers moist to wet conditions.

Hardiness Zones: 8 to 9.

Life Span: Long-lived; more than 150 years.

BEST FEATURES

Long-lived. Flood tolerant. Good wildlife food. Large size.

COMPANION PLANTS

Red maple (*Acer rubrum*), sweetbay (*Magnolia virginiana*), tupelos (*Nyssa* spp.), swamp bay (*Persea palustris*), buttonbush (*Cephalanthus occidentalis*), blue beech (*Carpinus caroliniana*).

DISADVANTAGES

Deciduous habit and large, hard fruit capsules require cleanup.

ALLERGENIC AND TOXIC PROPERTIES

Pollen may be an airborne allergen.

SIMILAR AND RELATED SPECIES

Most similar in appearance to the non-native pecan tree (*C. illinoinensis*). Several other hickories, most of which are mentioned below with pignut hickory (*C. glabra*), also occur in Florida.

Carya glabra

KA-ree-uh GLAY-bruh

Pignut Hickory

Family: Juglandaceae
Large tree
Height: 50 to 100 feet
Spread: 30 to 100 feet

LANDSCAPE USE

Serves well as a long-lived specimen or shade tree. Very good tree for upland restoration. Excellent where showy fall color is desired.

FORM

A large, straight-trunked tree with a broad, spreading crown of stout limbs.

NATIVE RANGE

Upland dry to mesic hammocks. Massachusetts southward to central peninsular Florida, and west to Iowa, eastern Kansas, and eastern Texas.

CHARACTERISTICS

Flowers: Tiny, borne in relatively inconspicuous, drooping catkins.

Leaves: Compound, usually with 5 or 7 leaflets, dark green above, paler below. Turning golden to burnt orange in autumn.

Fruit: A nut borne in a large, globose, 1- to 2-inch-long husk that splits along several seams at maturity. September and October.

Bark: Grayish; shallowly fissured with diamond-patterned ridges.

CULTURE

Soil: Does best in fertile, well-drained, slightly acid soil.

Exposure: Part sun to shade.

Water: Supplemental irrigation not required once established.

Hardiness Zones: 4 to 9.

Life Span: Slow growing and long-lived. Matures at about 200 years, and specimens to 400 years are known.

BEST FEATURES

Long-lived. Provides shade for humans and food for wildlife, especially squirrels. One of the faster growing hickories. Exceptionally beautiful fall color in October and November.

COMPANION PLANTS

Oaks (*Quercus* spp.), black walnut (*Juglans nigra*), basswood (*Tilia americana*), sourwood (*Oxydendrum arboreum*), beech (*Fagus grandifolia*), Florida sugar maple (*Acer saccharum* subsp. *floridanum*), sweetgum (*Liquidambar styraciflua*), spruce pine (*Pinus glabra*), winged and American elms (*Ulmus alata* and *U. americana*), sweetshrub (*Calycanthus floridus*), beautyberry (*Callicarpa americana*), American hophornbeam (*Ostrya virginiana*), red buckeye (*Aesculus pavia*).

DISADVANTAGES

Hickories are deciduous and drop both their large, coarse leaves and their large, hard fruits during the fall, the latter of which can do damage to mowers and may require removal. Should not be used in parking areas as the large fruit can cause damage to vehicles.

ALLERGENIC AND TOXIC PROPERTIES

Pollen may be an airborne allergen.

SIMILAR AND RELATED SPECIES

Several hickories occur in Florida. The mockernut (*C. alba*) is a large upland tree that is similar in form to the pignut but has very hairy leaves. The sand hickory (*C. pallida*) and scrub hickory (*C. floridana*), the latter of which is found only in Florida's central scrub, are smaller than the others and do best in well-drained sandy soils. The bitternut hickory (*C. cordiformis*) occurs in Florida only sparingly in the floodplains of larger rivers in the northern reaches of the panhandle. It and the shaggy-barked water hickory (*C. aquatica*), which is useful along retention ponds, prefer moist soils.

Castanea pumila

kas-TAY-nee-uh PEW-mi-luh

Chinquapin

Family: Fagaceae
Small to medium-sized tree or shrub
Height: 30 to 40 feet
Spread: 15 to 30 feet

LANDSCAPE USE

Used as a deciduous shade tree or, in its shrubby form, as a large, densely foliated shrub. Especially good for naturalistic settings.

FORM

A large shrub to medium-sized, deciduous tree with a straight trunk and coarsely toothed leaves, like those of a chestnut tree.

NATIVE RANGE

Dry hammocks and sandhills. Pennsylvania southward to central Florida, west to Texas.

CHARACTERISTICS

Flowers: Male and female flowers borne in the leaf axils in separate, narrow, elongated catkins. Spring.

Leaves: Alternate, simple, 3–5 inches long, 1½–2 inches wide, dark green above, whitish below, margins toothed. Similar to the American chestnut (*C. dentata*).

Fruit: A 1-inch-diameter, prickly, two-valved burr enclosing a small, shiny brown nutlet. Burrs borne in conspicuous clusters.

Bark: Gray and smoothish when young, becoming darker and moderately fissured with age.

CULTURE

Soil: Prefers sandy, well-drained soil.
Exposure: Full sun to light shade.
Water: Does best on dry, well-drained sites.
Hardiness Zones: 5 to 9.
Life Span: Relatively short-lived; less than 50 years.

BEST FEATURES

Fall color. Fruit is an excellent wildlife food. Leaves resemble those of a chestnut tree. Resistant to the blight that has decimated populations of the American chestnut (*C. dentata*).

COMPANION PLANTS

Longleaf pine (*Pinus palustris*), bluejack, turkey, post, and Chapman oaks (*Quercus incana, Q. laevis, Q. stellata,* and *Q. chapmanii*), sourwood (*Oxydendrum arboreum*), silver bluestem (*Andropogon ternarius*), Adam's needle (*Yucca filamentosa*).

DISADVANTAGES

Burrs can be a nuisance and may require removal from manicured landscapes.

CULTIVARS

None, though a shrubby, broad-spreading form with horizontal branches is common.

SIMILAR AND RELATED SPECIES

In the same botanical family with, but not similar to, the oak trees.

Celtis laevigata

SEL-tis lee-vi-GAY-tuh

Sugarberry, Hackberry

Family: Celtidaceae
Large tree
Height: 60 to 80 feet
Spread: 30 to 50 feet

J. C. Putnam H.

LANDSCAPE USE

Works well as a specimen or shade tree and is a good choice for parking lots and roadsides. It is attractive to wildlife, including butterflies, songbirds, and especially yellow-bellied sapsucker woodpeckers.

FORM

A large, spreading tree with a rounded crown and stout, zigzag branches.

NATIVE RANGE

Floodplain forests and calcareous river swamps. Indiana and Virginia southward, throughout Florida, and west to Texas.

CHARACTERISTICS

Flowers: Yellowish green, small, and inconspicuous.

Leaves: Alternate, simple, 2–5 inches long, minutely toothed on the margins, light green during summer but turning yellow in the fall, somewhat wedge shaped in overall outline and tapering to a long, often curving point.

Fruit: Reddish orange to yellowish drupes that turn dark in the fall.

Bark: Gray; sometimes with warty outgrowths, mostly from injury by woodpeckers, but often nearly as smooth as that of American beech (*Fagus grandifolia*).

CULTURE

Soil: Does best in moist, rich situations, but adapts well to a variety of soils from acid to alkaline and is very drought tolerant.

Exposure: Part shade to full sun.

Water: Irrigate to keep soil moist, but not wet, until established. Will adapt to drier sites.

Hardiness Zones: 4 to 10.

Life Span: Moderately long-lived; probably not exceeding 150 years.

BEST FEATURES

A relatively fast-growing tree that is excellent for alkaline soils. Its attractive grayish, warty bark makes it an interesting, attractive, and easy-to-grow shade tree. It does well in urban and suburban situations, and although deciduous it maintains its charm and beauty during winter. Its appearance improves with age. Does very well on disturbed soils.

COMPANION PLANTS

Oaks (*Quercus* spp.), American beech (*Fagus grandifolia*), sweetgum (*Liquidambar styraciflua*), blue beech (*Carpinus caroliniana*), gumbo limbo (*Bursera simaruba*), satinleaf (*Chrysophyllum oliviforme*), pignut hickory (*Carya glabra*), winged elm (*Ulmus alata*), redbud (*Cercis canadensis*), American hophornbeam (*Ostrya virginiana*), beautyberry (*Callicarpa americana*), Cherokee bean (*Erythrina herbacea*), witch hazel (*Hamamelis virginiana*), yaupon (*Ilex vomitoria*), needle palm (*Rhapidophyllum hystrix*), blue-stem palmetto (*Sabal minor*).

DISADVANTAGES

Hackberry has a shallow root system that may prevent other plants from growing beneath it.

CULTIVARS

'All Seasons' hackberry is a selection of *C. laevigata* but is not used in Florida.

SIMILAR AND RELATED SPECIES

The dwarf or Georgia hackberry (*C. tenuifolia*), which occurs naturally in Florida in rich, shaded woodlands of the northern peninsula and panhandle, is a small tree that resembles a miniature hackberry.

Cephalanthus occidentalis

se-fuh-LAN-thus ahk-si-den-TAY-lis

Buttonbush

Family: Rubiaceae
Large shrub or small tree
Height: 6 to 20 feet
Spread: 8 to 12 feet

J.C. Putnam H.

LANDSCAPE USE

Best in naturalistic settings along the edges of ponds, lakes, and wetland depressions. May also be used along decks, patios, and outdoor sitting areas in moist, rich soil. May be pruned to produce a more densely foliated plant. A very good choice for restoration areas. Should be more often used to hide unsightly retention ponds, drainage swales, and canal banks.

FORM

Typically a large shrub with spreading branches and dark, shiny green leaves. The crowns of younger plants tend to be somewhat rounded and densely vegetated. Those of older plants are more irregular and spreading.

NATIVE RANGE

Swamps, marshes, and the edges of ponds, swamps, and lakes across the entire eastern United States south to southernmost Florida, west to southern Minnesota, Oklahoma, Arizona, and central California (where it is called western buttonbush).

CHARACTERISTICS

Flowers: A rounded, creamy white, 2-inch-wide, pincushion-like head appearing in large numbers in summer.

Leaves: Opposite or sometimes whorled in groups of three at a node, to about 7 inches long and 3 inches wide, dark, shiny green above, paler below.

Fruit: Hard, round, reddish brown, ball-like clusters. Fall, but persisting through the winter.

Bark: Grayish brown to dark brown or nearly black; fissured and ridged.

CULTURE

Soil: Occurs naturally in wet soils; roots will tolerate complete submersion in water. Adapts well to disturbed soils.

Exposure: Full sun to part shade.

Water: Does best in moist to wet sites with poor drainage. Typically requires moderate irrigation, especially in drier situations.

Hardiness Zones: 5 to 11.

Life Span: Moderately long-lived for a shrub; likely more than 50 years.

BEST FEATURES

Fragrant flowers borne in profusion and attractive to both bees and butterflies. Foliage is attractive to deer. Irregular form is excellent for naturalistic gardens and landscapes. Does very well in disturbed soils.

COMPANION PLANTS

Yellow anise (*Illicium parviflorum*), dog-hobble (*Leucothoe axillaris*), fetterbush (*Lyonia lucida*), dahoon (*Ilex cassine*), swamp fern (*Blechnum serrulatum*), southern shield fern (*Dryopteris ludoviciana*), loblolly pine (*Pinus taeda*), titi (*Cyrilla racemiflora*), scarlet hibiscus (*Hibiscus coccineus*), Virginia willow (*Itea virginica*), swamp dogwood (*Cornus foemina*), swamp tupelo (*Nyssa sylvatica* var. *biflora*), red maple (*Acer rubrum*), cypresses (*Taxodium* spp.), yellow canna (*Canna flaccida*).

DISADVANTAGES

Foliage sometimes appears tattered. Will colonize much of the watery edge if left unattended along the edges of lakes or ponds. Older specimens become somewhat scraggly and irregular, may require pruning to maintain a compact form, and may not be appropriate for more manicured landscapes.

ALLERGENIC AND TOXIC PROPERTIES

Has reportedly caused vomiting, paralysis, and spasms in horses.

SIMILAR AND RELATED SPECIES

Vegetatively similar to the closely related fevertree (*Pinckneya bracteata*), which displays beautiful pinkish flowers.

Cercis canadensis

SIR-sis ka-nuh-DEN-sis

Redbud

Family: Fabaceae or Leguminosae
Small tree
Height: 15 to 30 feet
Spread: 10 to 35 feet

LANDSCAPE USE

Excellent as a flowering tree in lawns and along roadsides, as a small shade or specimen tree, or to offer height in a shrub border. Especially attractive when planted in a small group and in naturalistic settings. Should be planted with flowering dogwood (*Cornus florida*) for a beautiful complement of flower colors.

FORM

A relatively short, attractive, deciduous tree with a spreading to rounded crown, heart-shaped leaves, and arresting spring flowers.

NATIVE RANGE

Mesic hammocks. Connecticut and Michigan, southward to central Florida, and west to north-central Texas.

CHARACTERISTICS

Flowers: Tiny, irregular, typical of the pea family; bright magenta, displayed in profusion. Borne on old wood, often from trunk and larger branches. February to March, prior to the new leaves.

Leaves: Alternate, simple, heart shaped, dull green, 3–6 inches long, with prominent venation.

Fruit: A flattened, green to light brown, 4-inch-long pod, turning dark throughout the fall and persisting into winter.

Bark: Grayish, thin, mostly smooth.

CULTURE

Soil: Prefers well-drained, acid or basic soil, but will tolerate occasional short-term flooding.

Exposure: Full sun to shade.

Water: Supplemental irrigation not required once established.

Hardiness Zones: 4 to 9.

Life Span: Moderate to fast growing and short-lived; probably less than 50 years.

BEST FEATURES

Redbud can be magnificent during its early spring flowering season when it is clothed with thousands of magenta to rosy-pink flowers. Also excellent as a small tree and for its yellowish leaves in the fall.

COMPANION PLANTS

Flowering dogwood (*Cornus florida*), serviceberry (*Amelanchier arborea*), wild plums (*Prunus* spp.), American beech (*Fagus grandifolia*), sweetgum (*Liquidambar styraciflua*), blue beech (*Carpinus caroliniana*), pignut hickory (*Carya glabra*), winged elm (*Ulmus alata*), American hophornbeam (*Ostrya virginiana*), beautyberry (*Callicarpa americana*), Cherokee bean (*Erythrina herbacea*), witch hazel (*Hamamelis virginiana*), yaupon (*Ilex vomitoria*), needle palm (*Rhapidophyllum hystrix*), blue-stem palmetto (*Sabal minor*).

DISADVANTAGES

Some homeowners and landscapers object to the persistent fruit that stays on the tree into the winter. Some specimens are especially subject to stem canker, wilt, and root rot.

CULTIVARS

Numerous cultivars and varieties have been selected for varying shades of flower color. None are widely used in Florida.

SIMILAR AND RELATED SPECIES

No related species in Florida are similar to the redbud.

Chamaecyparis thyoides

ka-mee-SI-puh-ris thy-OY-deez

Atlantic White Cedar

Family: Cupressaceae
Large tree
Height: 15 to 60 feet
Spread: 10 to 20 feet

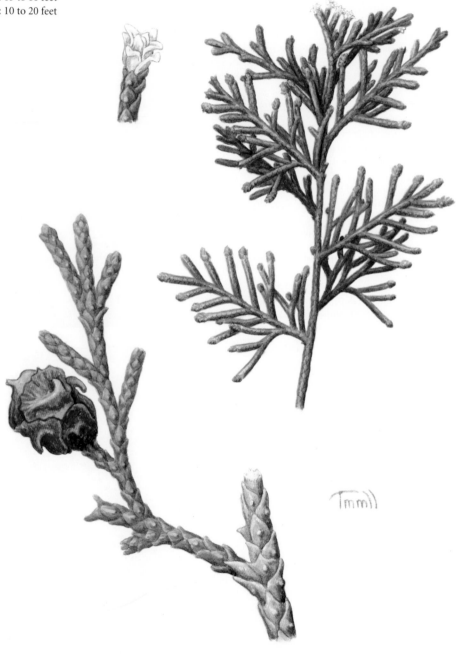

LANDSCAPE USE

Specimen tree. Also excellent for moist areas along bogs, swamps, and rivers.

FORM

An erect, typically straight-trunked tree with thin, reddish brown, irregularly ridged and furrowed bark, with a narrow, somewhat pyramidal crown and overlapping, dark green, scalelike leaves that are borne on laterally flattened branchlets.

NATIVE RANGE

Swamps, bogs, floodplains, and woodlands along spring runs. Eastern United States from Maine south to at least Lake County Florida, and west to Mississippi. Often found in pure stands.

CHARACTERISTICS

Leaves: Scalelike, dark green to bluish green, less than ¼ inch long, overlapping and pressed to the stem.
Fruit: A small, ¼-inch-diameter, bluish green cone.
Bark: Reddish brown to grayish; ridged, furrowed, and very attractive.

CULTURE

Soil: Prefers moist, sandy soils or shallow peat underlain by sand; may adapt to drier sites that lack hardwood competition.
Exposure: Full sun.
Water: Moist conditions are best.
Hardiness Zones: 4 to 8.
Life Span: To 100 years or more.

BEST FEATURES

The reddish brown, scaly, furrowed bark and evergreen, spraylike foliage are this species' most ornamental features.

COMPANION PLANTS

Red maple (*Acer rubrum*), cypresses (*Taxodium* spp.), black gum and tupelo (*Nyssa* spp.), Virginia willow (*Itea virginica*), laurel oak (*Quercus laurifolia*), swamp dogwood (*Cornus foemina*).

DISADVANTAGES

Will not tolerate competition from hardwoods.

CULTIVARS

More than 40 cultivars are reported. *C. thyoides* 'Okefenokee,' noted for rich green foliage, and *C. thyoides* 'Red Star,' which features a compact, dense, columnar crown, blue-green summer foliage, and purplish winter foliage, are available in Florida.

ALLERGENIC AND TOXIC PROPERTIES

Pollen known to be an airborne allergen.

SIMILAR AND RELATED SPECIES

Red cedar (*Juniperus virginiana*) is similar in some respects but has bluish, berrylike cones.

Chionanthus virginicus

ky-o-NAN-thus vir-JI-ni-kus

Fringetree

Family: Oleaceae
Small tree
Height: 15 to 30 feet
Spread: 8 to 20 feet

J.C. Putnam H.

LANDSCAPE USE

Normally used as a small specimen, flowering shrub, or small tree in yards, though it also performs quite well in naturalistic landscapes. May also be grouped in borders and along the foundations of buildings. A very good choice for showy roadside plantings. The fruit attracts birds.

FORM

A small, graceful, sometimes multitrunked, upright tree with a rounded crown and spreading lower branches. It is slow growing and sometimes retains a shrublike stature.

NATIVE RANGE

Wet hammocks, floodplain forests, and sandy uplands. An old and much-loved southern landscape plant ranging from Pennsylvania and New Jersey southward to northern Florida and west to Texas.

CHARACTERISTICS

Flowers: Showy clusters of delicate, creamy white, fragrant, fringelike or straplike petals borne in loose, dangling panicles. Early spring.

Leaves: Simple, opposite, elliptic in overall outline, 3–8 inches long.

Fruit: A blue drupe (green when immature) borne in pendent clusters. Summer and fall.

Bark: Grayish, slightly fissured.

CULTURE

Soil: Rich, moist to well-drained, acid soil with pH 5.5–6.5.

Exposure: Full sun for best flowering, but often occurs in nature in shady situations.

Water: Drought tolerant.

Hardiness Zones: 3 to 10. Pygmy fringetree (*C. pygmaeus*) is hardy in zones 5 to 10.

Life Span: Slow growing and moderately long-lived; well over 50 years.

BEST FEATURES

Most highly prized in spring for its conspicuous show of cream-colored flowers with fringelike petals, followed by dangling clusters of olivelike fruit. Other good features include its small size and drought tolerance. Among the most trouble-free small landscape trees.

COMPANION PLANTS

Red buckeye (*Aesculus pavia*), blue beech (*Carpinus caroliniana*), parsley haw (*Crataegus marshallii*), sugarberry (*Celtis laevigata*), summer haw (*Crataegus flava*), longleaf pine (*Pinus palustris*), pignut hickory (*Carya glabra*), Shumard oak (*Quercus shumardii*), sweetgum (*Liquidambar styraciflua*), basswood (*Tilia americana*), winged elm (*Ulmus alata*), American holly (*Ilex opaca*), American hophornbeam (*Ostrya virginiana*), beautyberry (*Callicarpa americana*), Cherokee bean (*Erythrina herbacea*), yaupon (*Ilex vomitoria*), needle palm (*Rhapidophyllum hystrix*), blue-stem palmetto (*Sabal minor*), redbud (*Cercis canadensis*), flowering dogwood (*Cornus florida*).

DISADVANTAGES

Somewhat nondescript during its nonflowering times and may go unnoticed. New leaves appear late in spring and drop early in fall. Large specimens are difficult to locate.

ALLERGENIC AND TOXIC PROPERTIES

Used medicinally, but overdoses can cause nausea, vomiting, severe headaches, weakness, and sore eyes.

SIMILAR AND RELATED SPECIES

Pygmy fringetree (*C. pygmaeus*), a closely related species

that is endemic to the central Florida scrub, is also used for landscaping. It is much smaller than *C. virginicus,* usually not exceeding about 12 feet tall, and has smaller but similar flowers. It occurs naturally in well-drained, deep sands but is quite hardy and has been used under cultivation as far north as Michigan and Delaware.

Chrysobalanus icaco

kri-so-BA-luh-nus i-KAH-ko

Cocoplum

Family: Chrysobalanaceae
Shrub or very small tree
Height: 10 to 30 feet
Spread: 10 to 20 feet

J. C. Putnam H.

LANDSCAPE USE
Will form dense hedges from the ground up in full sun and is excellent along property boundaries and for other situations where screening is desired.

FORM
A multitrunked, rounded to dome-shaped, densely foliated shrub of medium texture.

NATIVE RANGE
Coastal and tropical hammocks and edges in southernmost Florida and the West Indies.

CHARACTERISTICS
Flowers: Tiny, mostly inconspicuous, white, borne in spikes at the base of the leaves. Year-round.

Leaves: Alternate, rounded, leathery, shiny green, to about 3 inches long, twisted upward so as to appear to be borne on only one side of the branch.

Fruit: About 1½ inches in diameter. Purple to almost white, pulpy, edible, with an easily cracked nut with tasty meat. Year-round.

Bark: Brown.

CULTURE
Soil: Tolerant of a wide range of soils. The shrub form is salt tolerant.

Exposure: Full sun for best fruiting and dense vegetation. Forms a somewhat more thinly vegetated shrub in shady sites.

Water: Supplemental irrigation not required.

Hardiness Zones: 10 to 11.

Life Span: Moderate.

BEST FEATURES
Cocoplum is prized for its dense foliage, general hardiness, and edible fruit that can be made into jelly. It also provides very good cover and food for wildlife.

COMPANION PLANTS
Spicewood (*Calyptranthes pallens*), Jamaica caper (*Capparis cynophallophora*), Simpson's stopper (*Myrcianthes fragrans*), marlberry (*Ardisia escallonioides*), several of the stoppers (*Eugenia* spp.), Virginia willow (*Itea virginica*), leather fern (*Acrostichum danaeifolium*), wax myrtle (*Myrica cerifera*), beautyberry (*Callicarpa americana*), inkberry (*Ilex glabra*), staggerbushes (*Lyonia* spp.), eastern gamagrass (*Tripsacum dactyloides*), saw palmetto (*Serenoa repens*), muhly grass (*Muhlenbergia capillaris*), gopher apple (*Licania michauxii*).

CULTIVARS
At least two cocoplum cultivars are available. 'Red Tip' is an inland plant that is not salt tolerant. 'Horizontal' is a spreading form that may be used as a low, woody shrub that requires little or no pruning. Typical cocoplum will grow into a tree 20–30 feet tall.

SIMILAR AND RELATED SPECIES
Closely related to gopher apple (*Licania michauxii*), a low-growing ground cover that is found throughout Florida and is used as a landscape component in deep sand and poor soils.

Chrysophyllum oliviforme

kri-so-FI-lum ah-li-vi-FOR-mee

Satinleaf

Family: Sapotaceae
Small tree
Height: 15 to 30 feet
Spread: 10 to 30 feet

J.C. Putnam

LANDSCAPE USE

Lawn specimen, shrub border, accent, or in groups of three or more.

FORM

A small to medium-sized, graceful tree with fissured, roughened, grayish to reddish brown bark, slender, arching branches, and somewhat drooping leaves that are dark, shiny green above and rusty-coppery below.

NATIVE RANGE

Tropical hammocks of southernmost Florida and the West Indies.

CHARACTERISTICS

Flowers: Tiny, tubular, whitish, sweetly fragrant, with 5 petals. Year-round.

Leaves: Simple, alternate, oval, 4–6 inches long, dark, shiny green above, copper colored and satiny below.

Fruit: A 1-inch-long, oblong or elliptical, edible, purple berry similar in appearance to an olive. Spring.

Bark: Fissured, roughened, dark grayish brown to reddish brown.

CULTURE

Soil: Does best in slightly acid, fertile, organic soil; mildly salt tolerant.

Exposure: Full sun to shade; intolerant of freezing temperatures.

Water: Prefers rich, well-drained soils. May require watering until established.

Hardiness Zones: 10 to 11.

Life Span: Moderate.

BEST FEATURES

Prized most for the stark contrast between the shiny green upper surfaces and copper-colored lower surfaces of its leaves, which are especially attractive on breezy days. Good wildlife food.

COMPANION PLANTS

Gumbo limbo (*Bursera simaruba*), pigeon plum (*Coccoloba diversifolia*), marlberry (*Ardisia escallonioides*), spicewood (*Calyptranthes pallens*), cocoplum (*Chrysobalanus icaco*), Simpson's stopper (*Myrcianthes fragrans*), buttonwood (*Conocarpus erectus*), fiddlewood (*Citharexylum spinosum*), stoppers (*Eugenia* spp.), wild lime (*Zanthoxylum fagara*), Jamaica caper (*Capparis cynophallophora*), wild coffee (*Psychotria nervosa*), white indigoberry (*Randia aculeata*), Cherokee bean (*Erythrina herbacea*).

DISADVANTAGES

Brittle. Can be difficult to establish. Grows slowly.

SIMILAR AND RELATED SPECIES

At least one other, non-native, member of this genus is sometimes used in Florida, but it should be avoided in favor of the present species.

Citharexylum spinosum

si-thuh-REK-si-lum spy-NO-sum

Fiddlewood

Family: Verbenaceae
Large shrub or small tree
Height: 15 to 25 feet
Spread: To about 12 feet

J. C. Putnam H.

LANDSCAPE USE
Freestanding specimens in lawns, spaced along walkways, or as a street tree.

FORM
A single- to multi-stemmed evergreen shrub or small tree to about 36 feet tall, with square twigs and smooth brown bark.

NATIVE RANGE
Hammocks and pinelands. Southern Florida, the Florida Keys, and the West Indies.

CHARACTERISTICS
Flowers: White, tubular, sweetly fragrant, borne in long, showy, often pendent racemes; male and female flowers borne on separate plants. Year-round.

Leaves: Opposite, elliptical, shiny green above, paler below, 3–7 inches long.

Fruit: A rounded drupe, yellow at first, turning orange, then reddish brown, to about ½ inch in diameter. Year-round.

Bark: Light brown; smooth but sometimes becoming fissured with age.

CULTURE
Soil: Dry soils; both salt and drought tolerant once established.

Exposure: Sun to part shade.

Water: Supplemental irrigation not required.

Hardiness Zones: 10 to 11.

Life Span: Medium.

BEST FEATURES
Rugged and tolerant of poor conditions. Attractive, shiny green foliage. Fragrant flowers attract butterflies. Good wildlife food.

COMPANION PLANTS
Pigeon plum (*Coccoloba diversifolia*), gumbo limbo (*Bursera simaruba*), coontie (*Zamia pumila*), white indigoberry (*Randia aculeata*), mastic (*Sideroxylon foetidissimum*), marlberry (*Ardisia escallonioides*), spicewood (*Calyptranthes pallens*), cocoplum (*Chrysobalanus icaco*), Simpson's stopper (*Myrcianthes fragrans*), other stoppers (*Eugenia* spp.), saw palmetto (*Serenoa repens*).

DISADVANTAGES
Sometimes attacked by scales and caterpillars.

SIMILAR AND RELATED SPECIES
Fiddlewood is often found listed under the botanical name *Citharexylum fruticosum*.

Cladium jamaicense

KLAY-dee-um juh-may-KEN-see

Sawgrass

Family: Cyperaceae
Ground cover
Height: 3 to 10 feet
Spread: Forms large colonies by underground stems

Serves best along the edges of swamps, marshes, and shores; especially suitable to coastal situations.

FORM
A robust, grasslike, perennial sedge with large, stout, scaly runners and long, tapered leaves that have fine, sawlike teeth along their margins and midribs.

NATIVE RANGE
Swamps, marshes, and shores, mostly near the coast; the dominant plant of Everglades marshes. Virginia, southward to and throughout Florida, west to Texas; also West Indies and Mexico.

CHARACTERISTICS
Flowers: Tiny, but borne in a large, conspicuous, compound cyme that often stands far above the leaves when flowering and fruiting. Year-round.
Leaves: To about 1½ inches wide at the base, tapering to a narrow tip; lined along the margins and midrib with sharp, fine, sawlike teeth.
Fruit: A tiny, brownish, inconspicuous achene.

CULTURE
Soil: Wet to saturated, fertile soils.
Exposure: Full sun.
Water: Tolerates inundation.
Hardiness Zones: 8 to 10.
Life Span: Perennial.

BEST FEATURES
Tolerant of wet situations. Can cover large areas through spreading. Larval food source for a variety of butterflies and skippers.

COMPANION PLANTS
Water hyssop (*Bacopa monnieri*), yellow canna (*Canna flaccida*), horsetail (*Equisetum hyemale*), cinnamon and royal ferns (*Osmunda cinnamomea* and *O. regalis*), buttonbush (*Cephalanthus occidentalis*), scarlet hibiscus (*Hibiscus coccineus*), string lily (*Crinum americanum*), prairie blue flag (*Iris hexagona*), wild rice (*Zizania aquatica*).

DISADVANTAGES
Should not be planted in areas with high foot traffic due to sawlike blades.

SIMILAR AND RELATED SPECIES
Swamp sawgrass (*C. mariscoides*) occurs rarely in coastal counties of the central and western panhandle.

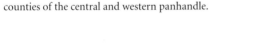

Clethra alnifolia

KLE-thruh ahl-ni-FO-lee-uh

Summersweet

Family: Clethraceae
Shrub
Height: 3 to 10 feet
Spread: 2 to 5 feet

LANDSCAPE USE

Excellent for naturalistic settings, as well as for shrub borders, shrub beds, hedges, and screening for patios and decks. Particularly useful where summer flowering is preferred.

FORM

An erect, deciduous shrub with coarse, toothed leaves and showy summer flower clusters.

NATIVE RANGE

Pinelands and coastal scrub. Throughout the eastern United States, from Maine southward to about central peninsular Florida and west to coastal Texas.

CHARACTERISTICS

Flowers: White, fragrant, borne in conspicuous, erect racemes at the tips of branches. Throughout the summer.

Leaves: Alternate, with conspicuous venation, toothed along the margins, somewhat coarse to the touch, 2–4 inches long.

Fruit: A tiny, hard, brown capsule.

Bark: Brown.

CULTURE

Soil: Prefers moist, acid soil, but will adapt to drier, less acid sites; slightly tolerant of salt spray.

Exposure: Full sun to shade.

Water: Moist conditions produce the best results.

Hardiness Zones: 3 to 9.

Life Span: Moderate.

BEST FEATURES

Fragrant white to pinkish flowers are showy, provide a sweet aroma, and are attractive to bees and butterflies. Shade tolerance, summer flowering, and erect form are other important features. Displays colorful fall foliage.

COMPANION PLANTS

Sweetbay (*Magnolia virginiana*), fetterbush (*Lyonia lucida*), inkberry (*Ilex glabra*), red maple (*Acer rubrum*), Walter's viburnum (*Viburnum obovatum*), native azaleas (*Rhododendron* spp.), highbush blueberries (*Vaccinium* spp.), buttonbush (*Cephalanthus occidentalis*), titi (*Cyrilla racemiflora*), Virginia willow (*Itea virginica*), yaupon (*Ilex vomitoria*), royal fern (*Osmunda regalis*).

DISADVANTAGES

Loses its leaves in winter but has an attractive winter form.

CULTIVARS

At least 15 cultivars are known, of which 'Hummingbird,' 'Anne Bidwell,' 'Cottondale,' 'Rosea,' and 'Ruby Spice' are available in Florida.

SIMILAR AND RELATED SPECIES

Summersweet is the only member of its family in Florida, but it is similar in many respects to, and sometimes confused with, Virginia willow (*Itea virginica*).

Coccoloba diversifolia

kah-ko-LO-buh dy-vir-si-FO-lee-uh

Pigeon Plum

Family: Polygonaceae
Medium-sized tree
Height: Ordinarily 30 to 40 feet; potentially to 60 feet
Spread: 10 to 20 feet

J. C. Putnam H.

LANDSCAPE USE

Massed along fences, roadsides, slopes, and shorelines, or to provide shade for patios. Compact crown makes it especially good for backyards or narrow openings between buildings and houses. Well suited for beautifying parking lots, highway medians, and road and powerline rights-of-way.

FORM

An erect, densely foliated, evergreen shrub or tree with ascending branches, a typically narrow, columnar outline, and mottled bark.

NATIVE RANGE

Subtropical hammocks. South-central to southernmost Florida and the West Indies.

CHARACTERISTICS

Flowers: Greenish white, individually tiny, but borne in conspicuous, elongated spikes. Mostly summer.
Leaves: Alternate, leathery, dark green and curled under along the edges, quite variable in size depending on suckering and shade, 4–12 inches long.
Fruit: Purple, juicy, acidic, edible, about ½ inch in diameter, borne in narrow, elongated clusters. Mostly fall.
Bark: Gray when young, becoming mottled, multicolored, and peeling in large plates with age.

CULTURE

Soil: Tolerates a wide range of soils but does best in sandy, organic soils; good salt tolerance.
Exposure: Full sun to part shade.
Water: Supplemental irrigation typically not required after becoming established.
Hardiness Zones: 10 to 11.
Life Span: Fast growing, but relatively long-lived.

BEST FEATURES

The upright, narrow form; attractive mottled, peeling bark; general hardiness; and prolific fruit, which is consumed by birds and other wildlife, make this an excellent landscape tree.

COMPANION PLANTS

Satinleaf (*Chrysophyllum oliviforme*), marlberry (*Ardisia escallonioides*), stoppers (*Eugenia* spp.), beautyberry (*Callicarpa americana*), gumbo limbo (*Bursera simaruba*), coontie (*Zamia pumila*), white indigoberry (*Randia aculeata*), mastic (*Sideroxylon foetidissimum*), spicewood (*Calyptranthes pallens*), cocoplum (*Chrysobalanus icaco*), Simpson's stopper (*Myrcianthes fragrans*), saw palmetto (*Serenoa repens*).

DISADVANTAGES

Sometimes attacked by chewing insects, especially on new growth.

SIMILAR AND RELATED SPECIES

Seagrape (*C. uvifera*) is a closely related and much-used landscape plant in southern Florida.

Coccoloba uvifera

kah-ko-LO-buh yew-VI-fe-ruh

Seagrape

Family: Polygonaceae
Large shrub or tree
Height: 3 to 35 feet
Spread: 10 to 50 feet

LANDSCAPE USE

Excellent as a large hedge, as a specimen shrub or tree, for soil stabilization, as an accent along entrances and roadsides, or near seashores and other salt-rich situations.

FORM

A single- to multistemmed, widely branching shrub or medium-sized tree with a broad, rounded crown, coarse limbs, and attractive mottled bark.

NATIVE RANGE

Edges of beaches, coastal hammocks. South-central and southern Florida, and West Indies.

CHARACTERISTICS

Flowers: Tiny, white to yellowish white, borne in 8- to 12-inch-long spikes. Year-round.

Leaves: Large, orbicular, to about 8 inches wide, leathery, dark shiny green above with reddish central and major lateral veins.

Fruit: Green when young but turning purplish, edible, to about 1 inch diameter, borne in conspicuous, 8- to 12-inch-long spikes. Year-round.

Bark: Mottled and peeling; various shades of brown.

CULTURE

Soil: Poor, sandy soils, extremely salt tolerant.

Exposure: Full sun to part shade.

Water: Irrigation not required, though irrigated plants tend to grow more rapidly.

Hardiness Zones: 9 to 11.

Life Span: Moderately long.

BEST FEATURES

The overall character, tropical look, general hardiness, and salt tolerance are the best features of this species. Fruit is useful to larger wildlife.

COMPANION PLANTS

Capers (*Capparis* spp.), necklace pod (*Sophora tomentosa*), stoppers (*Eugenia* spp.), Cherokee bean (*Erythrina herbacea*), white indigoberry (*Randia aculeata*), buttonwood (*Conocarpus erectus*), lancewood (*Ocotea coriacea*), myrtle-of-the-river (*Calyptranthes zuzygium*), fiddlewood (*Citharexylum spinosum*), marlberry (*Ardisia escallonioides*), myrsine (*Rapanea punctata*), maidenbush (*Savia bahamensis*).

DISADVANTAGES

The large leaves fall continuously, decay slowly, and require removal in formal landscapes.

SIMILAR AND RELATED SPECIES

Pigeon plum (*C. diversifolia*) is a close relative.

Coccothrinax argentata

kah-ko-THRY-naks ar-jen-TAY-tuh

Silver Palm

Family: Arecaceae or Palmae
Small tree or single-stemmed shrub
Height: 5 to 20 feet
Spread: 5 feet

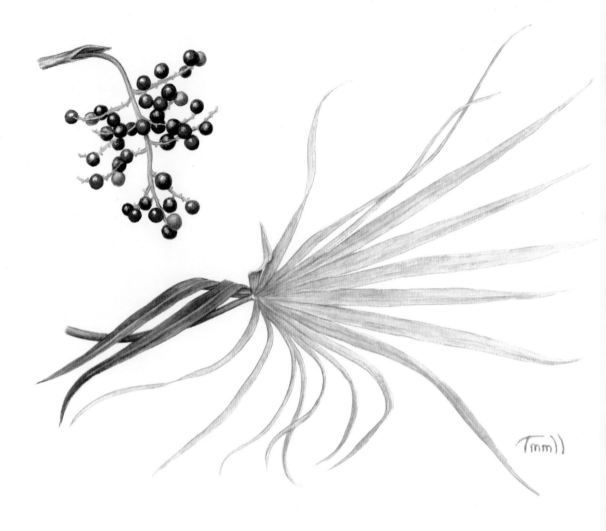

LANDSCAPE USE

An excellent specimen for its attractive leaves, which are green above and silvery below. May be used along property lines, in corners, or in other situations where a narrow, erect form is needed.

FORM

A short, erect tree with fan-shaped leaves and a smooth, grayish trunk.

NATIVE RANGE

Rocky pinelands and inland edges of sandy beaches. Southernmost Florida, from Palm Beach County southward; also West Indies.

CHARACTERISTICS

Flowers: Tiny, white, fragrant, borne in large, showy clusters. Spring.
Leaves: Fan shaped, about 2 feet wide, on 3-foot stalks; upper surface shiny green, lower silvery and very attractive.
Fruit: Black, ¼-inch-diameter, rounded.
Bark: Smooth, grayish, and very attractive.

CULTURE

Soil: Dry, well-drained soils of rocklands.
Exposure: Full sun.
Water: Prefers well-drained situations.
Hardiness Zones: 10 to 11.
Life Span: Slow growing and moderately long-lived; over 50 years.

BEST FEATURES

Attractive, delicate form, slow growth, and showy flower clusters make this a desirable small tree or shrub. Tolerates wind, drought, salt spray, and light freezes. The fruit is useful to wildlife.

COMPANION PLANTS

Cabbage palm (*Sabal palmetto*), southern slash pine (*Pinus elliottii* var. *densa*), white indigoberry (*Randia aculeata*), saw palmetto (*Serenoa repens*), broomsedge (*Andropogon virginicus*), lopsided Indiangrass (*Sorghastrum secundum*), coontie (*Zamia pumila*).

DISADVANTAGES

Old leaves require minor pruning.

CULTIVARS

Cultivars with small leaves are reported but are not readily available from native plant nurseries.

SIMILAR AND RELATED SPECIES

Perhaps most similar to young specimens of the brittle thatch palm (*Thrinax morrisii*), which also has leaves with silvery undersides.

Conocarpus erectus

ko-no-KAR-pus e-REK-tus

Buttonwood

Family: Combretaceae
Small tree
Height: 35 to 50 feet
Spread: 15 to 40 feet

J.C. Putnam H.

LANDSCAPE USE

Specimen tree, tree borders, oceanfront landscapes, shoreline plantings. Excellent as a single-trunked tree for road and highway medians.

FORM

An erect tree with a spreading, irregularly branched crown and a brown, roughened, often gnarled and twisted trunk.

NATIVE RANGE

Edges of tidal watercourses, near the mangrove zone, south-central to southernmost Florida and the West Indies.

CHARACTERISTICS

Flowers: Tiny, greenish, borne in dense, rounded clusters. Year-round; perhaps more prevalent during summer.

Leaves: Alternate, leathery, about 4 inches long, slimly elliptic in outline, pointed at the tip.

Fruit: Round, brown, buttonlike knobby balls borne in conelike collections. Year-round.

Bark: Brownish; flaking and shredding.

CULTURE

Soil: Poor, dry sands as well as wet, saline situations; very salt tolerant.

Exposure: Full sun to some shade.

Water: Irrigation not required except on very dry sites. Drought tolerant.

Hardiness Zones: 10 to 11.

Life Span: Long-lived.

BEST FEATURES

Salt and drought tolerant. Fast growing once established. Hardy at the edges of saline wetlands as well as dry sites with poor soil. Silver buttonwood, described below, is most valued for its silvery foliage.

COMPANION PLANTS

Seagrape (*Coccoloba uvifera*), necklace pod (*Sophora tomentosa*), coontie (*Zamia pumila*), white indigoberry (*Randia aculeata*), capers (*Capparis* spp.), stoppers (*Eugenia* spp.), Cherokee bean (*Erythrina herbacea*), lancewood (*Ocotea coriacea*), myrtle-of-the-river (*Calyptranthes zuzygium*), spicewood (*Calyptranthes pallens*), fiddlewood (*Citharexylum spinosum*), marlberry (*Ardisia escallonioides*), myrsine (*Rapanea punctata*), maidenbush (*Savia bahamensis*), saw palmetto (*Serenoa repens*).

DISADVANTAGES

Subject to scales and molds.

CULTIVARS

Two cultivars, including 'Momba' and 'Card Sound,' are available; see below, however.

SIMILAR AND RELATED SPECIES

Silver buttonwood (*C. erectus* var. *sericeus*) is a spreading, low-branching shrub or small tree usually not exceeding about 20 feet in height. This variety has grayish or silvery leaves that shimmer in the sun and wind. In addition to the uses listed above for green buttonwood, silver buttonwood may also be used as a shrub.

Conradina spp.

kahn-ruh-DY-nuh (but often pronounced kahn-ruh-DEE-nuh)

Scrub Mints

Family: Lamiaceae or Labiatae
Low shrub
Height: 2 to 5 feet
Spread: 2 to 4 feet

LANDSCAPE USE

Used as low ground-cover shrubs in sandy soils under full sun. Excellent for mixed herb and wildflower gardens.

FORM

Low, dense, bushy shrubs of the mint family with mostly needlelike, aromatic leaves and lavender to whitish, 2-lipped, aromatic flowers.

NATIVE RANGE

Scrub, sandhills, dunes, and sandy oak woodlands. Wild rosemary (*C. canescens*) occurs throughout northern Florida, southward to the south-central peninsula. Etonia rosemary (*C. etonia*) is limited in nature to north-central Florida but is cultivated more widely. Large-flowered rosemary (*C. grandiflora*) occurs along the eastern coast of central peninsular Florida.

CHARACTERISTICS

Flowers: Showy, 2-lipped, lavender to white or purplish, ½ to 1 inch long. Year-round.
Leaves: Needlelike, less than 1 inch long, grayish green, aromatic.
Fruit: Tiny, dry nutlets.
Bark: Thin and grayish.

CULTURE

Soil: Dry, sandy, well-drained, mostly neutral soils.
Exposure: Full sun.
Water: Prefers well-drained situations. May require supplemental irrigation until established.
Hardiness Zones: 8 to 9.
Life Span: More than 50 years if kept free from shading competition.

BEST FEATURES

Drought tolerant. Performs well in sandy, nutrient-poor soils. Profuse flowering over an extended period. Aromatic flowers and foliage. A good choice to replace non-native, low-growing junipers.

COMPANION PLANTS

Gopher apple (*Licania michauxii*), lopsided Indiangrass (*Sorghastrum secundum*), butterfly weed (*Asclepias tuberosa*), coral honeysuckle (*Lonicera sempervirens*), Chapman and myrtle oaks (*Quercus chapmanii* and *Q. myrtifolia*), calaminthas (*Calamintha* spp.), saw palmetto (*Serenoa repens*), coontie (*Zamia pumila*), staggerbushes (*Lyonia* spp.).

SIMILAR AND RELATED SPECIES

The endangered Apalachicola rosemary (*C. glabra*) occurs in Florida on sandhills in the central panhandle. Three lavender-flowered species of calamintha (*Calamintha* spp.) also occur in Florida and are sometimes confused with the several species of rosemary.

Cordia sebestena

KOR-dee-uh se-BES-tuh-nuh

Geiger Tree

Family: Boraginaceae
Small tree
Height: 10 to 30 feet
Spread: 10 to 15 feet

LANDSCAPE USE

Well suited as a freestanding specimen. Also useful along streets and avenues. Recommended for coastal settings.

FORM

An erect, irregularly branched small tree with a typically crooked trunk having great character, a dense, rounded crown of large, coarse leaves, and showy orange flowers.

NATIVE RANGE

Coastal hammocks. Southernmost Florida, Florida Keys, and the West Indies.

CHARACTERISTICS

Flowers: Bright orange to orange-red, funnel shaped, 1–2 inches long, borne in conspicuous, showy, open clusters.

Leaves: Coarse, heart shaped, 4–6 inches long, dark green, hairy.

Fruit: A white, egg-shaped drupe, 1–1½ inches long.

Bark: Dark; roughish.

CULTURE

Soil: Tolerant of sandy, alkaline soils, marl, and limestone.

Exposure: Full sun to part shade. Tolerant of salt and wind.

Water: Drought tolerant. Moderate watering improves performance.

Hardiness Zones: 10 to 11.

Life Span: 50 years or more.

BEST FEATURES

One of Florida's most colorful native flowering trees. Flowers are attractive to hummingbirds.

COMPANION PLANTS

Silver palm (*Coccothrinax argentata*), thatch palms (*Thrinax* spp.), long-stalked stopper (*Mosiera longipes*), white indigoberry (*Randia aculeata*), broomsedges (*Andrópogon* spp.), coontie (*Zamia pumila*).

DISADVANTAGES

Foliage is attacked by Geiger beetles, which chew the leaves, making them somewhat ragged, but cause no permanent harm to the plant. The beetles are colorful and attractive.

SIMILAR AND RELATED SPECIES

Some authorities believe that this species is not native to Florida. Two other native *Cordia* species occur in Florida. Bloodberry (*C. globosa*), which has small white flowers borne in small clusters, is also used in landscaping.

Coreopsis spp.

ko-ree-OP-sis

Tickseeds

Family: Asteraceae or Compositae
Wildflowers
Height: 1 to 3 feet
Spread: Spreads by self-sown seed

LANDSCAPE USE

The many species of *Coreopsis* are often-used components of mixed wildflower and butterfly gardens and are excellent for sunny roadsides, highway medians, and powerline easements. *C. leavenworthii* is especially good for roadsides.

FORM

Herbaceous wildflowers with showy, daisylike heads of bright yellow flowers (or lavender flowers, in *C. nudata*).

NATIVE RANGE

Disturbed sites, flatwoods, and sandhills. Two species are commonly available in Florida, both endemic to the state. Florida tickseed (*C. floridana*) occurs in wet flatwoods in the central panhandle as well as in the central and southern peninsula. Leavenworth's tickseed (*C. leavenworthii*) is found in flatwoods and disturbed areas throughout the state.

CHARACTERISTICS

Flowers: 1- to 2-inch-diameter heads composed of dark disk flowers and yellow ray flowers. Ray flowers typically with lobed apices. Year-round (primarily fall and winter for *C. floridana*).
Leaves: Basal and lowermost leaves with expanded blades; upper leaves narrow, sometimes divided (in *C. leavenworthii*), and few in number.
Fruit: A small, dry, inconspicuous achene.

CULTURE

Soil: Moist, acid soils.
Exposure: Full sun.
Water: The two species treated here prefer moist conditions.
Hardiness Zones: 8 to 11.
Life Span: Annual or short-lived perennials; reproducing by self-sown seed.

BEST FEATURES

Excellent for sunny, mixed-species butterfly gardens, roadsides, and highway medians.

COMPANION PLANTS

Virginia creeper (*Parthenocissus quinquefolia*), lopsided Indiangrass (*Sorghastrum secundum*), deer tongues (*Carphephorus* spp.), blazing stars (*Liatris* spp.), black-eyed Susans (*Rudbeckia* spp.), goldenrods (*Solidago* spp.), St. John's–worts (*Hypericum* spp.), broomsedge (*Andropogon virginicus*).

CULTIVARS

Numerous cultivars and hybrids of other *Coreopsis* species are available in the trade but are generally not available from native plant nurseries in Florida. Care should be taken to ensure that those used in the garden derive from native species.

SIMILAR AND RELATED SPECIES

At least 11 species of *Coreopsis* are native to Florida.

Cornus florida

KOR-nus FLO-ri-duh

Flowering Dogwood

Family: Cornaceae
Small tree
Height: 15 to 40 feet
Spread: 20 to 40 feet

J.C. Putnam H.

LANDSCAPE USE

An often-used spring-flowering street tree, specimen tree in yards and commercial landscapes, or background tree. Should be more widely used in street plantings. Very showy, once established.

FORM

An erect, low-branching, deciduous tree with a relatively open, spreading, densely vegetated crown and blocky bark.

NATIVE RANGE

Hammocks and upland woods. Throughout the eastern United States, from about Massachusetts southward to central Florida, west to Illinois, Oklahoma, and Texas.

CHARACTERISTICS

Flowers: Small, yellowish, borne in dense clusters above 4 large white bracts that are often mistaken for petals. Spring.
Leaves: Opposite, oval, 3–6 inches long, soft green, turning reddish in fall.
Fruit: Bright red, egg-shaped, showy, borne in conspicuous clusters. Attractive to birds. Fall.
Bark: Gray; blocky and broken into attractive small, grayish to blackish, platelike squares.

CULTURE

Soil: Well-drained, moist, acid soils with pH 5.5–6.5. Intolerant of over-fertilization and poorly drained sites with heavy soil.
Exposure: Full sun to part shade.
Water: Irrigation usually not required once established in favorable conditions. Roots are shallow and subject to stress during droughts. Should be heavily mulched with oak leaves or pine straw. Do not use cypress mulch.
Hardiness Zones: 5 to 9.
Life Span: Moderately long. Trees to 125 years are known, but cultivated specimens may be shorter lived.

BEST FEATURES

One of northern Florida's most attractive and well-loved trees. Valued for its delicate form, profuse spring flowering, attractive bark and foliage, and bright red clusters of fall fruit. Fruit attractive to wildlife, especially birds. A showy indicator of spring.

COMPANION PLANTS

Redbud (*Cercis canadensis*), fringetree (*Chionanthus virginicus*), American holly (*Ilex opaca*), sweetshrub (*Calycanthus floridus*), blueberries (*Vaccinium* spp.), black gum (*Nyssa sylvatica*), yaupon (*Ilex vomitoria*), red buckeye (*Aesculus pavia*), flatwoods plum (*Prunus umbellata*), wild olive (*Osmanthus americanus*), American hophornbeam (*Ostrya virginiana*), witch hazel (*Hamamelis virginiana*), mountain laurel (*Kalmia latifolia*), native azaleas (*Rhododendron* spp.), beautyberry (*Callicarpa americana*).

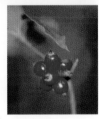

DISADVANTAGES

Susceptible to borers, root rot, petal and leaf spots, and leaf blight. Dogwood anthracnose has been reported in more northern areas but seems unable to survive Florida's hot summers. Subject to drought stress, and may struggle in roadside applications unless afforded watering and maintenance.

CULTIVARS

Nearly 100 cultivars, with flower colors ranging from white to pink, have been developed across the dogwood's range and are sometimes seen in Florida.

SIMILAR AND RELATED SPECIES

Several additional species of dogwood occur naturally in Florida and are available to landscapers, including pagoda dogwood (*C. alternifolia*), roughleaf dogwood (*C. asperifolia*), and swamp dogwood (*C. foemina,* including *C. stricta*).

Cornus foemina

KOR-nus FE-mi-nuh

Swamp Dogwood

Family: Cornaceae
Shrub or small tree
Height: 10 to 25 feet
Spread: 10 to 15 feet

LANDSCAPE USE

Used as a container, street, or yard tree, as a shrub along rivers, streams, and other wet areas, or to beautify retention ponds, drainage swales, and canal banks.

FORM

A multitrunked, deciduous shrub or small tree with opposite leaves and a spreading form.

NATIVE RANGE

Stream and marsh banks, cypress swamps, floodplains, low wet woodlands. Virginia and Missouri southward, nearly throughout Florida, west to Texas.

CHARACTERISTICS

Flowers: Small, bright white, borne in dense, flat-topped, showy, 2-inch-wide clusters at the ends of branches, in some respects quite similar to the flowers of *Viburnum*. Spring.

Leaves: Opposite, 2–4 inches long, mostly lance shaped to elliptic in outline.

Fruit: Branched clusters of bluish, ¼-inch-diameter drupes, appearing mostly summer to early fall.

Bark: Gray to brownish gray, with a knitted or plated appearance.

CULTURE

Soil: Moist to inundated, fertile, moderately acid soils.

Exposure: Full sun to shade.

Water: Prefers wet conditions, but will adapt to moist sites.

Hardiness Zones: 6 to 10.

Life Span: Relatively short-lived; probably less than 50 years.

BEST FEATURES

Showy white flower clusters. Fruit is attractive to birds. Tolerance of hydric conditions.

COMPANION PLANTS

Red maple (*Acer rubrum*), water hickory (*Carya aquatica*), sugarberry (*Celtis laevigata*), sweetbay (*Magnolia virginiana*), laurel oak (*Quercus laurifolia*), American elm (*Ulmus americana*), Simpson's stopper (*Myrcianthes fragrans*), strangler fig (*Ficus aurea*), swamp bay (*Persea palustris*), royal palm (*Roystonea regia*), swamp fern (*Blechnum serrulatum*), firebush (*Hamelia patens*).

DISADVANTAGES

Relatively short-lived.

CULTIVARS

A few selections have been made, but these are not widely available in Florida.

SIMILAR AND RELATED SPECIES

Roughleaf dogwood (*C. asperifolia*) and silky dogwood (*C. amomum*) are similar, and both occur in Florida. Roughleaf dogwood has rough leaves and occurs in well-drained hammocks. Silky dogwood occurs sparingly in wetlands of the central and western panhandle.

Crataegus flava

kruh-TEE-gus FLAY-vuh

Summer Haw

Family: Rosaceae
Small tree
Height: 3 to 20 feet
Spread: 3 to 8 feet

J.C. Putnam H.

LANDSCAPE USE

As a group, the haws can be used as specimen plants, large shrubs in naturalistic landscapes, and to provide cover for nesting birds. A very good choice for highway plantings, especially in northern Florida and the western panhandle. Also does well in other difficult situations, such as to beautify parking lots.

FORM

An erect, densely foliated, deciduous shrub or small tree with a somewhat crooked trunk, rounded crown of thorny branches, and grayish bark. Forms derived from the Florida panhandle (sometimes called *C. lacrimata*) often display "weeping" branches.

NATIVE RANGE

Most species of *Crataegus* that occur in Florida are confined to the northern peninsula and panhandle. These and numerous other species occur across the eastern United States.

CHARACTERISTICS

Flowers: Showy, fragrant, white with greenish yellow anthers, about 1 inch wide, appearing in profusion. Spring.
Leaves: Alternate, simple, 1–2 inches long, widest above the middle, with toothed margins.
Fruit: A red pome, ⅝ inch in diameter and borne in clusters on long stalks. Attractive to songbirds. Summer.
Bark: Medium to light gray; fissured and roughened.

CULTURE

Soil: Dry, well-drained, sandy soils.
Exposure: Prefers full sun, but will tolerate light shade.
Water: Supplemental irrigation not required after becoming established.
Hardiness Zones: 6 to 9.
Life Span: Hardy and at least moderately long-lived, likely reaching an age of 50 to 100 years.

BEST FEATURES

Valued for its profuse spring flowering, dense, soft green foliage, often "weeping" habit, and hardiness in dry sands.

COMPANION PLANTS

Yaupon (*Ilex vomitoria*), lowbush blueberries (*Vaccinium* spp.), pignut hickory (*Carya glabra*), sparkleberry (*Vaccinium arboreum*), silver bluestem (*Andropogon ternarius*), myrtle oak (*Quercus myrtifolia*), rusty lyonia (*Lyonia ferruginea*), Chickasaw plum (*Prunus angustifolia*), gopher apple (*Licania michauxii*), lopsided Indiangrass (*Sorghastrum secundum*), Adam's needle (*Yucca filamentosa*), Carolina jessamine (*Gelsemium sempervirens*), coral honeysuckle (*Lonicera sempervirens*), redbud (*Cercis canadensis*), flowering dogwood (*Cornus florida*), fringetrees (*Chionanthus* spp.).

DISADVANTAGES

Many haws bear sharp thorns on the branches and/or trunks. Cedar-apple rust may also pose a problem in some localities.

CULTIVARS

There are numerous cultivars and natural forms and varieties of haws across eastern North America. In the past, more than 1,200 species have been recognized, though the actual number of species may be closer to 100.

SIMILAR AND RELATED SPECIES

As many as ten species of *Crataegus* are listed as occurring in Florida, depending upon the authority cited. Two native species, besides summer haw, are available in the trade in Florida. May haw (*C. aestivalis*) is a wetland plant that blooms prolifically in spring and is adaptable to upland, average soils. Cockspur haw (*C. crus-galli*) is an upland plant that prefers alkaline soils.

Crinum americanum

KRY-num uh-me-ri-KAY-num

String Lily

Family: Amaryllidaceae
Wildflower, ground cover
Height: 2 to 3 feet
Spread: 2 to 3 feet; spreads into large patches by self-sown seed

LANDSCAPE USE

Excellent for wetland edges and marshes, including retention ponds, drainage swales, and canal banks.

FORM

A dark green, perennial herb with conspicuous, straplike leaves, showy white flowers, and a succulent bulb.

NATIVE RANGE

Swamps, marshes, stream shores, wet hammocks. Coastal Plain of Georgia, throughout Florida, west along the coast to east Texas.

CHARACTERISTICS

Flowers: Showy bright white, with 6 straplike, 5-inch-long petals and conspicuous stamens. Spring and summer.

Leaves: Straplike, dark green, 1–2 feet long, and arising from a succulent bulb.

Fruit: A thin-walled capsule containing large, fleshy seeds.

CULTURE

Soil: Prefers rich, wet soils.

Exposure: Sun to part shade; often found in very shaded river swamps.

Water: Prefers wet conditions.

Hardiness Zones: 8 to 10.

Life Span: Perennial.

BEST FEATURES

Dark green leaves. Showy white flowers. Tolerant of wet conditions.

COMPANION PLANTS

Swamp dogwood (*Cornus foemina*), red maple (*Acer rubrum*), climbing aster (*Symphyotrichum carolinianum*), royal and cinnamon ferns (*Osmunda regalis* and *O. cinnamomea*), sweetbay (*Magnolia virginiana*), laurel oak (*Quercus laurifolia*), American elm (*Ulmus americana*), Simpson's stopper (*Myrcianthes fragrans*), strangler fig (*Ficus aurea*), swamp bay (*Persea palustris*), royal palm (*Roystonea regia*), swamp fern (*Blechnum serrulatum*), wood ferns (*Thelypteris* spp.), sword ferns (*Nephrolepis* spp.), firebush (*Hamelia patens*), eastern gamagrass (*Tripsacum dactyloides*).

SIMILAR AND RELATED SPECIES

Similar in habitat and general appearance to the spider lilies (*Hymenocallis* spp.), which are also used as native landscape plants. Differing by the flower lacking the central cup (corona-like tube) that is characteristic of spider lilies.

Cyrilla racemiflora

sy-RI-luh ray-see-mi-FLO-ruh

Titi

Family: Cyrillaceae
Large shrub or small tree
Height: 10 to 30 feet
Spread: 6 to 15 feet

J.C. Putnam H.

LANDSCAPE USE
An excellent shrub along watercourses or in wet, acid soils, particularly in naturalistic landscapes. Also makes an effective hedge. A very good choice for moist roadsides and for beautifying the edges of retention ponds.

FORM
An erect, densely foliated shrub or small tree with a short, sometimes crooked and gnarly trunk and an irregular, spreading crown of twisted branches.

NATIVE RANGE
Swamps, bayheads, and streams. Southeastern Coastal Plain from about Virginia, southward to south-central Florida, and west to Texas.

CHARACTERISTICS
Flowers: White, individually small but borne in conspicuous clusters of 3- to 6-inch-long, showy racemes. Spring to early summer.
Leaves: Shiny green, variable in size from plant to plant, some plants having very small leaves not exceeding about 2 inches in length, others with leaves 3–4 inches long.
Fruit: Small, brownish capsules borne in conspicuous racemes. Summer, but persisting into the winter.
Bark: Smooth to somewhat peeling; tan.

CULTURE
Soil: Prefers poorly drained, acid soils, but will adapt to dry situations and a wide range of soils.
Exposure: Full sun to part shade.
Water: May require irrigation until established, but will adapt to drier conditions.
Hardiness Zones: 6 to 10.
Life Span: Long-lived; well over 100 years.

BEST FEATURES
Blooms profusely in late spring and early summer. Attractive to bees. Can be pruned and shaped. Thicket forming. Showy flowers.

COMPANION PLANTS
Inkberry (*Ilex glabra*), fetterbush (*Lyonia lucida*), red maple (*Acer rubrum*), loblolly bay (*Gordonia lasianthus*), sweetbay (*Magnolia virginiana*), cabbage palm (*Sabal palmetto*), buttonbush (*Cephalanthus occidentalis*), summersweet (*Clethra alnifolia*), Virginia willow (*Itea virginica*), highbush blueberry (*Vaccinium corymbosum*), royal fern (*Osmunda regalis*), dahoon (*Ilex cassine*), swamp bay (*Persea palustris*), tupelos (*Nyssa* spp.).

SIMILAR AND RELATED SPECIES
Black titi (*Cliftonia monophylla*), which blooms earlier and produces buckwheatlike fruit, occurs with titi and is sometimes confused with it.

Diospyros virginiana

dee-ahs-PY-rus vir-ji-nee-AY-nuh (or dy-AHS-pi-rus)

Persimmon

Family: Ebenaceae
Medium-sized tree
Height: 30 to 60 feet
Spread: 15 to 25 feet

LANDSCAPE USE

Performs well as a specimen tree, in poor soil along roads and fence lines, or in naturalistic landscapes. Also a good choice for parks and golf courses.

FORM

An erect, straight-trunked, deciduous tree with a typically oval form, spreading branches, brightly colored fruit, and dark, blocky, bark that is high in character.

NATIVE RANGE

Hammocks, flatwoods, fields, upland woods, bottomlands. Southern New England west to Ohio, south to and nearly throughout Florida, and west to eastern Texas.

CHARACTERISTICS

Flowers: Whitish to greenish or yellowish green, inconspicuous, borne in small clusters in the leaf axils. Male and female flowers borne mostly on separate trees. Spring.
Leaves: Alternate, simple, to about 6 inches long, glossy above, hairy below, turning golden or reddish in fall.
Fruit: A several-seeded, globose, yellowish, 1- to 2-inch-diameter, fleshy berry. Edible but very sour and pungent before fully ripe. Mature fruit is very sweet.
Bark: Dark brown; that of mature trees divided into small, attractive, rectangular blocks.

CULTURE

Soil: Very adaptable from wet to dry, poor soil.
Exposure: Full sun to part shade.
Water: Performs well in moist to quite dry situations.
Hardiness Zones: 4 to 10.
Life Span: Long-lived; at least 100 years.

BEST FEATURES

The bark of older trees has great character. Fruit is relished by wildlife. Adapts to relatively poor soil. Fast growing. Fall color.

COMPANION PLANTS

Sourwood (*Oxydendrum arboreum*), sugarberry (*Celtis laevigata*), flowering dogwood (*Cornus florida*), redbud (*Cercis canadensis*), fringetree (*Chionanthus virginicus*), red bay

(*Persea borbonia*), American holly (*Ilex opaca*), wild olive (*Osmanthus americanus*), sand live oak (*Quercus geminata*), sparkleberry (*Vaccinium arboreum*), wild lime (*Zanthoxylum fagara*).

DISADVANTAGES

Subject to leaf spot and tent caterpillars. Plants that produce heavy fruit crops require cleanup in formal landscapes. Difficult to transplant due to a large taproot.

CULTIVARS

Numerous cultivars are known, but few are available from Florida native plant growers.

SIMILAR AND RELATED SPECIES

Few native trees can be confused with the persimmon, although black cherry (*Prunus serotina*) and flowering dogwood (*Cornus florida*) also have blocky bark.

Distichlis spicata

dis-TIK-lis spy-KAY-tuh

Saltgrass

Family: Poaceae or Gramineae
Ground cover
Height: 1 to 2 feet
Spread: Potentially spreading by underground runners
and forming large colonies

LANDSCAPE USE
Especially well suited for brackish edges, salt flats, and the margins of salt marshes.

FORM
A low, rhizomatous, meadow-forming perennial grass with upright culms, spreading leaves, and a densely flowered, terminal inflorescence.

NATIVE RANGE
Brackish marshes and salt flats. Gulf of St. Lawrence southward along the Atlantic coast, nearly throughout coastal Florida, and west along the coast to Texas.

CHARACTERISTICS
Flowers: A dense, spikelike panicle of 5–15 flattened spikelets.
Leaves: Blades folded or rolled, stiff, spreading and ascending in a plane (2-ranked) along the stem, reminiscent of the form of a feather; sheaths overlapping each other, at least on the lower stem.
Fruit: A tiny, inconspicuous grain.

CULTURE
Soil: Saline soils of coastal marshes and salt flats; highly salt tolerant.
Exposure: Full sun.
Water: Prefers moist to wet, saline situations.
Hardiness Zones: 6 to 10.
Life Span: Perennial.

BEST FEATURES
Very salt tolerant. Spreads by underground runners, potentially creating large colonies.

COMPANION PLANTS
Salt bush (*Baccharis halimifolia*), black needlerush (*Juncus roemerianus*), switchgrass (*Panicum virgatum*), sawgrass (*Cladium jamaicense*), water hyssop (*Bacopa monnieri*), seashore paspalum (*Paspalum vaginatum*), cordgrasses (*Spartina* spp.), leather fern (*Acrostichum danaeifolium*), marsh elder (*Iva frutescens*).

SIMILAR AND RELATED SPECIES
Several grasses have spreading-ascending leaves. Seashore dropseed (*Sporobolus virginicus*), which occurs in similar habitats, is vegetatively similar but has a narrow inflorescence.

Echinacea purpurea

e-ki-NAY-shuh pir-PEW-ree-uh

Purple Coneflower

Family: Asteraceae or Compositae
Wildflower
Height: 2 to 3 feet
Spread: 2 to 3 feet

LANDSCAPE USE

An excellent addition to mixed wildflower gardens, along walkways, or bordering shrub beds.

FORM

A hardy perennial with erect stems topped with showy lavender flowers.

NATIVE RANGE

Limestone glades and clearings in calcareous hammocks. Southeastern United States from Virginia to the Ozarks and west to Texas; occurring naturally only rarely in Florida in Gadsden and Jackson Counties, but widely used in landscaping.

CHARACTERISTICS

Flowers: A complex, rounded head of brownish purple disk flowers surrounded by numerous lavender, showy ray flowers. Spring to fall.

Leaves: Somewhat coarse, dark green, 3–6 inches long, alternate, simple, lance shaped, typically with toothed margins.

Fruit: A tiny, inconspicuous achene.

CULTURE

Soil: Prefers well-drained, calcareous soils, but adapts to a variety of well-drained situations.

Exposure: Full sun to part shade.

Water: Drought tolerant. Well-drained situations are essential.

Hardiness Zones: 7 to 10.

Life Span: Perennial.

BEST FEATURES

Hardy. Perennial. Showy; blooms profusely throughout an extended flowering period. Attractive to butterflies.

COMPANION PLANTS

A variety of wildflowers, including blazing stars (*Liatris* spp.), poppy mallow (*Callirhoe papaver*), tickseeds (*Coreopsis* spp.), asters (*Symphyotrichum* spp.), and yellow coneflower (*Ratibida pinnata*).

DISADVANTAGES

Requires minor attention to removing old flower heads to ensure a long flowering period.

CULTIVARS

Numerous cultivars and hybrids are available. A white form is reported.

SIMILAR AND RELATED SPECIES

Swamp coreopsis (*Coreopsis nudata*) also has lavender flower heads, but it occurs in wetland habitats and lacks the large, toothed leaves of purple coneflower.

Eleocharis spp.

e-lee-AH-kuh-ris

Spikerushes

Family: Cyperaceae
Aquatic
Height: 1 to 3 feet
Spread: 1 to 2 feet; some species spread by runners

LANDSCAPE USE

Several species of spikerush are available from Florida native nurseries and are commonly used on wet sites, some in brackish situations and others along freshwater marshes and shores.

FORM

Erect to clump-forming, mostly perennial herbs with narrow, rounded stems and an expanded flowering tip.

NATIVE RANGE

Brackish and freshwater marshes and shores (depending upon species). Most species available in Florida occur widely across the Coastal Plain from North Carolina southward throughout Florida.

CHARACTERISTICS

Flowers: Inconspicuous; borne in dense clusters at the tip of the quill-like stem.

Leaves: Leaves are limited to bladeless sheaths at the base of the culm.

Fruit: A tiny, inconspicuous achene.

CULTURE

Soil: Moist to wet soils.

Exposure: Full sun to part shade, depending upon species.

Water: All species of spikerush grow in wet situations, often in standing water.

Hardiness Zones: 7 to 10.

Life Span: Herbaceous perennial.

BEST FEATURES

Tolerant of inundation. Perennial.

COMPANION PLANTS

Salt bush (*Baccharis halimifolia*), black needlerush (*Juncus roemerianus*), switchgrass (*Panicum virgatum*), sawgrass (*Cladium jamaicense*), water hyssop (*Bacopa monnieri*), seashore paspalum (*Paspalum vaginatum*), cordgrasses (*Spartina* spp.), leather fern (*Acrostichum danaeifolium*), marsh elder (*Iva frutescens*), maidencane (*Panicum hemitomon*), cinnamon and royal ferns (*Osmunda cinnamomea* and *O. regalis*), scarlet and swamp hibiscus (*Hibiscus coccineus* and *H. grandiflorus*), yellow canna (*Canna flaccida*), string lily (*Crinum americanum*).

DISADVANTAGES

Not particularly showy. Does not adapt to well-drained situations.

SIMILAR AND RELATED SPECIES

At least 28 species of spikerush are native to Florida. Those available in the native plant trade include *E. baldwinii, E. cellulosa, E. geniculata, E. interstincta,* and *E. vivipara.*

Equisetum hyemale

e-kwi-SEE-tum hy-uh-MAY-lee

Horsetail, Scouring Rush

Family: Equisetaceae
Aquatic
Height: 1 to 4 feet
Spread: Individually narrow but typically spreading into expansive colonies

LANDSCAPE USE

Ideal for wet areas and marshy edges, along the banks of alluvial rivers, and along borders of retention ponds and drainage canals.

FORM

An erect, clump-forming, rushlike, herbaceous, nonflowering, fern ally with a hollow, conspicuously jointed stem topped by a conelike structure that resembles a tiny pineapple. Evergreen in south Florida, but dies to the ground during cold winters in north Florida.

NATIVE RANGE

Marshes, ditches, and banks and bars of alluvial rivers. Throughout the United States and Florida.

CHARACTERISTICS

Leaves: Reduced to scalelike structures surrounding the blackened stem joints.

Fruit: Microscopic spores shed from the conelike stem tip.

CULTURE

Soil: Wet to saturated silty soils.

Exposure: Full sun.

Water: Prefers and does best in standing water.

Hardiness Zones: 4 to 10, though 7 to 10 are best.

Life Span: Perennial.

BEST FEATURES

Easy to root and grow. Excellent as a submerged pot plant. Tolerant of continuous inundation. Fast growth and spreading habit make it excellent for bank stabilization and erosion control.

COMPANION PLANTS

Softrush (*Juncus effusus*), buttonbush (*Cephalanthus occidentalis*), pickerelweed (*Pontederia cordata*), lizard's tail (*Saururus cernuus*), string lily (*Crinum americanum*), yellow canna (*Canna flaccida*), blue flags (*Iris* spp.).

DISADVANTAGES

Rapid growth can be difficult to control. May become a pest plant in ideal habitats.

CULTIVARS

A dwarf form is available.

SIMILAR AND RELATED SPECIES

Similar in some respects to the rushes; otherwise, quite distinctive.

Eragrostis spp.

e-ruh-GRAHS-tis

Lovegrasses

Family: Poaceae or Gramineae
Accent, specimen, ground cover, grass
Height: 1 to 3 feet
Spread: Spreads by underground stems
and self-seeding as allowed

J.C. Putnam H.

LANDSCAPE USE

Elliott lovegrass (*E. elliottii*) and purple lovegrass (*E. spectabilis*) are used in Florida landscaping. Both make excellent borders and accent plants and are attractive in massed plantings, especially when mixed with wildflowers. They are also very good choices for showy roadside plantings in the no-mowing zone.

FORM

A clump-forming, tufted grass with stiff, erect to spreading leaves and diffuse flowering panicles with a distinctive purple (*E. spectabilis*), pale tan, or grayish (*E. elliottii*) cast.

NATIVE RANGE

Elliott lovegrass occurs in dry, sandy habitats across the southeastern Coastal Plain, west to Texas, and throughout Florida. Purple lovegrass occurs in sandy sites throughout the southeast, southward to southern peninsular Florida, and west to Arizona and Mexico.

CHARACTERISTICS

Flowers: Borne in delicate, wispy, fragile, pale lavender, tan, or purplish panicles. Mainly fall, but potentially all year.
Leaves: Fine, bluish or silvery green, borne in spreading clumps.
Fruit: Small, hard, inconspicuous grains.

CULTURE

Soil: Both species of *Eragrostis* tolerate a range of conditions but do best in dry to moist, sandy soils.
Exposure: Full sun or light shade.
Water: Supplemental irrigation not required.
Hardiness Zones: 5 to 10, depending upon species.
Life Span: Perennial.

BEST FEATURES

The graceful, delicate, wispy, lavender-beige to purple flowering stems make it notable in the fall, but the leaves are attractive year-round. Both species may be used in dry arrangements. Both also make excellent soil binders and are useful in erosion control. Both are excellent choices for steep roadside banks.

COMPANION PLANTS

A variety of wildflowers and other grasses, muhly grass (*Muhlenbergia capillaris*), scarlet hibiscus (*Hibiscus coccineus*), salt bush (*Baccharis halimifolia*), cordgrasses (*Spartina* spp.).

SIMILAR AND RELATED SPECIES

Muhly grass (*Muhlenbergia capillaris*) has similar flowering stems but is taller.

Ernodea littoralis

ir-NO-dee-uh li-tuh-RAY-lis

Golden Creeper

Family: Rubiaceae
Low shrub, ground cover
Height: 1 to 2 feet
Spread: 2 to 6 feet or more, potentially spreading into large colonies

LANDSCAPE USE
Excellent as a hardy ground-cover shrub for dry, sandy or rocky coastal areas and similarly inhospitable situations. Especially useful in difficult situations such as parking lots, medians, powerline easements, and sunny rights-of-way.

FORM
A low, mat-forming shrub with arching stems, fleshy leaves, and pinkish, tubular flowers with recurved petals.

NATIVE RANGE
Dunes and beaches. Central and southern peninsular Florida, West Indies, Mexico, Central America, and northern South America.

CHARACTERISTICS
Flowers: Small, tubular, pinkish to white, ½ inch long, typically with tightly recurved petals. Year-round.

Leaves: Opposite, green to yellowish green, essentially stalkless, 1½ inches long, fleshy, lance shaped.

Fruit: A rounded to oval, yellowish, single-seeded, ¼-inch-diameter drupe.

CULTURE
Soil: Coarse, well-drained sands of beaches and dunes.

Exposure: Full sun to very light shade.

Water: Dry sites are preferred. Intolerant of overwatering.

Hardiness Zones: 9 to 11.

Life Span: Colonies can persist for many years.

BEST FEATURES
Tolerant of sun, drought, and arid situations. Good erosion control for shifting sands. Mat-forming habit.

COMPANION PLANTS
Muhly grass (*Muhlenbergia capillaris*), coontie (*Zamia pumila*), saltgrass (*Distichlis spicata*), gopher apple (*Licania michauxii*), prickly pears (*Opuntia* spp.), necklace pod (*Sophora tomentosa*), bay cedar (*Suriana maritima*), seashore paspalum (*Paspalum vaginatum*), sea purslane (*Sesuvium portulacastrum*), beach bean (*Canavalia rosea*).

SIMILAR AND RELATED SPECIES
Coker's beach creeper (*E. cokeri*), a rare species of Miami-Dade County, is very similar but not available in the native plant trade.

Eryngium spp.

e-RIN-jee-um

Snakeroots

Family: Apiaceae or Umbelliferae
Wildflowers
Height: 1 to 4 feet
Spread: 2 to 4 feet

Used in mixed wildflower beds, especially in wetter sections of such beds (depending upon species).

FORM
Erect, clump-forming herbs with tall, essentially leafless stems topped with a 1-inch-diameter, globular head of greenish to bluish flowers.

NATIVE RANGE
Marshes, bogs, edges of cypress ponds, flatwoods, floodplain forests. Three species are used in native plant landscaping. *E. aquaticum* ranges from New Jersey south to south-central Florida. *E. yuccifolium* occurs from Minnesota and Connecticut south throughout Florida, and west to Kansas and Oklahoma. *E. integrifolium* ranges from North Carolina south to northern Florida and west to Mississippi.

CHARACTERISTICS
Flowers: Borne in dense, rounded heads at the tip of the stem and its main branches. Those of *E. aquaticum* and *E. integrifolium* are commonly blue. Those of *E. yuccifolium* are white, often tinged pale green.
Leaves: Basal leaves of *E. yuccifolium* narrow and tapering to a sharp tip, 1–3 feet long, with bristlelike teeth along the margins, resembling the leaves of yucca; those of *E. aquaticum* linear, 1–2 feet long, entire or only finely toothed along the margins; and those of *E. integrifolium* broadly lance shaped to oval and toothed along the margins.
Fruit: Borne in several-seeded heads.

CULTURE
Soil: Moist, acid soil is preferred. Will tolerate basic soil. *E. yuccifolium* will adapt to well-drained soils.
Exposure: Full sun.
Water: *E. aquaticum* and *E. integrifolium* do best in moist to wet situations. *E. yuccifolium* is tolerant of a wide range of moisture regimes.
Hardiness Zones: 6 to 10.
Life Span: Perennial.

BEST FEATURES
Interesting flowers. Toothed, yuccalike leaves of *E. yuccifolium.* Tolerance of moist conditions and full sun. Excellent addition to mixed wildflower beds.

COMPANION PLANTS
Black-eyed Susans (*Rudbeckia* spp.), mist flower (*Conoclinium coelestinum*), pineland hibiscus (*Hibiscus aculeata*), tickseeds (*Coreopsis* spp.).

SIMILAR AND RELATED SPECIES
No plants are closely similar in appearance to these three species. Few other members of the Apiaceae, or carrot family, are used in landscaping.

Erythrina herbacea

e-ri-THRY-nuh hir-BAY-see-uh

Cherokee Bean

Family: Fabaceae or Leguminosae
Small tree, shrub, or perennial
Height: 3 to 20 feet
Spread: 5 to 10 feet

J.C. Putnam H.

LANDSCAPE USE

An excellent shrub for naturalistic landscapes as well as along sunny wooded borders. Particularly effective in curtailing foot traffic.

FORM

A spiny, irregular, sometimes viney, herbaceous to woody, multistemmed shrub in northern Florida, sometimes reaching the dimensions of a small tree in southern Florida.

NATIVE RANGE

Dry, open woods, sandy roadsides, and clearings. North Carolina south throughout Florida and west to Texas.

CHARACTERISTICS

Flowers: Narrow, long, bright red, borne in conspicuous upright spikes. Late spring and summer.
Leaves: Attractively divided into 3 triangular leaflets with pointed tips.
Fruit: Brown pods that split to expose several attractive, bright red seeds.
Bark: Smooth green when young, turning light brown with age.

CULTURE

Soil: Tolerates a wide range of soil conditions, but does best in dry, fertile sands.
Exposure: Full sun to part shade.
Water: Supplemental irrigation not required.
Hardiness Zones: 8 to 10.
Life Span: Dies back in winter in colder locations; short-lived.

BEST FEATURES

Most enjoyed for the spikes of bright red, showy flowers and its bright red seeds, but also for its interesting, 3-parted leaves. Cherokee bean is pest free except for occasional attacks by stem tip borers.

COMPANION PLANTS

Summer haw (*Crataegus flava*), beautyberry (*Callicarpa americana*), St. John's–worts (*Hypericum* spp.), Carolina jessamine (*Gelsemium sempervirens*), coral honeysuckle (*Lonicera sempervirens*), cocoplum (*Chrysobalanus icaco*), Simpson's and other stoppers (*Myrcianthes fragrans* and *Eugenia* spp.), wild coffee (*Psychotria nervosa*), white indigoberry (*Randia aculeata*), witch hazel (*Hamamelis virginiana*), American holly (*Ilex opaca*), needle palm (*Rhapidophyllum hystrix*).

DISADVANTAGES

The bright red, poisonous seeds are attractive to children. Dies back to the ground in winter in northern Florida.

CULTIVARS

Cherokee bean takes on many forms but lacks recognized cultivars.

ALLERGENIC AND TOXIC PROPERTIES

The seeds are toxic and have been used as rat poison in Mexico.

SIMILAR AND RELATED SPECIES

Cherokee bean is unique among Florida's native shrubs.

Eugenia spp.

yew-JEE-nee-uh

Stoppers

Family: Myrtaceae
Large shrub, small tree
Height: 10 to 30 feet, depending upon species
Spread: 5 to 20 feet, depending upon species

LANDSCAPE USE

Stoppers are used as ornamental specimen trees, as densely vegetated shrubs in hedges, as shrub components in shady gardens, or as screening and background plants.

FORM

Four species of stoppers are native to Florida, including the white stopper (*E. axillaris*) and Spanish stopper (*E. foetida*), both of which are quite common, and the rarer red stopper (*E. rhombea*) and redberry stopper (*E. confusa*). All are small, erect, attractive, evergreen trees with relatively narrow to somewhat spreading crowns, opposite leaves, and mostly grayish to grayish brown single to multistemmed trunks.

NATIVE RANGE

Subtropical hardwood hammocks. Central to southernmost peninsular Florida and the West Indies.

CHARACTERISTICS

Flowers: White, hairy, tiny, and inconspicuous. Year-round.
Leaves: Opposite, dark to shiny bright green (depending upon species), 1–3 inches long, typically with a pointed tip.
Fruit: Rounded, black to reddish or purplish, about ¼ inch in diameter.
Bark: Grayish to grayish brown; smooth to somewhat flaking.

CULTURE

Soil: Tolerant of a wide range of soils. Spanish and white stoppers are salt tolerant.
Exposure: Full sun to part shade. Intolerant of freezing temperatures, except for Simpson's stopper, which grows in zone 9.
Water: Supplemental irrigation not required once established.
Hardiness Zones: 9 to 11.
Life Span: Moderate.

BEST FEATURES

Stoppers are easy to propagate and produce dense, attractive foliage. Their typically narrow crowns also make them excellent for constricted spaces. Fruits are attractive to birds.

COMPANION PLANTS

Gumbo limbo (*Bursera simaruba*), satinleaf (*Chrysophyllum oliviforme*), pigeon plum (*Coccoloba diversifolia*), red bay (*Persea borbonia*), marlberry (*Ardisia escallonioides*), Simpson's stopper (*Myrcianthes fragrans*), fiddlewood (*Citharexylum spinosum*), myrtle-of-the-river and spicewood (*Calyptranthes zuzygium* and *C. pallens*), wild lime (*Zanthoxylum fagara*), Jamaica and limber capers (*Capparis cynophallophora* and *C. flexuosa*), wild coffees (*Psychotria* spp.), white indigoberry (*Randia aculeata*), coontie (*Zamia pumila*).

DISADVANTAGES

The leaves of white stopper emit a skunklike aroma, especially during summer, that some find objectionable. As a group, stoppers are slow growing.

Euonymus americanus

yew-AH-ni-mus uh-me-ri-KAY-nus

Strawberry Bush

Family: Celastraceae
Large shrub or small tree
Height: 3 to 6 feet
Spread: 3 feet

J. C. Putnam H.

LANDSCAPE USE

An excellent shrub for moist, shaded understory gardens in naturalistic settings.

FORM

A deciduous, upright, irregular, diffusely branched, multistemmed shrub with green, ascending or arching branches.

NATIVE RANGE

Moist hammocks and woodlands, stream banks. New York, southward to central Florida, and west to Texas.

CHARACTERISTICS

Flowers: Small, white to yellowish green, 5-petaled. March and April.
Leaves: Opposite, simple, toothed, 1–3 inches long; turning reddish in fall.
Fruit: A conspicuous, reddish, warty, 1-inch-diameter, strawberry-like capsule that splits at maturity to expose several reddish orange seeds that dangle on reddish, threadlike attachments. September and October.
Bark: Greenish; smooth to somewhat flaking.

CULTURE

Soil: Prefers moist, deep, fertile, well-drained soils with high organic content.
Exposure: Shade to part shade.
Water: Requires moist but not wet conditions.
Hardiness Zones: 6 to 9.
Life Span: Short; approximately ten years or a little more.

BEST FEATURES

The diffusely branched habit; interesting, strawberry-like fruit; and the tendency to form dense colonies are the best features. An excellent food source for white-tailed deer.

COMPANION PLANTS

River birch (*Betula nigra*), red maple (*Acer rubrum*), sweetgum (*Liquidambar styraciflua*), Virginia willow (*Itea virginica*), Carolina jessamine (*Gelsemium sempervirens*), buttonbush (*Cephalanthus occidentalis*), anises (*Illicium* spp.), wax myrtle (*Myrica cerifera*), blue-stem palmetto (*Sabal minor*), eastern gamagrass (*Tripsacum dactyloides*), highbush blueberries (*Vaccinium* spp.), Walter's viburnum (*Viburnum obovatum*), cinnamon and royal ferns (*Osmunda cinnamomea* and *O. regalis*), sweetshrub (*Calycanthus floridus*).

DISADVANTAGES

Probably not appropriate for manicured gardens. Fruit sometimes aborts before maturing.

ALLERGENIC AND TOXIC PROPERTIES

Toxicity unknown, but close relatives in the same genus are known to cause vomiting, diarrhea, and weakness.

SIMILAR AND RELATED SPECIES

Burning bush (*E. atropurpureus*), a shrub or small tree of the eastern United States, occurs very rarely in the central panhandle.

Ficus aurea

FY-kus AW-ree-uh

Strangler Fig

Family: Moraceae
Medium-sized to large tree
Height: 40 to 60 feet
Spread: 30 to 50 feet

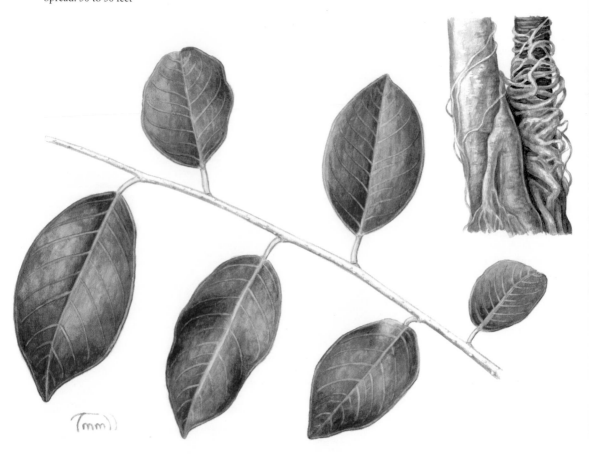

(mm)

LANDSCAPE USE
The large size makes this species most useful as a shade tree in parks and parking lots and along streets. Appropriate only for large residential sites.

FORM
A large, erect, evergreen, canopy tree with a stout trunk. Often starting as an epiphyte on the trunks of cabbage palms and other trees and forming a latticelike trunk that eventually surrounds and strangles its host, hence the common name.

NATIVE RANGE
Tropical hammocks and mangrove edges. Central and southern peninsular Florida.

CHARACTERISTICS
Flowers: Tiny, inconspicuous, borne in the leaf axils. Spring and summer.
Leaves: Dark lustrous green, thick and leathery, to about 5 inches long, pointed at the apex.
Fruit: A rounded, fleshy, juicy, ¾-inch-diameter fig, ranging in color from red to brownish or yellow.
Bark: Smooth; dark to very light gray.

CULTURE
Soil: Tolerant of a wide range of soil types.
Exposure: Shade to part sun.
Water: Irrigation not required.
Hardiness Zones: 9 to 11.
Life Span: Long-lived; perhaps 100 years.

BEST FEATURES
Spreading canopy provides shade in parks, along roadsides, and in very large suburban yards. Fast growing.

COMPANION PLANTS
Red maple (*Acer rubrum*), royal palm (*Roystonea regia*), red mulberry (*Morus rubra*), Simpson's stopper (*Myrcianthes fragrans*), marlberry (*Ardisia escallonioides*), wild coffee (*Psychotria nervosa*), firebush (*Hamelia patens*), swamp fern (*Blechnum serrulatum*).

DISADVANTAGES
Will sometimes start as an epiphyte in a host tree, eventually killing it. Fallen fruit may create problems if planted near walks and driveways.

ALLERGENIC AND TOXIC PROPERTIES
Toxicity unknown. Related species in the genus are known to cause photodermatitis. Sensitive persons sometimes feel a burning sensation when exposed to the sun after contact.

SIMILAR AND RELATED SPECIES
Shortleaf fig (*F. citrifolia*) is similar in overall appearance and use, but its fruits are stalked rather than stalkless like those of strangler fig. The figs are in the same family as the native red mulberry (*Morus rubra*), which is also used in landscaping. Numerous non-native figs are sold and cultivated in Florida, but they should be avoided in favor of these two native species.

Forestiera segregata

fo-res-tee-E-ruh se-gruh-GAY-tuh

Florida Privet

Family: Oleaceae
Large shrub, small tree
Height: 4 to 15 feet
Spread: 3 to 12 feet

Jean C. Putnam H.

LANDSCAPE USE

Good for hedges and for screening patios and outside sitting areas. Excellent for slope erosion control and shorelines.

FORM

A large, erect, densely foliated shrub or small, much-branched tree.

NATIVE RANGE

Coastal woodlands. Extreme southeastern Georgia, coastal South Carolina, south throughout much of coastal peninsular Florida and the West Indies.

CHARACTERISTICS

Flowers: Small, yellowish to yellowish green, and borne in clusters along the branches in early spring with the appearance of new leaves.

Leaves: Small, opposite, 1–3 inches long, shiny green above, paler below.

Fruit: Black, egg shaped, olivelike, about ½ inch long and about half as broad, dangling from stalks along the branches.

Bark: Smooth; pale gray.

CULTURE

Soil: Prefers moist, sandy loam, but will adapt to a variety of soil and moisture situations.

Exposure: Light shade to sun.

Water: Moist to dry conditions.

Hardiness Zones: 8 to 11.

Life Span: Moderate.

BEST FEATURES

The dainty and tidy habit; thick, dense, evergreen foliage; drought and salt tolerance; and edible fruit, which are a superb food source for songbirds, make Florida privet an excellent landscape plant. Tolerates pruning and shaping.

COMPANION PLANTS

Beautyberry (*Callicarpa americana*), fiddlewood (*Citharexylum spinosum*), stoppers (*Eugenia* spp.), yaupon (*Ilex vomitoria*), saw palmetto (*Serenoa repens*), Simpson's stopper (*Myrcianthes fragrans*), myrsine (*Rapanea punctata*), spicewood (*Calyptranthes pallens*), Cherokee bean (*Erythrina herbacea*), coontie (*Zamia pumila*), cocoplum (*Chrysobalanus icaco*), white indigoberry (*Randia aculeata*), wild lime (*Zanthoxylum fagara*), marlberry (*Ardisia escallonioides*), paradise tree (*Simarouba glauca*).

DISADVANTAGES

Subject to a few insect pests, but not seriously so.

CULTIVARS

Pineland privet—sometimes considered a distinct variety (*F. segregata* var. *pinetorum*) or as a

cultivar (Florida privet 'pineland')—is a shorter, somewhat more compact shrub with small, gray-green leaves.

SIMILAR AND RELATED SPECIES

Eastern swamp privet (*F. acuminata*), Godfrey's privet (*F. godfreyi*), and upland swamp privet (*F. ligustrina*) also occur in Florida.

Fraxinus caroliniana

FRAK-si-nus ka-ro-li-nee-AY-nuh

Pop Ash

Family: Oleaceae
Small to medium-sized tree
Height: 30 to 50 feet
Spread: 20 to 35 feet

LANDSCAPE USE

Highly tolerant of inundation and excellent for the borders of retention ponds, drainage swales, canal banks, and wet roadsides.

FORM

A relatively small, erect to leaning, often multitrunked tree with a rounded crown.

NATIVE RANGE

Swamps, flatwoods depressions, floodplain forests. Virginia, south nearly throughout Florida, and west to Arkansas and Texas.

CHARACTERISTICS

Flowers: Very small, inconspicuous, without petals. Spring.

Leaves: Compound, 6–12 inches long, with 5–7 leaflets.

Fruit: A winged samara, often widest near the middle and somewhat diamond shaped in outline, but variable.

Bark: Grayish; thin and scaly when young, becoming roughened and furrowed with age.

CULTURE

Soil: Wet, acid soils of swamps and riverbanks.

Exposure: Shade to part sun.

Water: Prefers moist to wet conditions. Tolerant of inundation.

Hardiness Zones: 8 to 10.

Life Span: Relatively short-lived; about 50 years.

BEST FEATURES

Very good for concealing unsightly retention ponds and drainage canals. Tolerates regular inundation.

COMPANION PLANTS

Red maple (*Acer rubrum*), dahoon (*Ilex cassine*), swamp tupelo (*Nyssa sylvatica* var. *biflora*), Coastal Plain willow (*Salix caroliniana*), pond apple (*Annona glabra*), swamp dogwood (*Cornus foemina*), Virginia willow (*Itea virginica*), buttonbush (*Cephalanthus occidentalis*), climbing aster (*Symphyotrichum carolinianum*), Virginia creeper (*Parthenocissus quinquefolia*), string lily (*Crinum americanum*).

ALLERGENIC AND TOXIC PROPERTIES

Oils from these plants may cause allergic dermatitis in rare cases.

SIMILAR AND RELATED SPECIES

Two other ash trees occur in Florida, both of which are used in landscaping. Green ash (*F. pennsylvanica*) is a large, long-lived tree of river floodplains. White ash (*F. americana*) is an upland species that does best in well-drained situations.

Fraxinus pennsylvanica

FRAK-si-nus pen-sil-VA-ni-kuh

Green Ash

Family: Oleaceae
Medium-sized to large tree
Height: 50 to 100 feet
Spread: 30 to 70 feet

LANDSCAPE USE

Highly adaptable. Often used in parks and golf courses, along streets, and in suburban lawns. Performs best on continually moist or seasonally wet sites.

FORM

A large, erect, single-trunked, deciduous tree with an irregular, spreading crown.

NATIVE RANGE

Floodplain forests, swamps, and wet woodlands. Quebec and Manitoba, southward to central peninsular Florida, and west to east Texas.

CHARACTERISTICS

Flowers: Small, green to reddish purple, borne in panicles before new leaf growth. Spring.

Leaves: Opposite, pinnately compound, to about 12 inches long, with 5–7 ovate, 2- to 5-inch-long leaflets.

Fruit: A 1- to 2-inch-long, single-seeded, narrowly winged samara.

Bark: Ashy gray to brownish, with interlacing, often diamond-shaped furrows and ridges.

CULTURE

Soil: Prefers rich, moist soils, but adapts to most soil conditions.

Exposure: Full sun to shade.

Water: Wet to moist conditions are preferred. Will tolerate regular flooding.

Hardiness Zones: 3 to 9.

Life Span: Long-lived; at least 100 years.

BEST FEATURES

Adaptable to a wide variety of soil types and moisture regimes. Shade tolerant. Produces fall color. Excellent for shade. Will tolerate inundation. Fast growing once established.

COMPANION PLANTS

Box elder and red maple (*Acer negundo* and *A. rubrum*), water hickory (*Carya aquatica*), loblolly bay (*Gordonia lasianthus*), sweetbay (*Magnolia virginiana*), loblolly pine (*Pinus taeda*), laurel oak (*Quercus laurifolia*), blue beech (*Carpinus caroliniana*), dahoon (*Ilex cassine*), cinnamon and royal ferns (*Osmunda cinnamomea* and *O. regalis*), climbing aster (*Symphyotrichum carolinianum*), mist flower (*Conoclinium coelestinum*), string lily (*Crinum americanum*), cardinal flower (*Lobelia cardinalis*).

DISADVANTAGES

Some specimens fruit heavily and shed large quantities of winged fruit, which can be very messy in early summer.

CULTIVARS

At least two dozen cultivars and selections are reported for green ash, none of which are currently available from Florida's native plant nurseries and growers.

SIMILAR AND RELATED SPECIES

Two other ash trees occur in Florida, both of which are used in landscaping.

Pop ash (*F. caroliniana*) is a relatively small, multitrunked tree of swamps and floodplains. White ash (*F. americana*) is an upland species that does best in well-drained situations.

Gaillardia pulchella

gay-LAR-dee-uh pul-KE-luh

Blanket Flower

Family: Asteraceae or Compositae
Wildflower
Height: 1 to 2 feet
Spread: 1 to 2 feet

LANDSCAPE USE

Well suited to sunny and sandy roadsides, beaches, and wildflower gardens. Also useful in difficult situations, such as sandy medians in parking lots.

FORM

A 1- to 2-foot-tall, herbaceous wildflower with brightly colored flowers and narrow leaves.

NATIVE RANGE

Roadsides, sandy fields, and beaches. Coastal North Carolina and south nearly throughout Florida.

CHARACTERISTICS

Flowers: Brightly colored, showy, ½-inch-wide, daisylike flowers with a deep, purplish disk and reddish to maroon rays that are tipped in yellow. Spring through summer in northern Florida; year-round in the southern peninsula.

Leaves: Alternate, narrowly lance shaped, and hairy.

Fruit: A tiny, inconspicuous achene.

CULTURE

Soil: Coarse, well-drained sands.

Exposure: Full sun. Somewhat salt tolerant. May be used in coastal landscapes.

Water: Dry conditions are preferred. Will not tolerate moist or poorly drained situations.

Hardiness Zones: 8 to 11.

Life Span: Annual to short-lived perennial.

BEST FEATURES

Showy flowers. Tolerant of dry conditions and poor soil. Extended flowering period. Particularly well suited to coastal sands.

COMPANION PLANTS

Yellowtop (*Flaveria linearis*), coontie (*Zamia pumila*), golden creeper (*Ernodea littoralis*), gopher apple (*Licania michauxii*), sea oats (*Uniola paniculata*), beach bean (*Canavalia rosea*), white indigoberry (*Randia aculeata*), necklace pod (*Sophora tomentosa*), bay cedar (*Suriana maritima*), beach morning glory (*Ipomoea imperati*).

DISADVANTAGES

Will not tolerate shading. May become infected with fungi if planted in wet sites.

CULTIVARS

Several cultivars are known, including rayless forms, forms with tubular rays, and forms with variously colored flowers.

ALLERGENIC AND TOXIC PROPERTIES

May cause contact dermatitis in some people.

SIMILAR AND RELATED SPECIES

Numerous members of the Asteraceae occur in Florida, many of which are also used in landscaping and wildflower gardening. None have the two-toned red and yellow flowers of blanket flower.

Garberia heterophylla

gar-BE-ree-uh he-tuh-ro-FI-luh (or he-tuh-RAH-fi-luh)

Garberia

Family: Asteraceae or Compositae
Shrub
Height: 1 to 6 feet
Spread: 2 to 5 feet

LANDSCAPE USE
Useful as a freestanding shrub, in mixed shrub beds, and in butterfly gardens. Ideal for difficult dry, sunny areas along highway rights-of-way.

FORM
An evergreen, densely foliated, fall-flowering shrub with oval, gray-green leaves and showy lavender to pinkish flowers.

NATIVE RANGE
Oak and sand pine scrub. Endemic to the Florida scrub of the northern and central peninsula.

CHARACTERISTICS
Flowers: Pink to lavender, tubular, without rays, borne in conspicuous, showy heads.
Leaves: Alternate, oval, grayish green, 1–2 inches long, erect to ascending along the stem.
Fruit: A tiny, inconspicuous achene.
Bark: Grayish; thin.

CULTURE
Soil: Coarse, well-drained, sandy soils.
Exposure: Full sun to light shade.
Water: Occurs naturally in dry, well-drained situations. Irrigation not required.
Hardiness Zones: 8 to 9.
Life Span: Moderately long-lived, 25 to 50 years.

BEST FEATURES
Grayish green, evergreen leaves. Dense form. Attractive lavender flowers. Excellent nectar plant for butterflies.

COMPANION PLANTS
Chickasaw plum (*Prunus angustifolia*), saw palmetto (*Serenoa repens*), gopher apple (*Licania michauxii*), milkweeds (*Asclepias* spp.), pawpaws (*Asimina* spp.), beautyberry (*Callicarpa americana*), shiny blueberry (*Vaccinium myrsinites*), scrub mints (*Conradina* spp.), coontie (*Zamia pumila*).

SIMILAR AND RELATED SPECIES
Few shrubs are similar to garberia when in flower. Tarflower (*Bejaria racemosa*) is somewhat similar vegetatively.

Gelsemium sempervirens

jel-SE-mee-um sem-pir-VY-renz

Carolina Jessamine

Family: Gelsemiaceae
Vine
Height: Climbing to more than 20 feet
Spread: To several feet along fences

J. C. Putnam H.

LANDSCAPE USE

Used to conceal chain-link and other fences. Excellent for use on mailboxes, trellises, arbors, and other such structures. Effective as a ground cover and in window boxes and planters. An excellent choice for woodland and naturalistic landscapes.

FORM

A sparsely to densely foliated, potentially high-climbing, twining, multistemmed, somewhat aggressive, evergreen vine with opposite, dark green leaves, a reddish brown wiry stem, and bright yellow flowers.

NATIVE RANGE

Woodland edges, hammocks, and flatwoods. Virginia, southward to central Florida, and west to Texas.

CHARACTERISTICS

Flowers: Trumpet shaped, bright yellow, 1–1½ inches long, fragrant, showy. Late winter and early spring.
Leaves: Opposite, lance shaped, dark green and shiny above, pointed at the tip, 1–4 inches long, evergreen.
Fruit: An ellipsoid capsule, about ½ inch long.
Bark: Reddish brown.

CULTURE

Soil: Prefers well-drained, acid soil, but adapts to a variety of soil conditions.
Exposure: Full sun to part shade, but flowers better in full sun.
Water: Supplemental irrigation not required.
Hardiness Zones: 6 to 9.
Life Span: Moderately long-lived.

BEST FEATURES

Bright yellow flowers and winter and early spring blooming season. Pleasant, but sometimes strong, odor. Twining habit. Evergreen. Fast growth. Relatively pest free. Attractive to both hummingbirds and butterflies. Particularly effective when used alongside coral honeysuckle (*Lonicera sempervirens*) for a contrast of colors. An excellent replacement for Chinese wisteria (*Wisteria sinensis*).

COMPANION PLANTS

Beautyberry (*Callicarpa americana*), yaupon (*Ilex vomitoria*), lopsided Indiangrass (*Sorghastrum secundum*), oaks (*Quercus* spp.), coral honeysuckle (*Lonicera sempervirens*), lowbush and highbush blueberries (*Vaccinium* spp.), broomsedges and bluestems (*Andropogon* spp.), dahoon (*Ilex cassine*), inkberry (*Ilex glabra*), pine trees (*Pinus* spp.).

DISADVANTAGES

Aggressive habit may make some plants difficult to control and require pruning; otherwise trouble free.

CULTIVARS

Several cultivars have been selected, including at least two that have double flowers, but none are readily available in Florida.

ALLERGENIC AND TOXIC PROPERTIES

All parts of the plant are poisonous if swallowed but not to the touch. Symptoms are many. Ingesting the roots may be deadly.

SIMILAR AND RELATED SPECIES

Swamp jessamine (*G. rankinii*), an odorless, wetland species that flowers somewhat later than *G. sempervirens,* also occurs in northern Florida but is not readily available in the nursery trade.

Gordonia lasianthus

gor-DO-nee-uh la-see-AN-thus

Loblolly Bay

Family: Theaceae
Large tree
Height: 30 to 60 feet
Spread: 20 to 30 feet

J.C.Putnam H.

LANDSCAPE USE
Useful as a canopy, understory, or specimen tree. Also a good restoration tree that should be more often used to beautify retention ponds. Best suited for lake and pond margins.

FORM
A straight-trunked tree with dark green leaves, a pyramidal crown, and deeply furrowed bark at maturity.

NATIVE RANGE
Swamps and bayheads. Virginia, southward to south-central Florida, and west to Louisiana.

CHARACTERISTICS
Flowers: Five creamy white petals surrounding a yellow center; showy, 3–4 inches wide. Spring and summer; may produce flowers over several months.

Leaves: Dark green, leathery, 2–5 inches long, bluntly toothed along the margins. Older leaves sometimes turn red, which can be an aid to identification.

Fruit: An ovoid capsule.

Bark: Dark brown to grayish; old trees develop deeply furrowed, rough-textured bark.

CULTURE
Soil: Prefers, if not requires, moist, acid, fertile soil. May adapt to drier, sandy sites but is likely very short-lived and susceptible to nematode damage in such situations.

Exposure: Full sun to part shade.

Water: Should be watered frequently during first year, with moderate watering thereafter.

Hardiness Zones: 7 to 9.

Life Span: Relatively short-lived in planted landscapes, maybe even only a few years, unless perfectly situated. Perhaps exceeding an age of 100 years under natural conditions.

BEST FEATURES
Dark, evergreen leaves. Showy white flowers, in an extended blooming season that lasts throughout the summer. Deeply furrowed bark has much character.

COMPANION PLANTS
Sweetbay (*Magnolia virginiana*), red bays (*Persea* spp.), blueberries (*Vaccinium* spp.), Virginia willow (*Itea*

virginica), titi (*Cyrilla racemiflora*), wax myrtle (*Myrica cerifera*), dahoon (*Ilex cassine*), sugarberry (*Celtis laevigata*), swamp bay (*Persea palustris*), elms (*Ulmus* spp.), pipestem (*Agarista populifolia*), red maple (*Acer rubrum*), river birch (*Betula nigra*), fringetree (*Chionanthus virginicus*), native azaleas (*Rhododendron* spp.).

DISADVANTAGES
Slow growth rate. Can be difficult under cultivation unless grown in moist situations. Low salt tolerance.

SIMILAR AND RELATED SPECIES
The white flowers are sometimes described as similar to those of the magnolias, but the two are not closely related.

Hamamelis virginiana

ha-muh-ME-lis vir-ji-nee-AY-nuh

Witch Hazel

Family: Hamamelidaceae
Small tree
Height: 10 to 25 feet
Spread: 6 to 10 feet

LANDSCAPE USE

Serves well in naturalistic landscapes, in shrub borders, in shaded areas near houses and buildings, and along woodland edges.

FORM

A small, upright, deciduous tree or large shrub with an oval to irregularly spreading crown of crooked, horizontal branches.

NATIVE RANGE

Wet hammocks, moist slopes, upland woods, creek swamps, and floodplains. New England, southward to central peninsular Florida, and west to Texas.

CHARACTERISTICS

Flowers: Small, yellowish to richly yellow, slightly fragrant, about ¾ inch long, with thin, ribbonlike petals. Appearing in autumn with or after leaf drop.

Leaves: Alternate, simple, with scalloped edges and coarse texture, 3–6 inches long, 2–4 inches wide, pale green.

Fruit: A hard, irregularly shaped, conelike capsule, maturing in summer.

Bark: Smooth; gray to grayish brown.

CULTURE

Soil: Prefers deep, rich, moist, slightly acid soil, but is adaptable to a variety of soil types.

Exposure: Will tolerate deep shade, but flowers best in filtered sun.

Water: Prefers moist conditions, but will adapt to drier sites once established.

Hardiness Zones: 4 to 9.

Life Span: Relatively long-lived; to 100 years.

BEST FEATURES

Fall and winter flowers are a main attraction. Produces fall color and interesting fruit. Irregular branching is very attractive.

COMPANION PLANTS

Oakleaf hydrangea (*Hydrangea quercifolia*), beautyberry (*Callicarpa americana*), highbush blueberries (*Vaccinium* spp.), arrowwood (*Viburnum dentatum*), Ashe magnolia (*Magnolia macrophylla* var. *ashei*), Florida and pinxter azaleas (*Rhododendron austrinum* and *R. canescens*), Carolina jessamine (*Gelsemium sempervirens*), purple coneflower (*Echinacea purpurea*).

SIMILAR AND RELATED SPECIES

Few other native shrubs or small trees have leaves or flowers similar to witch hazel. The closely related witch alder (*Fothergilla gardenii*) is also used in landscaping, but its flowers are borne in conspicuous, densely flowered spikes.

Hamelia patens

huh-ME-lee-uh PAY-tenz

Firebush

Family: Rubiaceae
Small to moderate shrub
Height: 3 to 10 feet (taller in southernmost Florida)
Spread: 3 to 6 feet

J.C. Putnam H

LANDSCAPE USE

An excellent shrub for barriers, borders along boardwalks, paths, and sidewalks, or for massing in mixed or single-species shrub beds.

FORM

A multistemmed, spreading shrub or small tree with a rounded form, slender branches, and opposite or whorled foliage.

NATIVE RANGE

Coastal hammocks and shell middens. Central and southern Florida.

CHARACTERISTICS

Flowers: Bright orange-red, tubular, about 1½ inches long, filled with nectar, which attracts hummingbirds and butterflies. Year-round.

Leaves: Whorled with up to 7 leaves per node, 5–8 inches long, shiny green above with reddish veins.

Fruit: Red to purplish black, juicy, rounded, about 1¼ inches in diameter. A food source for songbirds.

Bark: Brownish.

CULTURE

Soil: Prefers dry, sandy, somewhat alkaline soils, but will adapt to a variety of conditions. Only slightly salt tolerant.

Exposure: Shade to sun. Foliage is usually more attractive in shady situations. Not cold tolerant. Flowers best in full sun.

Water: Irrigate two to three times per year during droughts. Otherwise, irrigation not required after establishment.

Hardiness Zones: 8B to 11.

Life Span: Moderate.

BEST FEATURES

Bright red, showy flowers appear year-round. Attractive foliage. Flowers and fruit are attractive to butterflies, hummingbirds, and songbirds.

COMPANION PLANTS

Eastern gamagrass (*Tripsacum dactyloides*), red mulberry (*Morus rubra*), Simpson's stopper (*Myrcianthes fragrans*), wild coffees (*Psychotria* spp.), marlberry (*Ardisia escallonioides*), red maple (*Acer rubrum*).

DISADVANTAGES

Intolerant of cold. Will die back in locations subject to freezing temperatures but will return in spring. Known pests include scales, whiteflies, chewing insects, and mites. Tends to spread by seeds transported by birds.

CULTIVARS

H. patens 'Compacta' is a compact form of firebush that has recently been recognized by some as a new species.

SIMILAR AND RELATED SPECIES

Of the many members of its family that occur in Florida, none have the appearance or similar horticultural uses of firebush.

Helianthus spp.

hee-lee-AN-thus

Sunflowers

Family: Asteraceae or Compositae
Wildflowers
Height: 2 to 6 feet
Spread: Spreading by self-sown seed or thin, underground stems

LANDSCAPE USE

At least 14 species of native sunflowers occur in Florida, three of which are commonly available in Florida's native plant trade. All are well suited for mixed wildflower beds, borders along walkways, or sunny butterfly gardens. Beach or dune sunflower (*H. debilis*) makes an excellent roadside wildflower in central and southern Florida.

FORM

Herbaceous wildflowers producing showy, bright yellow, daisylike flowers or dark, purplish heads of rayless flowers.

NATIVE RANGE

Flatwoods, marshes, and coastal dunes. Narrowleaf sunflower (*H. angustifolius*) occurs in the northern third of the state, rayless sunflower (*H. radula*) occurs nearly statewide, and beach sunflower (*H. debilis*) occurs in coastal dunes along Florida's east coast.

CHARACTERISTICS

Flowers: Those of *H. angustifolius* and *H. debilis* are medium to large in size, bright yellow, and showy. Those of *H. radula* have a purplish head and few to no ray flowers.
Leaves: Those of *H. angustifolia* are very narrow, rough to the touch, and up to 8 inches long. Those of *H. debilis* are broad at the base, long-stalked, with expanded blade tissue. Those of *H. radula* are confined mostly to a cluster at the base of the plant.
Fruit: A tiny achene.

CULTURE

Soil: Moist to wet, acid soils are best for *H. angustifolius* and *H. radula*. *H. debilis* prefers the well-drained soils of beaches and dunes.
Exposure: Full sun to light shade.
Water: *H. angustifolius* and *H. radula* prefer moist conditions. *H. debilis* does best in well-drained situations.
Hardiness Zones: 8 to 10.
Life Span: Perennial.

BEST FEATURES

H. debilis is an excellent shrubby ground cover for beaches and dunes and is especially attractive when used in mixed plantings with blanket flower (*Gaillardia pulchella*). The large, bright yellow flowers and large size commend *H. angustifolius* for mixed wildflower gardens.

COMPANION PLANTS

Depending upon the species of *Helianthus* selected, companion plants may include: St. John's–worts (*Hypericum* spp.), mist flower (*Conoclinium coelestinum*), blanket flower (*Gaillardia pulchella*), railroad vine (*Ipomoea pescaprae*), tickseeds (*Coreopsis* spp.), muhly grass (*Muhlenbergia capillaris*), wiregrass (*Aristida stricta* var. *beyrichiana*), and bluestems (*Andropogon* spp.).

DISADVANTAGES

H. debilis will develop a fungus if planted in wet areas.

SIMILAR AND RELATED SPECIES

Many of the 14 native sunflowers have similar flowers. Numerous non-native species of *Helianthus* are also sold in Florida, but these should be avoided in favor of those native to the state.

Hibiscus coccineus

hi-BIS-kus kahk-SI-nee-us

Scarlet Hibiscus

Family: Malvaceae
Large, semiwoody shrub or herbaceous perennial
Height: 4 to 6 feet
Spread: 2 to 5 feet

J. C. Putnam H.

LANDSCAPE USE

Used in moist soils along patios and as a background plant. A very good choice for wet roadsides; it blooms almost all summer and can be mowed in early fall.

FORM

An upright to sprawling, stout, somewhat open, perennial subshrub.

NATIVE RANGE

Edges of swamps and wetlands. Coastal South Carolina, southward to south-central Florida, and west to Texas.

CHARACTERISTICS

Flowers: Large, bright red, showy, 4–8 inches in diameter, with 5 well-separated petals.
Leaves: Palmately veined and deeply divided into 3–5 lobes. Unique and showy.
Fruit: An egg-shaped capsule, 1–2 inches long.
Bark: Brownish.

CULTURE

Soil: Prefers moist to wet, fertile soils, but will adapt to most well-drained soils if kept moist.
Exposure: Full sun to part shade.
Water: Prefers moist to wet conditions.
Hardiness Zones: 8 to 11.
Life Span: Not fully cold tolerant but will return year after year.

BEST FEATURES

Large, red flowers are showy in spring and summer. Relatively easy to grow, pest free, with a fast growth rate.

COMPANION PLANTS

Swamp hibiscus (*Hibiscus grandiflorus*), yellow canna (*Canna flaccida*), prairie blue flag (*Iris hexagona*), softrush (*Juncus effusus*), buttonbush (*Cephalanthus occidentalis*), sand cordgrass (*Spartina bakeri*).

DISADVANTAGES

Normally dies back during cold winters. May require pruning if not winter killed for several years.

CULTIVARS

None known, but may hybridize with *H. grandiflorus*.

SIMILAR AND RELATED SPECIES

Swamp hibiscus (*H. grandiflorus*) is a large wetland shrub with pink flowers. Rose mallow (*H. moscheutos*) has large, creamy white flowers with red centers.

Hydrangea quercifolia

hy-DRAYN-jee-uh kwir-si-FO-lee-uh

Oakleaf Hydrangea

Family: Saxifragaceae
Large shrub
Height: 4 to 8 feet
Spread: 4 to 8 feet

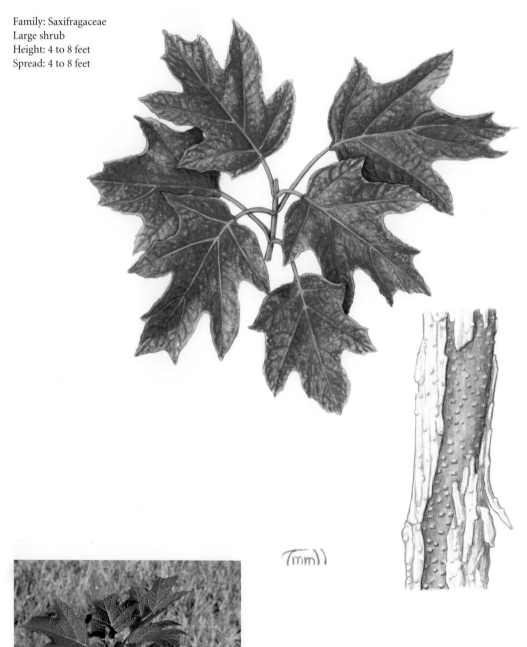

(7mm))

LANDSCAPE USE

Excellent as a specimen or massed in shaded, naturalistic gardens. Serves well in shrub borders, as a background plant in large shrub beds, or to soften the corners of houses.

FORM

An erect, deciduous, irregularly branching shrub with a rounded, somewhat open crown, large coarse leaves, and spectacular flower clusters.

NATIVE RANGE

Bluffs and ravine slopes, especially along streams. Southern New England, southward to central peninsular Florida, and west to eastern Texas.

CHARACTERISTICS

Flowers: Borne profusely in numerous 12-inch-long, 4-inch-wide clusters. White to creamy white when fresh, turning progressively pinkish, to purplish, to light brown and persisting on the plant for several months. Late spring and early summer.

Leaves: Opposite, simple, ovate in overall outline, 3- to 7-lobed and toothed along the edges, to about 8 inches long, greenish above, whitish below, very attractive.

Fruit: A brownish capsule, often persisting throughout the winter.

Bark: Light brown and high in character, exfoliating in strips to expose lighter inner bark.

CULTURE

Soil: Does best on rich, acid soils, but adapts well to drier mixtures of sand and silts.

Exposure: Full to part shade. Will tolerate temperatures to -25 degrees F.

Water: Requires well-drained situations with moist but not wet soil. Plants sited in the southern parts of the state may require supplemental water.

Hardiness Zones: 5 to 9.

Life Span: Colonies may persist for many years by extension from underground stems; individual aboveground stems may live to 50 years.

BEST FEATURES

The numerous large, showy clusters of whitish flowers; the large leaves, which provide excellent fall color; and the beautiful, exfoliating bark make this one of Florida's most ornamental native shrubs. Easy to grow. Seeds attractive to wildlife.

COMPANION PLANTS

Red buckeye (*Aesculus pavia*), redbud (*Cercis canadensis*), fringetree (*Chionanthus virginicus*), American hophornbeam (*Ostrya virginiana*), beautyberry (*Callicarpa americana*), needle palm (*Rhapidophyllum hystrix*), witch hazel (*Hamamelis virginiana*), maidenhair fern

(*Adiantum capillus-veneris*), arrowwood (*Viburnum dentatum*), Carolina jessamine (*Gelsemium sempervirens*), Christmas fern (*Polystichum acrostichoides*).

DISADVANTAGES

Loses its leaves and has a coarse appearance in winter. Subject to disease if poorly sited.

CULTIVARS

Over 20 cultivars are reported across the southeastern United States, none of which are regularly available in Florida.

ALLERGENIC AND TOXIC PROPERTIES

May cause restlessness, abdominal pain, and diarrhea in cows and horses.

SIMILAR AND RELATED SPECIES

Mountain hydrangea (*H. arborescens*) also occurs rarely, in Liberty and Walton Counties, but it is not used in Florida landscaping. Several non-native members of the genus are also used in landscaping and should not be confused with the native species.

Hymenocallis latifolia

hy-me-no-KA-lis la-tuh-FO-lee-uh

Spider Lily

Family: Amaryllidaceae
Wildflower
Height: 2 to 3 feet
Spread: Multiplies and spreads rapidly by underground bulbs

J.C. Putnam H.

LANDSCAPE USE
Popular in beds, along borders, as a ground cover, or as an accent plant.

FORM
A clump-forming perennial with dark green, straplike leaves.

NATIVE RANGE
Coastal dunes and swales, the more elevated parts of mangrove thickets, open rocky sites, beaches and sand ridges, flatwoods. South-central and southern Florida; also West Indies.

CHARACTERISTICS
Flowers: White, about 5 inches in diameter, with 6 narrow petals surrounding a depressed, funnel-like or cuplike center and 6 elongated stamens tipped with showy golden anthers. Borne spring though fall in clusters at the tip of an elongated scape.

Leaves: Dark green, straplike, arising from ground level in a dense, erect to arching clump.

Fruit: A fleshy capsule.

CULTURE
Soil: Adaptable to most soil types. Salt tolerant.

Exposure: Full sun to some shade.

Water: Supplemental irrigation not required under normal conditions.

Hardiness Zones: 9 to 11.

Life Span: Plantings may take 1 to 3 years to become well established, but are subsequently self-sustaining.

BEST FEATURES
The large, showy white flowers make this species unique. Requires little maintenance or care.

COMPANION PLANTS
Broomsedge (*Andropogon virginicus*), white indigoberry (*Randia aculeata*), muhly grass (*Muhlenbergia capillaris*), necklace pod (*Sophora tomentosa*), Adam's needle (*Yucca filamentosa*), saltgrass (*Distichlis spicata*).

DISADVANTAGES
Leaves are sometimes chewed by grasshoppers.

ALLERGENIC AND TOXIC PROPERTIES
May be toxic to grazing livestock and other animals.

SIMILAR AND RELATED SPECIES
String lily (*Crinum americanum*), an excellent plant for wet sites in zones 8 to 10, also has dark green, straplike leaves and white flowers with narrow petals, but it lacks the central funnel-shaped structure in the center of its blossoms. Ten other native species of *Hymenocallis* occur in Florida, all of which are similar and difficult to distinguish from one another.

Hypericum spp.

hy-PE-ri-kum

St. John's–Worts, St. Andrew's–Crosses

Family: Clusiaceae or Guttiferae
Small shrubs
Height: 1 to 8 feet, depending upon species
Spread: 2 to 4 feet, depending upon species

J. C. Putnam H.

LANDSCAPE USE

Excellent for naturalistic landscapes, especially in understory colonies, in sunny shrub beds along foundations, or to conceal the edges of backyard decks. Excellent for golf courses and roadside retention ponds. Also used as a specimen shrub.

FORM

At least five species of *Hypericum* are available in the native plant trade. These include *H. fasciculatum, H. galioides, H. hypericoides, H. lissophloeus,* and *H. reductum.* The first four are erect woody shrubs with small linear to oblong leaves and bright yellow flowers. *H. reductum* is a reclining woody species that ordinarily does not exceed about 1 foot in height.

NATIVE RANGE

H. fasciculatum and *H. hypericoides* occur throughout Florida and the southeast. *H. galioides* and *H. reductum* occur naturally mostly from the central peninsula north to North Carolina and west to at least Mississippi, though *H. reductum* is planted nearly statewide. *H. lissophloeus* is a Florida specialty that is endemic only to a few counties in the central panhandle.

CHARACTERISTICS

Flowers: Yellow, less than 1 inch across, with 4 or 5 petals and masses of yellow stamens. Spring to fall, depending upon species. Most species are prolific and showy bloomers.

Leaves: Short, linear, and needlelike in some species; wider in other species. Mostly less than 2 inches long and mostly evergreen.

Fruit: A brown capsule that splits to expose numerous very tiny seeds. The capsules are showy in late fall and early winter.

Bark: Mostly reddish brown and sloughing off in thin strips. The bark of *H. lissophloeus* is silvery gray.

CULTURE

Soil: Most species do best in moist, organic, acid soil, but will adapt to a variety of conditions. *H. reductum* occurs in scrub and is particularly suited for drier sites.

Exposure: Full sun to part shade, depending upon species.

Water: Most species require moist conditions for best performance. *H. hypericoides* and *H. reductum* adapt well to very dry sites.

Hardiness Zones: 7 to 10, depending upon species.

Life Span: Mostly short-lived; considerably less than 50 years.

BEST FEATURES

Hardy, easy to grow, and requires little maintenance. Judicious use of the several species of *Hypericum* will ensure yellow flowers nearly year-round.

COMPANION PLANTS

Sparkleberry (*Vaccinium arboreum*), lowbush and highbush blueberries (*Vaccinium* spp.), summersweet (*Clethra alnifolia*), wax myrtle (*Myrica cerifera*), broomsedges and bluestems (*Andropogon* spp.), lopsided Indiangrass (*Sorghastrum secundum*), Cherokee bean (*Erythrina herbacea*), Adam's needle (*Yucca filamentosa*), inkberry (*Ilex glabra*), staggerbush (*Lyonia fruticosa*), pines (*Pinus elliottii, P. palustris,* and *P. serotina*).

DISADVANTAGES

Short-lived.

ALLERGENIC AND TOXIC PROPERTIES

Many species are used medicinally. Some species may be toxic to livestock.

SIMILAR AND RELATED SPECIES

At least 29 species of *Hypericum,* including the 5 mentioned above, occur in Florida. Many are woody, though some are herbaceous annuals.

Ilex cassine

EYE-leks kuh-SEE-nuh (or kuh-SEEN)

Dahoon

Family: Aquifoliaceae
Small tree
Height: 20 to 40 feet
Spread: 8 to 30 feet

LANDSCAPE USE

Useful as a specimen tree, especially in narrow spaces, or as a large shrub. May be grouped with other male and female holly trees to ensure maximum fruit set. Well suited for such difficult sites as road and powerline rights-of-way, medians, the edges of retention ponds, and the borders of drainage swales and canal banks. Performs best in continually moist to seasonally wet areas.

FORM

An erect, evergreen tree with slender, spreading to ascending branches and a densely foliated, relatively narrow crown. Sometimes shrublike.

NATIVE RANGE

Edges of swamps, ponds, and wet hammocks. Virginia, south throughout Florida, and west to Louisiana.

CHARACTERISTICS

Flowers: White, individually small and inconspicuous, but borne in dense, showy clusters. Male and female flowers borne on separate trees. Spring.
Leaves: Alternate, oblong, leathery, shiny medium green above, paler below, to 5 inches long.
Fruit: A reddish orange to bright red drupe, ¼ inch in diameter, borne in dense, showy clusters on female plants. Winter, but may persist for several months.
Bark: Smooth; light gray.

CULTURE

Soil: Prefers moist to wet, boggy, acid to slightly acid soil with pH 3.5–6.5. Tolerant of low soil oxygen but can adapt to moist sites.
Exposure: Full sun to part shade. Somewhat tolerant of salt air and quite shade tolerant.
Water: Irrigate and fertilize after transplanting. Plants situated in dry sites may require supplemental irrigation.
Hardiness Zones: 7 to 11.
Life Span: Moderate to short; less than 50 years.

BEST FEATURES

Showy, red-orange or bright red fruit, evergreen habit, narrow form, dense foliage, and tolerance of low soil oxygen.

COMPANION PLANTS

Red bays (*Persea* spp.), scarlet hibiscus (*Hibiscus coccineus*), buttonbush (*Cephalanthus occidentalis*), Virginia willow (*Itea virginica*), sweetbay (*Magnolia virginiana*), red maple (*Acer rubrum*), swamp fern (*Blechnum serrulatum*), pipestem (*Agarista populifolia*), blue beech (*Carpinus caroliniana*), swamp dogwood (*Cornus foemina*), Simpson's stopper (*Myrcianthes fragrans*), Walter's viburnum (*Viburnum obovatum*).

DISADVANTAGES

Spittlebugs and scales are sometimes bothersome. Otherwise hardy. Fruit production requires the presence of both a female and male plant.

CULTIVARS

Myrtle-leaved holly (*Ilex myrtifolia*) is sometimes considered a variety of *I. cassine.*

ALLERGENIC AND TOXIC PROPERTIES

Fruit is reportedly poisonous to humans, but is eaten by birds.

SIMILAR AND RELATED SPECIES

At least 11 hollies are native to Florida. At least 6 species are used in landscaping, including possumhaw holly (*I. decidua*), myrtle-leafed holly (*I. myrtifolia*), and Krug's holly (*I. krugiana*), the last of which is a south Florida specialty.

Ilex glabra

EYE-leks GLAY-bruh

Inkberry, Gallberry

Family: Aquifoliaceae
Small shrub
Height: 3 to 7 feet
Spread: 2 to 4 feet

J. C. Putnam H.

LANDSCAPE USE

Typically used as a foundation or screening plant or as a component in naturalistic landscapes. Can be pruned to maintain a compact form.

FORM

An erect, evergreen, mostly multistemmed, colony-forming shrub with an irregular, mostly informal form.

NATIVE RANGE

Swamps, flatwoods, bayheads, and wet areas. Massachusetts, south nearly throughout Florida, and west to Mississippi.

CHARACTERISTICS

Flowers: White, small, and inconspicuous. Spring. Male and female flowers borne on separate plants.

Leaves: Alternate, shiny green above, 1–3 inches long, the tip notched with several small, blunt teeth.

Fruit: A showy, round, black, ¼-inch-diameter, hard drupe. Fall and winter.

Bark: Smooth; gray.

CULTURE

Soil: Prefers moist to wet, acid soil with pH 4.5–7.0. Tolerant of low soil oxygen. Moderately salt tolerant.

Exposure: Full sun to shade.

Water: Soil should be kept moist.

Hardiness Zones: 5 to 10.

Life Span: Plantings may be long-lived due to inkberry's clonal tendencies.

BEST FEATURES

Generally hardy and trouble free. Shiny black fruit is showy and useful for wildlife. Flowers attract bees. Excellent for wet, acidic sites.

COMPANION PLANTS

Fetterbush (*Lyonia lucida*), saw palmetto (*Serenoa repens*), beautyberry (*Callicarpa americana*), lowbush blueberries (*Vaccinium* spp.), wiregrass (*Aristida stricta* var. *beyrichiana*), St. John's–worts (*Hypericum galioides* and *H. hypericoides*), tarflower (*Bejaria racemosa*), possum haw (*Viburnum nudum*), wax myrtle (*Myrica cerifera*), broomsedges (*Andropogon* spp.).

DISADVANTAGES

Difficult to transplant and sometimes subject to both root rot and leaf spot. Tends to spread by underground stems.

CULTIVARS

I. glabra 'Compacta' is a compact, oval form of inkberry.

SIMILAR AND RELATED SPECIES

Large, sweet gallberry (*I. coriacea*) is similar to inkberry but has larger fruit and typically prefers very wet sites.

Ilex opaca

EYE-leks o-PAY-kuh

American Holly

Family: Aquifoliaceae
Medium-sized tree
Height: 30 to 50 feet
Spread: 15 to 30 feet

G.C. Putnam H.

LANDSCAPE USE

An excellent evergreen specimen tree. Equally useful in groupings of male and female trees in open sun or understory shade. Also a good choice for beautifying parking lots.

FORM

An erect, evergreen, extremely attractive tree with spiny leaves, horizontal branches, and a pyramidal form. Densely foliated. Low branching in open situations.

NATIVE RANGE

Moist hammocks. Massachusetts, southward to central Florida, and west to Texas.

CHARACTERISTICS

Flowers: White, tiny, inconspicuous. Male and female flowers borne on separate plants. Spring to summer.

Leaves: Alternate, shiny green, spiny toothed along the margins, elliptical in outline, 2–4 inches long.

Fruit: Rounded, showy, bright red, ½-inch-diameter drupes. Fall and winter.

Bark: Smooth; light gray.

CULTURE

Soil: Does best in fertile, well-drained, acid to slightly acid soil with pH 4.0–6.0. Tolerates low soil oxygen.

Exposure: Full sun to shade.

Water: Supplemental irrigation not required unless situated on very dry sites.

Hardiness Zones: 5 to 9.

Life Span: Moderately long-lived; trees over 100 years old are known.

BEST FEATURES

Valued for its shiny, spiny-toothed, dark green leaves, evergreen habit, and showy bright red fruit.

COMPANION PLANTS

Red buckeye (*Aesculus pavia*), sweetshrub (*Calycanthus floridus*), several species of haw (*Crataegus* spp.), Shumard oak (*Quercus shumardii*), redbud (*Cercis canadensis*), fringetree (*Chionanthus virginicus*), red cedar (*Juniperus virginiana*), wild olive (*Osmanthus americanus*), wild lime (*Zanthoxylum fagara*), Hercules club (*Zanthoxylum clava-herculis*), sand live oak (*Quercus geminata*), wild coffee (*Psychotria nervosa*).

DISADVANTAGES

Slow growing. Leaf miners and scales can be a problem. Cannot tolerate alkaline soils. Both male and female trees are needed to ensure adequate fruit set.

CULTIVARS

At least 300 cultivars are listed for this species across its range; few if any of these are used in Florida.

SIMILAR AND RELATED SPECIES

Scrub holly (*I. opaca* var. *arenicola*) is endemic to well-drained, sandy scrub sites in the northern and central Florida peninsula.

Ilex vomitoria

EYE-leks vah-mi-TO-ree-uh

Yaupon

Family: Aquifoliaceae
Small to large shrub
Height: 8 to 25 feet
Spread: 5 to 15 feet

J.C. Putnam H.

LANDSCAPE USE

Equally effective as a large specimen shrub or in pruned hedges along patios, walkways, and roadsides. Numerous forms of yaupon are available for varying landscape requirements. Underutilized, but useful as a single-trunked specimen for median plantings.

FORM

An upright, densely foliated, multistemmed, evergreen shrub with irregular branching, an oval form, and slender, grayish branches.

NATIVE RANGE

Hammocks, swamps, floodplains, and dunes. New Jersey, southward to south-central peninsular Florida, and west to Texas.

CHARACTERISTICS

Flowers: Tiny, white, and borne in dense clusters. Spring. Male and female flowers are borne on separate plants.

Leaves: Alternate, dark green, leathery, oval to oblong, with scalloped margins. To about 1 inch long.

Fruit: A bright red, ½-inch-diameter drupe. Fall and winter. Produced on female trees only. Most cultivars produce showy fruit that persists well into winter.

Bark: Grayish white and smooth.

CULTURE

Soil: Prefers some moisture and good drainage, but will tolerate a wide range of soils. Salt tolerant.

Exposure: Shade to part sun.

Water: Soil should be kept moist but well drained.

Hardiness Zones: 7 to 10.

Life Span: Long-lived and moderately fast growing.

BEST FEATURES

Bright red fruit and evergreen habit. General hardiness. Wildlife food.

COMPANION PLANTS

Wax myrtle (*Myrica cerifera*), sparkleberry (*Vaccinium arboreum*), Simpson's stopper (*Myrcianthes fragrans*), red cedar (*Juniperus virginiana*), coontie (*Zamia pumila*), wild coffee (*Psychotria nervosa*), stoppers (*Eugenia* spp.), marlberry (*Ardisia escallonioides*), magnolia (*Magnolia grandiflora*), live oak (*Quercus virginiana*), pignut hickory (*Carya glabra*), summer haw (*Crataegus flava*), highbush and lowbush blueberries (*Vaccinium* spp.), beautyberry (*Callicarpa americana*).

DISADVANTAGES

Fruit production requires both male and female plants.

CULTIVARS

More than 30 cultivars are known, 8 of which are available in Florida. The most important of these are considered on the succeeding pages.

SIMILAR AND RELATED SPECIES

Several species of holly are native to Florida; yaupon is the most widely used.

Ilex vomitoria Cultivars

'Pendula' and 'Weeping Yaupon' are weeping forms with pendent branches similar to those of the weeping willow (*Salix babylonica*). They will reach heights of 10–25 feet with spreads of 6–8 feet. They are typically erect when young but become more spreading with age and are excellent as accent or specimen plants. They do well in wet to dry soils and readily adapt to alkaline conditions. Many nurseries grow 'Weeping Yaupon,' a showy plant with bright red berries that persist into late winter.

'Nana' is a dwarf, compact, female form, 3–5 feet tall and up to 10 feet wide. It tolerates a variety of soils in full sun to part shade and is virtually pest free. Its dense foliage, tolerance for adverse conditions, and rounded shape make it an excellent and often-used landscape shrub for hedges, foundations, and planters. An excellent substitute for boxwood (*Buxus* spp.).

'Schellings Dwarf' is a dwarf male with an even more compact form than 'Nana,' smaller leaves, and a somewhat more upright habit. It is rounded in outline. At maturity it is about 3–4 feet both tall and wide. The new stem growth has an attractive purplish tinge. 'Schellings Dwarf' is probably the best of the compact forms for Florida landscaping. This is a very good plant for roadway medians, parking lot borders, and other areas that require evergreen, drought-tolerant, low-growing plants.

'Will Fleming' is an upright male with a columnar form. It will reach heights of 12–18 feet. Its narrow form makes it very useful where height is needed but where lateral space is limited. An excellent replacement for Italian cypress (*Cupressus sempervirens*).

'Shadows Bigleaf,' 'Mobile,' and 'Pride of Houston' are not as readily available in Florida as 'Schellings Dwarf.' 'Shadows Bigleaf' is a large, dark green female with bright red fruit and an upright stature. 'Pride of Houston' is a moderately sized female to about 12 feet tall that has been selected for heavy and showy fruit production.

Ilex x *attenuata* 'East Palatka'

EYE-leks uh-te-new-AY-tuh

East Palatka Holly

Family: Aquifoliaceae
Small to medium-sized tree
Height: 15 to 25 feet
Spread: 10 to 15 feet

LANDSCAPE USE

A very nice specimen tree. Also works very well as a hedge plant, especially where heavy fruiting is desired.

FORM

A relatively small, single-trunked, evergreen holly with an open crown of lustrous, dark green leaves.

NATIVE RANGE

The first wild specimens were discovered in 1927 near Palatka, Florida, hence the cultivar and common names.

CHARACTERISTICS

Flowers: Small, white, relatively inconspicuous; male and female flowers borne on separate plants. Spring.

Leaves: Dark, lustrous green, margins toothed or entire.

Fruit: A bright red, ¼-inch-diameter drupe, borne in conspicuous, showy clusters in late fall and winter.

Bark: Thin, pale gray, typical of the hollies.

CULTURE

Soil: Well-drained to slightly moist, acid soil.

Exposure: Full sun for best fruit productions, but tolerant of light shade. Less cold tolerant than some of the other cultivars and selections of *Ilex* x *attenuata*.

Water: Somewhat drought tolerant. Supplemental irrigation required only on well-drained sites.

Hardiness Zones: 8 to 10.

Life Span: More than 50 years.

BEST FEATURES

Female plants produce large crops of bright red drupes. Dark, lustrous green foliage is attractive year-round. Branches and twigs are useful in Christmas decorations. Easy to cultivate and adaptable to a wide variety of situations. Fruit eaten by birds and other wildlife. Slow to moderate growth rate.

COMPANION PLANTS

Dahoon and American holly (*Ilex cassine* and *I. opaca*), flowering dogwood (*Cornus florida*), beautyberry (*Callicarpa americana*), hickories (*Carya* spp.).

DISADVANTAGES

Prone to *Sphaeropsis* knot disorder.

CULTIVARS

I. x *attenuata* is a cross between dahoon (*I. cassine*) and American holly (*I. opaca*). East Palatka holly is one of about 16 cultivars or forms of this hybrid. Other cultivars available in Florida include *I. attenuata* 'Fosteri' and *I. attenuata* 'Savannah,' both of which are cold hardy across the southeastern United States.

SIMILAR AND RELATED SPECIES

At least 11 native hollies occur in Florida, several of which are used regularly in landscaping. This large number of native species offers many substitutes for non-native hollies.

Illicium spp.

i-LI-see-um

Anises

Family: Illiciaceae
Large shrub or small tree
Height: 6 to 20 feet
Spread: 3 to 6 feet

J. C. Putnam tt

LANDSCAPE USE

Two species of anise occur in Florida: Florida or red anise (*I. floridanum*) and yellow anise (*I. parviflorum*). Both are commonly used as hedges, for screening, in naturalistic understory thickets, to soften corners of buildings, or as large background shrubs. Florida anise is also used to help conceal or beautify retention ponds, drainage swales, and canal banks, though it is not very tolerant of drought or full sun and does better in moist shady areas.

FORM

Both species of anise are erect, evergreen, densely foliated shrubs with dark green, leathery leaves, and a rounded shape. Should be trimmed heavily when young to maintain this shape.

NATIVE RANGE

Florida anise occurs along woodland streams and in low, rich areas along the lower Coastal Plain from Florida to Louisiana. Yellow anise is restricted to wet hammocks and swamps of north-central Florida but is widely used in cultivation far outside of its narrow natural range. It is appropriate for zones 6 to 9 and can survive temperatures as low as -9 degrees F.

CHARACTERISTICS

Flowers: Those of Florida anise are deep red with numerous ribbonlike petals. Those of yellow anise are smaller and yellowish. Spring.
Leaves: Alternate, elliptical, leathery, dark green, very aromatic, with an aroma similar to licorice when crushed or bruised.
Fruit: A brownish, star-shaped capsule, for which it is sometimes called "star anise." Late summer and fall.
Bark: Brown.

CULTURE

Soil: Both species prefer moist, sandy, acid soils and benefit from mulching. Yellow anise, in particular, will adapt to drier sites.
Exposure: Shade to semishade. Yellow anise tends to tolerate more sun. Not salt tolerant.
Water: Thrives best in moist soils.
Hardiness Zones: 7 to 10.
Life Span: Moderate.

BEST FEATURES

Hardy and relatively pest free. Evergreen habit. Dark green leathery leaves. Interesting red flowers of Florida anise. Shade tolerant. Reportedly highly resistant to deer damage.

COMPANION PLANTS

Strawberry bush (*Euonymus americanus*), red buckeye (*Aesculus pavia*), Walter's viburnum (*Viburnum obovatum*), climbing aster (*Symphyotrichum carolinianum*), several species of oaks (*Quercus* spp.), pipestem (*Agarista populifolia*), sweetshrub (*Calycanthus floridus*), needle palm (*Rhapidophyllum hystrix*), blue beech (*Carpinus caroliniana*), sweetbay (*Magnolia virginiana*), loblolly bay (*Gordonia lasianthus*), red maple (*Acer rubrum*), river birch (*Betula nigra*), cabbage palm (*Sabal palmetto*).

DISADVANTAGES

May require pruning to maintain compact form.

CULTIVARS

I. floridanum 'Alba' is a white-flowered form of Florida anise.

SIMILAR AND RELATED SPECIES

Though not closely related, the several species of bay trees (*Persea* spp.) have leaves similar in shape to those of the two anise trees.

Ipomoea imperati

eye-po-MEE-uh im-puh-RAH-ty

Beach Morning Glory

Family: Convolvulaceae
Trailing vine
Height: 6 inches
Spread: 10 to 50 feet

LANDSCAPE USE

Often used in beach restoration and stabilization. Excellent for beachfront homes and coastal landscaping, especially in nutrient-poor, sandy soils.

FORM

A low-growing, trailing, nonclimbing vine with fleshy leaves and showy flowers. Spreading by shallow belowground stems and often forming dense mats on coastal dunes and beaches.

NATIVE RANGE

Beaches. North and South Carolina, southward to central Florida, and west to Mississippi.

CHARACTERISTICS

Flowers: Funnel shaped, about 2 inches long, white with a yellow center, showy. Summer and fall.

Leaves: 1–2 inches long, leathery, oval to oblong, dark green.

Fruit: A ½-inch-diameter capsule.

CULTURE

Soil: Well-drained sands of beaches and dunes.

Exposure: Full sun.

Water: Very drought tolerant.

Hardiness Zones: 8 to 10.

Life Span: Perennial.

BEST FEATURES

Drought and sun tolerance. Tolerance of beach and dune conditions. Showy flowers. Quick growth and mat-forming habit make this species especially useful for beach restoration and stabilization.

COMPANION PLANTS

Saltgrass (*Distichlis spicata*), railroad vine (*Ipomoea pes-caprae*), seaside elder (*Iva imbricata*), gopher apple (*Licania michauxii*), muhly grass (*Muhlenbergia capillaris*), Simpson's stopper (*Myrcianthes fragrans*), cocoplum (*Chrysobalanus icaco*), saw palmetto (*Serenoa repens*), jointgrasses and knotgrasses (*Paspalum* spp.), seaside oxeye (*Borrichia frutescens*).

ALLERGENIC AND TOXIC PROPERTIES

Some species in this genus are known to be toxic to humans.

SIMILAR AND RELATED SPECIES

At least a dozen native morning glories occur in Florida, as well as numerous non-native species. Railroad vine (*Ipomoea pes-caprae*), with deep lavender flowers, is also used in landscaping.

Ipomoea pes-caprae

eye-po-MEE-uh pes-KA-pree

Railroad Vine

Family: Convolvulaceae
Vine
Height: 6 inches
Spread: Spreading to at least 100 feet by aboveground runners

LANDSCAPE USE

Often used in beach restoration and stabilization. Excellent for beachfront homes and coastal landscaping, especially in nutrient-poor, sandy soils.

FORM

A ground-hugging, spreading vine with bright green, fleshy leaves, magenta to pink flowers, and aboveground runners that can reach nearly 100 feet in length.

NATIVE RANGE

Beaches and dunes. Georgia, south along the Atlantic and Gulf coasts throughout peninsular Florida, and west along the coast to Texas.

CHARACTERISTICS

Flowers: Large, funnel shaped, lavender, tinged with magenta, showy. Year-round.

Leaves: Fleshy, oblong, often reflexed upward from the midrib.

Fruit: A brown, ½-inch-diameter capsule.

CULTURE

Soil: Well-drained sands of beaches and dunes.

Exposure: Full sun.

Water: Very drought tolerant.

Hardiness Zones: 8 to 11.

Life Span: Perennial.

BEST FEATURES

Attractive to beach butterflies. Quickly spreading. Tolerant of full sun and xeric beach conditions. Can be effectively used in beach and dune restoration and seaside landscaping.

COMPANION PLANTS

Saltgrass (*Distichlis spicata*), seaside elder (*Iva imbricata*), gopher apple (*Licania michauxii*), muhly grass (*Muhlenbergia capillaris*), Simpson's stopper (*Myrcianthes fragrans*), cocoplum (*Chrysobalanus icaco*), saw palmetto (*Serenoa repens*), jointgrasses and knotgrasses (*Paspalum* spp.), sea oxeye (*Borrichia frutescens*), blanket flower (*Gaillardia pulchella*).

ALLERGENIC AND TOXIC PROPERTIES

Ingesting large amounts may cause nausea and diarrhea.

SIMILAR AND RELATED SPECIES

At least a dozen native morning glories occur in Florida, as well as numerous non-native species. Beach morning glory (*Ipomoea imperati*), with white flowers, is also used in landscaping.

Iris spp.

EYE-ris

Blue Flag Iris and Prairie Blue Flag Iris

Family: Iridaceae
Aquatic or wetland plant
Height: 3 to 5 feet
Spread: Forms colonies by underground stems

LANDSCAPE USE

Two species of native irises are used in Florida: blue flag (*I. virginica*) and prairie blue flag (*I. hexagona*). Both are aquatic species that are especially effective along the edges of shallow ponds and marshy sites. Excellent for the edges of retention ponds and drainage swales.

FORM

Erect herbs with dark green, sword- or strap-shaped leaves and showy blue flowers.

NATIVE RANGE

Swamps, marshes, and wet prairies. Virginia, southward to central peninsular Florida, and west to Texas.

CHARACTERISTICS

Flowers: Showy; petals 4–5 inches long, blue, sometimes marked with bold, yellowish orange spots (depending upon species) and white stripes. Spring.

Leaves: Large, to about 2 feet long, erect, swordlike, dark green, and leathery.

Fruit: A conspicuous ridged, oval pod. Summer.

CULTURE

Soil: Prefers wet, rich soil with pH 4.8–7.3. Tolerant of low soil oxygen.

Exposure: Sun to part shade.

Water: Needs moist to wet conditions.

Hardiness Zones: 7 to 10.

Life Span: Perennial.

BEST FEATURES

Showy blue flowers and dark green leaves. Aquatic habit. Elegant appearance. Shade tolerance.

COMPANION PLANTS

Yellow canna (*Canna flaccida*), buttonbush (*Cephalanthus occidentalis*), scarlet hibiscus (*Hibiscus coccineus*), spider lily (*Hymenocallis latifolia*).

DISADVANTAGES

Relatively short flowering period. Will spread beyond its planting if left untended.

ALLERGENIC AND TOXIC PROPERTIES

Several species of iris are known to cause abdominal pain, nausea, diarrhea, and vomiting. At least one species has caused the death of calves. May cause contact dermatitis in some people.

SIMILAR AND RELATED SPECIES

Zigzag iris (*I. brevicaulis*), copper iris (*I. fulva*), savanna iris (*I. tridentata*), and dwarf violet iris (*I. verna*) also occur in Florida but are not readily available in the native plant trade.

Itea virginica

eye-TEE-uh vir-JI-ni-kuh

Virginia Willow

Family: Iteaceae
Large shrub
Height: 3 to 8 feet
Spread: 2 to 4 feet

J. C. Putnam H.

LANDSCAPE USE

Excellent shrub for naturalistic settings, along decks and patios, in mixed shrub beds, or along streams, ponds, or wetland depressions. Also suitable for use along the borders of retention ponds, drainage swales, and canals.

FORM

An erect to spreading, multistemmed, clump-forming shrub with an open form and arching branches.

NATIVE RANGE

Swamps, stream banks, and wet hammocks. Virginia, southward to central Florida, and west to Texas.

CHARACTERISTICS

Flowers: White, individually small, but borne profusely in numerous showy, 4- to 6-inch-long, compact racemes. Spring.
Leaves: Alternate, elliptical, 2–3 inches long, finely toothed along the margins.
Fruit: A small, brownish capsule. Late summer and fall.
Bark: Brownish.

CULTURE

Soil: Occurs naturally in wet, acid soils with pH 4.0–7.5, but will adapt to surprisingly dry conditions. Tolerates low soil oxygen.
Exposure: Shade to full sun.
Water: Performs best with moderate moisture.
Hardiness Zones: 5 to 9.
Life Span: At least ten years.

BEST FEATURES

Most prized for its showy flower clusters and somewhat long flowering period, as well as for its colorful fall leaves. General hardiness.

COMPANION PLANTS

Titi (*Cyrilla racemiflora*), buttonbush (*Cephalanthus occidentalis*), climbing aster (*Symphyotrichum carolinianum*), scarlet hibiscus (*Hibiscus coccineus*), pop ash (*Fraxinus caroliniana*), Coastal Plain willow (*Salix caroliniana*), cypresses (*Taxodium* spp.), swamp tupelo (*Nyssa sylvatica* var. *biflora*), red maple (*Acer rubrum*), dahoon (*Ilex cassine*), swamp dogwood (*Cornus foemina*), yellow canna (*Canna flaccida*), prairie blue flag (*Iris hexagona*).

DISADVANTAGES

Leaf-eating insects are a minor pest. Otherwise mostly carefree except for occasional pruning. Will produce suckers from underground stems.

CULTIVARS

'Henry's Garnet,' with brighter, larger flowers, and 'Sarah Eve' are both used in Florida.

SIMILAR AND RELATED SPECIES

Most often confused with summersweet (*Clethra alnifolia*).

Iva spp.

EYE-vuh

Seaside Elder and Marsh Elder

Family: Asteraceae or Compositae
Shrubs
Height: 2 to 6 feet
Spread: 1 to 4 feet

7mm))

Seaside elder (*I. imbricata*) and marsh elder (*I. frutescens*) are excellent shrubs for sandy, coastal landscapes, the edges of salt marshes, and dune restoration and stabilization.

FORM

Branched, mostly woody shrubs (sometimes herbaceous above) with narrow, lance-shaped, fleshy leaves and erect, terminal spikes of small, greenish flowers. Spreads by numerous underground stems. *I. imbricata*, in particular, may encourage the formation of low, rounded dunes in beach settings.

NATIVE RANGE

Dunes and edges of salt marshes. Virginia, southward to central peninsular Florida, and west to Mississippi.

CHARACTERISTICS

Flowers: Small, greenish, fragrant, borne in erect spikes at the ends of branches. Summer to fall.

Leaves: Lance shaped, narrow, fleshy, about 2 inches long, commonly toothed along the margins.

Fruit: A tiny, inconspicuous achene.

Bark: Pale gray to light brown but typically obscured by the dense foliage.

CULTURE

Soil: Well-drained sands of beaches and dunes.

Exposure: Full sun. Extremely salt tolerant.

Water: Tolerant of xeric to moist, salty environments. Supplemental irrigation not required.

Hardiness Zones: 8 to 10.

Life Span: Colonies can persist for many years.

BEST FEATURES

Salt tolerance. First-year seedlings are easily transplanted in spring. Excellent for dune stabilization and restoration. Spreads by underground runners.

COMPANION PLANTS

Sea oxeye (*Borrichia frutescens*), railroad vine (*Ipomoea pescaprae*), prickly pears (*Opuntia* spp.), sea oats (*Uniola paniculata*), beach morning glory (*Ipomoea imperati*), seashore paspalum (*Paspalum vaginatum*), beach panic grass (*Panicum amarum*), saw palmetto (*Serenoa repens*), Christmasberry (*Lycium carolinianum*), blanket flower (*Gaillardia pulchella*), beach sunflower (*Helianthus debilis*).

ALLERGENIC AND TOXIC PROPERTIES

Wind pollinated and may cause allergic reactions in some people.

SIMILAR AND RELATED SPECIES

Salt bush (*Baccharis halimifolia*) is also a member of the aster family and occurs in similar habitats.

Juncus effusus

JUN-kus e-FEW-sus

Softrush

Family: Juncaceae
Tall ground cover, large aquatic rush
Height: 1 to 4 feet
Spread: 1 to 2 feet

LANDSCAPE USE

Used at the edges of ponds, wetland depressions, and water gardens, or to stabilize wet roadsides, shorelines, and stream banks.

FORM

A grasslike, clump-forming, perennial herb with numerous arching to erect, smooth, green, hollow culms and brownish flower clusters.

NATIVE RANGE

Fresh to brackish marshes, pond and lake edges, stream banks, ditches, and seasonal wetlands. Throughout the eastern United States and Florida.

CHARACTERISTICS

Flowers: Small, brownish, borne in dense clusters. Summer.
Leaves: Soft, green, quill-like, to about 4 feet long.
Fruit: A small, brownish capsule. Fall.

CULTURE

Soil: Prefers rich, finely textured, wet soils with pH 4.0–6.0.
Exposure: Full sun to part shade.
Water: Requires wet conditions for best performance. Prefers shallow water to about 6 inches deep.
Hardiness Zones: 4 to 10.
Life Span: Perennial.

BEST FEATURES

Most valued as an accent along ponds. Excellent for sediment accretion, shoreline restoration and stabilization, and erosion control. Provides both food and cover for wildlife.

COMPANION PLANTS

Buttonbush (*Cephalanthus occidentalis*), yellow canna (*Canna flaccida*), blue flags (*Iris* spp.), sand cordgrass (*Spartina bakeri*), climbing aster (*Symphyotrichum carolinianum*), bulrushes (*Scirpus* spp.).

SIMILAR AND RELATED SPECIES

Black needlerush (*J. roemerianus*), the common rush of coastal saline wetlands, and nearly 20 other species of *Juncus* occur naturally in Florida.

Juniperus virginiana

joo-NI-puh-rus vir-ji-nee-AY-nuh

Red Cedar

Family: Cupressaceae
Medium-sized tree
Height: 20 to 60 feet
Spread: 10 to 30 feet

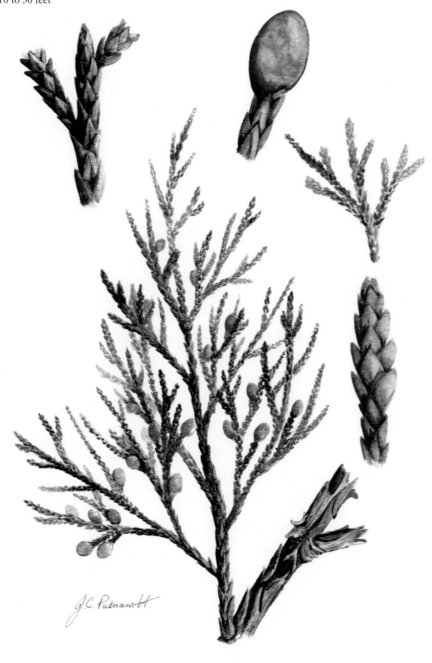

J.C. Putnam lt

LANDSCAPE USE

Used as a specimen tree, in groves, and to provide cover, food, and nest sites for birds and other wildlife. Especially useful along streets, on roadsides, in cemeteries, and as a tall, thick hedge along property borders.

FORM

An erect, conical, densely foliated, very low-branching, evergreen tree.

NATIVE RANGE

Pioneering in disturbed sites, along fields, and on roadsides. Throughout eastern North America, southward to central peninsular Florida.

CHARACTERISTICS

Leaves: Small, green, scalelike, crowded around the twigs and branches.

Fruit: Borne in bluish, rounded, berrylike female cones that are produced in profuse, showy clusters in late summer and fall. Male cones yellowish.

Bark: Reddish brown; exfoliating in thin, shaggy strips.

CULTURE

Soil: Especially well adapted to neutral and alkaline soils, but will adapt to almost any soil. Preferred pH 5.0–8.0. Salt tolerant.

Exposure: Full sun.

Water: Drought tolerant. Irrigation typically not required. Site should be well drained.

Hardiness Zones: 3 to 9.

Life Span: Long-lived.

BEST FEATURES

Evergreen habit, conical shape, dense foliage, bluish female cones, usefulness to wildlife, and exceptional tolerance of alkaline soil.

COMPANION PLANTS

Live oak and sand live oak (*Quercus virginiana* and *Q. geminata*), American holly (*Ilex opaca*), coontie (*Zamia pumila*), yaupon (*Ilex vomitoria*), fringetree (*Chionanthus virginicus*), American hophornbeam (*Ostrya virginiana*), blue beech (*Carpinus caroliniana*), redbud (*Cercis canadensis*), witch hazel (*Hamamelis virginiana*), needle palm (*Rhapidophyllum hystrix*), winged elm (*Ulmus alata*).

DISADVANTAGES

Susceptible to a number of insect pests. Host of cedar-apple rust; should not be grown near crabapple (*Malus angustifolia*) or haws (*Crataegus* spp.).

CULTIVARS

A number of red cedar cultivars have been selected, but none are much used in Florida.

ALLERGENIC AND TOXIC PROPERTIES

May cause dermatitis in some people and digestive upset to cattle; airborne pollen may cause respiratory problems in some people.

SIMILAR AND RELATED SPECIES

Some have recognized southern red cedar (*J. silicicola*) as a variety, subspecies, or separate species, though it is more likely that it and *J. virginiana* are one and the same.

Krugiodendron ferreum

KRU-gee-o-DEN-drawn FE-ree-um

Black Ironwood

Family: Rhamnaceae
Medium-sized tree
Height: 15 to 25 feet
Spread: 10 to 20 feet

LANDSCAPE USE

May be used as a small specimen tree in residential landscapes, as a street tree, or as a large shrub or small tree in the background or along shady borders.

FORM

An erect, densely foliated, evergreen tree with glossy green, oval leaves and an oval form.

NATIVE RANGE

Coastal hammocks. Brevard County south along the coast. More common in the Florida Keys; also West Indies, Bahamas, Mexico, and Central America.

CHARACTERISTICS

Flowers: Small, greenish, borne in clusters in the leaf axils. Spring and summer.

Leaves: Opposite, short-stalked, oval to egg shaped in outline, 1½–2½ inches long, shiny green above, flattened or notched at the apex. New growth is often reddish.

Fruit: A black, single-seeded, ¼-inch-diameter drupe.

Bark: Rough, furrowed, light to dark gray; trunk often contorted in maturity.

CULTURE

Soil: Organic, mostly neutral soils of coastal hammocks; pH 6.5–7.5.

Exposure: Shade to sun.

Water: Prefers moist, well-drained situations.

Hardiness Zones: 10 to 11.

Life Span: Slow growing and long-lived; likely more than 100 years.

BEST FEATURES

Dense form and attractive glossy, green, oval leaves. Reddish early growth. Slow growth rate. Fruit eaten by birds and other wildlife.

COMPANION PLANTS

Gumbo limbo (*Bursera simaruba*), satinleaf (*Chrysophyllum oliviforme*), pigeon plum (*Coccoloba diversifolia*), strangler fig (*Ficus aurea*), marlberry (*Ardisia escallonioides*), spicewood (*Calyptranthes pallens*), stoppers (*Eugenia* spp.), white indigoberry (*Randia aculeata*), wild coffee (*Psychotria nervosa*), Florida gamagrass (*Tripsacum floridanum*).

DISADVANTAGES

Fallen fruit can be a nuisance on paved surfaces.

SIMILAR AND RELATED SPECIES

Darling plum (*Reynosia septentrionalis*) is somewhat similar but has stiff, less shiny leaves.

Lachnanthes caroliana

lak-NAN-theez ka-ro-lee-AY-nuh

Redroot

Family: Haemodoraceae
Herbaceous wildflower
Height: 1 to 3 feet
Spread: 1 foot, but forming colonies by underground stems

LANDSCAPE USE

Especially useful in wet gardens in conjunction with and in front of irises and other wetland wildflowers. Will spread by underground runners to form large patches in wet savannas or along wetland borders.

FORM

An erect, perennial herb, 1–2 feet tall, with flat, long-tapering leaves and a conspicuous cluster of whitish yellow flowers.

NATIVE RANGE

Wet flatwoods, bogs, savannas, and coastal swales. Nova Scotia, south nearly throughout Florida, and west to Louisiana.

CHARACTERISTICS

Flowers: Creamy yellow; borne in conspicuous, 4-inch-wide clusters at the top of an erect stem.

Leaves: Erect, flat, 1–2 feet tall, tapering to a long-pointed tip. Similar in general form to those of the irises.

Fruit: A globular capsule bearing flat, brown seeds.

CULTURE

Soil: Wet, sandy, very acid soils, preferably overlaying impervious hardpan.

Exposure: Full sun to part shade.

Water: Occurs naturally in moist to wet situations. Tolerates inundation. Should be kept wet, especially during summer.

Hardiness Zones: 6 to 10.

Life Span: Perennial wildflower.

BEST FEATURES

Tolerates inundation and excellent for acid-rich bogs. Attractive to birds. Grasslike leaves visible for most of the growing season.

COMPANION PLANTS

Slash and longleaf pines (*Pinus elliottii* and *P. palustris*), bays (*Persea* spp.), tarflower (*Bejaria racemosa*), lyonias (*Lyonia* spp.), wax myrtle (*Myrica cerifera*), wiregrass (*Aristida stricta* var. *beyrichiana*), lowbush blueberries (*Vaccinium* spp.), broomsedge (*Andropogon virginicus*), saw palmetto (*Serenoa repens*), Florida paintbrush (*Carphephorus corymbosus*).

DISADVANTAGES

Does not tolerate dry sites.

ALLERGENIC AND TOXIC PROPERTIES

Toxicity unknown. Extracts from the roots are reported to cause dizziness and headache.

SIMILAR AND RELATED SPECIES

Goldcrest (*Lophiola aurea*) is very similar in form and habitat but is not used in native plant landscaping. Redroot is vegetatively similar to the irises and can be used in conjunction with them.

Laguncularia racemosa

luh-gun-kew-LA-ree-uh ray-si-MO-suh

White Mangrove

Family: Combretaceae
Large shrub
Height: 30 to 40 feet
Spread: 20 to 30 feet

LANDSCAPE USE

Used as a hedge in saline areas, as a windbreak, and to stabilize shorelines. An essential component in mangrove restoration projects. One of Florida's three true mangrove species. It and the red and black mangroves (*Rhizophora mangle* and *Avicennia germinans*) are extremely valuable for protecting south Florida's shoreline. All three, especially when used together, are excellent for controlling and reducing coastal erosion and related damage from hurricanes, winter storms, and high tides. All three are also essential for coastal and inland waterway restoration projects.

FORM

An erect, often multistemmed, irregularly branched, evergreen tree.

NATIVE RANGE

Brackish waters of low-energy shorelines. South Florida, the West Indies, and tropical America.

CHARACTERISTICS

Flowers: Tiny, white, fragrant, borne in short, simple or branched racemes near the ends of the branches. Year-round, but mostly March to September.

Leaves: Opposite, oval, thick, stiff, pale grayish green, 2–3 inches long.

Fruit: A greenish to reddish, ribbed capsule, narrow at the base, widening toward the tip, about 1 inch long. Year-round, mostly fall.

Bark: Light brown and ridged.

CULTURE

Soil: Wet, often salt-rich soils. Exceptionally salt tolerant.

Exposure: Full sun.

Water: Will adapt to freshwater situations. Soil should be kept moist.

Hardiness Zones: 9 to 11.

Life Span: Moderate.

BEST FEATURES

Dense foliage. Salt tolerance. Effectiveness in stabilizing and protecting saltwater shorelines.

COMPANION PLANTS

Red mangrove (*Rhizophora mangle*), black mangrove (*Avicennia germinans*), buttonwood (*Conocarpus erectus*), leather fern (*Acrostichum danaeifolium*), string lily (*Crinum americanum*), sea oxeyes (*Borrichia* spp.), saltwort (*Batis maritima*).

SIMILAR AND RELATED SPECIES

The several mangroves that occur in Florida are mentioned above.

Lantana involucrata

lan-TA-nuh in-vah-lew-KRAY-tuh

Wild Sage

Family: Verbenaceae
Medium shrub
Height: 3 to 5 feet
Spread: 1 to 5 feet

LANDSCAPE USE

An excellent shrub for tropical and subtropical gardens from about south-central Florida southward. It is especially attractive to butterflies and makes an excellent addition to butterfly gardens.

FORM

An upright, freely branching, woody shrub with attractive clusters of whitish to cream-colored flowers.

NATIVE RANGE

Dunes, coastal hammocks, and edges of thickets and coastal scrubs. South-central Florida and south; also West Indies, Bermuda, Mexico, and Central America.

CHARACTERISTICS

Flowers: Whitish; individually small, but borne in conspicuous clusters. Year-round.

Leaves: Opposite, simple, egg shaped to elliptic, sometimes more nearly oval, 1–2 inches long, a little more than 1 inch wide, rough to the touch, aromatic when crushed.

Fruit: A small, rounded, blue or purple drupe.

Bark: Thin; brownish.

CULTURE

Soil: Thin, well-drained, coastal soils.

Exposure: Full sun to very light shade.

Water: Drought tolerant.

Hardiness Zones: 8 to 11.

Life Span: Relatively short; perhaps less than 20 years in most situations.

BEST FEATURES

Attractive flower clusters. Attractive to butterflies. Long flowering period. Drought tolerance.

COMPANION PLANTS

Broomsedge (*Andropogon virginicus*), silver palm (*Coccothrinax argentata*), white indigoberry (*Randia aculeata*), coontie (*Zamia pumila*), saw palmetto (*Serenoa repens*).

DISADVANTAGES

May become sprawling and leggy if not adequately pruned.

CULTIVARS

A variety of *Lantana* cultivars and forms are available, almost all of which derive from the non-native and weedy *L. camara*. Some of these selections are dwarf forms and produce bright yellow flowers similar to the native trailing pineland lantana (*L. depressa*), with which they are often confused, even in native nurseries. *L. camara* should be avoided due to its invasive nature.

ALLERGENIC AND TOXIC PROPERTIES

The fruit of some species of *Lantana* is poisonous. The toxicity of *L. involucrata* is unknown; caution is advised.

SIMILAR AND RELATED SPECIES

Several species of *Lantana* are native to Florida; see the discussion of cultivars above.

Liatris spp.

ly-AY-tris

Blazing Stars, Gayfeathers

Family: Asteraceae or Compositae
Wildflowers
Height: 2 to 7 feet
Spread: Individually narrow, less than 1 foot, but potentially forming large colonies

Excellent additions to wildflower and butterfly gardens as well as open meadows. Most attractive when used in massed plantings. Excellent for roadside plantings.

FORM

About 15 species and varieties of blazing star occur in Florida, at least 5 of which are available from native plant nurseries. Most are slender herbs with narrow leaves and erect stems. The upper third of the stem produces a showy, elongated spike of lavender flowers.

NATIVE RANGE

Sandhills, flatwoods, scrub, and dunes. North and South Carolina, south nearly throughout Florida, and west to Mississippi.

CHARACTERISTICS

Flowers: Lavender, pinkish, rose-purple, or sometimes whitish, borne in showy, 2- to 4-foot-long spikes along the upper third of the stem. Summer through fall.

Leaves: Typically narrow with those lower on the stem spreading and ascending, those along the upper stem often shorter and pressed to the stem, depending upon species.

Fruit: A tiny, inconspicuous achene.

CULTURE

Soil: Typically sandy, moist to dry, slightly acid to neutral soils.

Exposure: Full sun.

Water: Prefer slightly moist to dry conditions. Supplemental irrigation not required when properly sited.

Hardiness Zones: 6 to 10.

Life Span: Perennial, persisting in the garden by self-sown seed.

BEST FEATURES

Showy flower spikes. Hardy, undemanding, and easy to grow. Flowers are attractive to a host of butterflies.

COMPANION PLANTS

Goldenrods (*Solidago* spp.), rayless and narrowleaf sunflowers (*Helianthus radula* and *H. angustifolia*), golden aster (*Pityopsis graminifolia*), Florida paintbrush (*Carphephorus corymbosus*), butterfly weed (*Asclepias tuberosa*), coral honeysuckle (*Lonicera sempervirens*), beautyberry (*Callicarpa americana*), lopsided Indiangrass (*Sorghastrum secundum*).

CULTIVARS

Several named cultivars or selections featuring various flower colors are reported.

SIMILAR AND RELATED SPECIES

Florida's several species of *Carphephorus* are somewhat similar and make excellent companion plants. They also have purple to lavender flowers, but their inflorescences are generally broader than those of the blazing stars. The several species of blazing stars available in Florida include *L. chapmanii, L. gracilis, L. spicata,* and two varieties of *L. tenuifolia.* Several non-native species are sometimes available in nurseries and should be avoided.

Licania michauxii

ly-KAY-nee-uh mi-SHO-ee-eye

Gopher Apple

Family: Chrysobalanaceae
Ground cover
Height: 1 to 1½ feet
Spread: Will spread over many square feet by underground stems

LANDSCAPE USE

Used primarily as a ground cover and soil stabilizer in poor, dry, sandy soils, especially in coastal settings and along roadsides.

FORM

A low-growing, spreading, woody subshrub that forms dense populations.

NATIVE RANGE

Sand ridges, sandy pinelands, and stabilized dunes. South Carolina, south throughout Florida, and west to Louisiana.

CHARACTERISTICS

Flowers: White, small, borne in erect, 4-inch-long terminal cymes.

Leaves: Alternate, stiff, pale green, finely but conspicuously veined, 1–4 inches long, sometimes conspicuously whitish on the lower surface.

Fruit: A creamy white to brownish, ellipsoid, 1- to 2-inch-long drupe.

Bark: Aboveground stems brownish.

CULTURE

Soil: Dry, thin, poor, sandy, well-drained soils of coastal dunes and pine rocklands.

Exposure: Full sun.

Water: Irrigation not required.

Hardiness Zones: 8 to 11.

Life Span: Colonies are long-lived.

BEST FEATURES

An exceptionally hardy ground cover for dry, sandy soils. Bright white flowers. Fruit is attractive to wildlife.

COMPANION PLANTS

Broomsedge (*Andropogon virginicus*), highbush and lowbush blueberries (*Vaccinium* spp.), sparkleberry (*Vaccinium arboreum*), coontie (*Zamia pumila*), garberia (*Garberia heterophylla*), wiregrass (*Aristida stricta* var. *beyrichiana*), lopsided Indiangrass (*Sorghastrum secundum*), Adam's needle (*Yucca filamentosa*), wild rosemary (*Conradina canescens*), summer haw (*Crataegus flava*), scrub oaks (*Quercus* spp.).

SIMILAR AND RELATED SPECIES

Gopher apple is in the same family as cocoplum (*Chrysobalanus icaco*) but is not similar to it.

Liquidambar styraciflua

li-kwi-DAM-bar sty-ruh-SI-floo-uh (or sty-ra-si-FLOO-uh)

Sweetgum

Family: Altingiaceae
Large tree
Height: 40 to 125 feet
Spread: 20 to 60 feet

LANDSCAPE USE

Excellent as a specimen or to provide shade and fall color. Excellent for reclaiming old fields and disturbed sites. Good to excellent for roadside plantings.

FORM

A large, single-trunked, deciduous tree with spreading branches, a conical shape, and star-shaped leaves.

NATIVE RANGE

Old fields, roadsides, bottomland woods, edges of swamps, and floodplains. Throughout the southeastern United States, southward to about central peninsular Florida, and west to Mexico.

CHARACTERISTICS

Flowers: Small, greenish yellow, emerging prior to the new leaves. Male flowers borne in upright clusters; female flowers borne in hanging, spherical clusters.
Leaves: Alternate, about 5 inches wide, shiny green above, star shaped with 3–7 lobes, toothed along the margins. Showy in fall when leaves turn yellow, maroon, or wine red.
Fruit: A spherical "gum ball" with hornlike or spiny projections.
Bark: Grayish; furrowed into narrow, distinctive ridges and grooves.

CULTURE

Soil: Prefers deep, moist, acid soil, but will adapt to dry sites, though the growth may be somewhat slower under dry conditions.
Exposure: Sun to part shade.
Water: If situated in moist soil, supplemental irrigation is not required. On drier sites, it should be irrigated until well established.
Hardiness Zones: 6 to 9.
Life Span: Long-lived; more than 75 years.

BEST FEATURES

Grows very quickly and can produce shade in as little as five years. Fall color. Tolerates a variety of soils, even those with low oxygen. Good wildlife food.

COMPANION PLANTS

Oaks (*Quercus* spp.), pignut hickory (*Carya glabra*), yaupon (*Ilex vomitoria*), magnolia (*Magnolia grandiflora*), red buckeye (*Aesculus pavia*), beautyberry (*Callicarpa americana*), Cherokee bean (*Erythrina herbacea*), loblolly pine (*Pinus taeda*).

DISADVANTAGES

Fallen fruit decomposes slowly and produces an untidy appearance in manicured landscapes. Wood is somewhat brittle, which may lead to wind damage.

CULTIVARS

A number of cultivars are known. 'Rotundiloba,' selected for reduced fruit production, is the only one available in Florida.

SIMILAR AND RELATED SPECIES

Sweetgum resembles the maples in leaf shape and fall color. Witch hazel (*Hamamelis virginiana*) and witch alder (*Fothergilla gardenii*) are in the same botanical family but are not similar.

Liriodendron tulipifera

lee-ree-o-DEN-drawn too-li-PI-fuh-ruh

Tulip Poplar

Family: Magnoliaceae
Large tree
Height: 60 to 100 feet
Spread: 35 to 50 feet

Useful as a street, shade, or ornamental tree in parks and large landscapes. Good for retention pond borders. Grows to large size and may not be suitable for residential or other small landscapes. Performs best in moist areas.

FORM

A large, erect, fast-growing, deciduous tree with a single trunk, slightly ascending branches, and pyramidal form.

NATIVE RANGE

Rich hammocks. New England, southward to central peninsular Florida, and west to east Texas.

CHARACTERISTICS

Flowers: Large, fragrant, tuliplike, with yellowish green petals and an orange center; borne high in the crown. Spring to summer.

Leaves: Alternate, simple, 3–8 inches both long and broad, 4-lobed, truncate at both base and apex, with a deep apical notch; turning a showy pale to bright yellow in fall.

Fruit: A 3- to 4-inch-long, conelike structure that opens at maturity into a vase-shaped structure with overlapping scales.

Bark: Ridged and furrowed; ashy gray to dark brown.

CULTURE

Soil: Moist, fertile, acid to neutral, well-drained, loose-textured soil with pH 4.5–7.5.

Exposure: Full sun to part shade.

Water: Moist, well-drained situations are preferred. Cannot tolerate excessively wet or dry situations.

Hardiness Zones: 4 to 9.

Life Span: Generally long-lived. Individual specimens may live 200 years in natural situations. Cultivated specimens may not exceed 100 years, especially if sited in wet conditions.

BEST FEATURES

Tulip poplar's best features include its rapid growth rate, handsome flowers, interesting fruit, resistance to disease, unusual leaves, and brightly colored fall foliage.

COMPANION PLANTS

Basswood (*Tilia americana*), Florida sugar maple (*Acer saccharum* subsp. *floridanum*), winged elm (*Ulmus alata*), Shumard oak (*Quercus shumardii*), magnolia (*Magnolia grandiflora*), hickories (*Carya* spp.), red buckeye (*Aesculus pavia*), red mulberry (*Morus rubra*), needle palm (*Rhapidophyllum hystrix*), Florida azalea (*Rhododendron austrinum*).

DISADVANTAGES

Yellow-poplar weevil, two cankers, and powdery mildews may pose problems. Will develop root rot and die if planted on wet sites. Young, fast-growing trees may have brittle wood.

CULTIVARS

Nearly a dozen cultivars are reported but are not generally available in Florida.

SIMILAR AND RELATED SPECIES

Tulip poplar is actually not a poplar, but a member of the magnolia family. Its unique flowers and leaves set it apart from all other Florida trees.

Lobelia cardinalis

lo-BE-lee-uh kar-di-NAY-lis (or lo-BEE-lee-uh, or kar-di-NA-lis)

Cardinal Flower

Family: Campanulaceae
Perennial wildflower
Height: 2 to 4 feet
Spread: Less than 1 foot

LANDSCAPE USE

Excellent in moist wildflower gardens, along small streams, and for beautifying the edges of retention ponds, canal banks, and drainage swales.

FORM

An erect, perennial, potentially thick-stemmed wildflower topped with a conspicuous, showy raceme of numerous bright red flowers.

NATIVE RANGE

Floodplain forests, wet edges of streams, and spring runs. Virginia, southward to central Florida, and west to Mississippi.

CHARACTERISTICS

Flowers: Scarlet red, showy, irregularly shaped with an enlarged lower lip; about 1 inch long and borne in an erect raceme at the stem tip.
Leaves: Alternate, lance shaped, to about 8 inches long and 2 inches wide.
Fruit: A small capsule.

CULTURE

Soil: Rich, acid, poorly drained soils.
Exposure: Full sun to part shade.
Water: Prefers moist to wet conditions.
Hardiness Zones: 3 to 10.
Life Span: Perennial, though plants sometimes die after flowering.

BEST FEATURES

The brilliant scarlet red flowers are attractive to both humans and hummingbirds. Very tolerant of wet situations.

COMPANION PLANTS

String lily (*Crinum americanum*), mist flower (*Conoclinium coelestinum*), box elder and red maple (*Acer negundo* and *A. rubrum*), green ash (*Fraxinus pennsylvanica*), sweetbay (*Magnolia virginiana*), dahoon (*Ilex cassine*), netted chain fern (*Woodwardia areolata*), cinnamon and royal ferns (*Osmunda cinnamomea* and *O. regalis*).

DISADVANTAGES

Though perennial, plants sometimes die after flowering.

ALLERGENIC AND TOXIC PROPERTIES

Although the toxicity of this species is unknown, caution is advised. Death has occurred from overdoses of related species. Symptoms include nausea, vomiting, headache, rapid pulse, tremors, and headache.

SIMILAR AND RELATED SPECIES

The closely related *L. glandulosa* is also used in landscaping but has blue flowers.

Lonicera sempervirens

lah-NI-suh-ruh sem-pir-VY-renz

Coral Honeysuckle

Family: Caprifoliaceae
Climbing vine
Height: Climbing stems reach 15 feet
Spread: Scrambling to several feet

An excellent vine for fences, arbors, and trellises. Not aggressive like the closely related but non-native pest, Japanese honeysuckle (*L. japonica*). Used extensively as a ground cover in highway medians.

FORM

A twining, climbing vine scrambling over fences, arbors, trees, shrubs, and other structures. Will become a weak shrub if not trained to a structure.

NATIVE RANGE

Rich hammocks, sandhills, open woodlands, thickets. Eastern United States, from Connecticut southward to central Florida and west to Texas.

CHARACTERISTICS

Flowers: Scarlet red to more or less orange, tubular and trumpet shaped, about 2 inches long, showy, and attractive to butterflies and hummingbirds. Mainly spring and summer; often into the fall.

Leaves: Opposite, oval to oblong, 1–3 inches long, dark green with smooth margins, those below the flowers usually completely clasping the stem.

Fruit: A scarlet red berry, ¼ inch in diameter. Late summer and fall.

Bark: Straw-colored.

CULTURE

Soil: Fertile, moist, rich, acid to slightly alkaline soils.

Exposure: Full sun to part shade.

Water: Well-drained, moderately dry conditions are best.

Hardiness Zones: 4 to 11.

Life Span: Will colonize and reproduce for many years.

BEST FEATURES

Foliage is showy and ornamental. Bright red to orange-red flowers are showy, have an extended blooming season, and attract butterflies and hummingbirds. Berries are both showy and attractive to wildlife. Twines rather than clasps.

COMPANION PLANTS

Gopher apple (*Licania michauxii*), summer haw (*Crataegus flava*), trumpet creeper (*Campsis radicans*), beautyberry (*Callicarpa americana*), Carolina jessamine (*Gelsemium sempervirens*), Cherokee bean (*Erythrina herbacea*), wax myrtle (*Myrica cerifera*), lopsided Indiangrass (*Sorghastrum secundum*), yaupon (*Ilex vomitoria*).

CULTIVARS

Several cultivars have been selected, none of which are readily available in Florida.

ALLERGENIC AND TOXIC PROPERTIES

Caution is advised. Fruit and leaves of some species have caused death to livestock.

SIMILAR AND RELATED SPECIES

Trumpet creeper (*Campsis radicans*) and cross vine (*Bignonia capreolata*), both of which are not closely related to coral honeysuckle, also have tubular red flowers.

Lycium carolinianum

LI-see-um ka-ro-li-nee-AY-num

Christmasberry

Family: Solanaceae
Shrub
Height: 3 to 9 feet
Spread: 3 to 5 feet

LANDSCAPE USE
Useful in coastal landscaping, especially along the salty edges of coastal marshes.

FORM
An erect to sprawling, loosely branched, woody shrub with somewhat thorny branches, beautiful blue flowers, and bright red fruit.

NATIVE RANGE
Edges of salt marshes and salt flats. Along the coast from Georgia to southern peninsular Florida and west to Texas.

CHARACTERISTICS
Flowers: Stalked, 4- to 5-lobed, blue to lavender, rarely almost white, borne individually in the leaf axils. Fall.
Leaves: Alternate, narrow, linear, succulent, bright green, borne in clusters along the branches.
Fruit: A bright red, ellipsoid berry borne in December, hence the common name.
Bark: Thin; grayish.

CULTURE
Soil: Moist, saline soils of coastal marshes.
Exposure: Full sun.
Water: Christmasberry is an obligate wetland species and performs best in wet situations. Salt tolerant.
Hardiness Zones: 8 to 11.
Life Span: Hardy and moderately long-lived; perhaps to 50 years.

BEST FEATURES
Beautiful blue flowers. Bright red fruit at Christmastime. Overall hardiness. Exceptional tolerance of saline situations.

COMPANION PLANTS
Sea oxeye (*Borrichia frutescens*), marsh and seaside elders (*Iva frutescens* and *I. imbricata*), railroad vine (*Ipomoea pes-caprae*), prickly pears (*Opuntia* spp.), sea oats (*Uniola paniculata*), beach morning glory (*Ipomoea imperati*), seashore paspalum (*Paspalum vaginatum*), beach panic grass (*Panicum amarum*), saw palmetto (*Serenoa repens*), blanket flower (*Gaillardia pulchella*), beach sunflower (*Helianthus debilis*).

ALLERGENIC AND TOXIC PROPERTIES
Christmasberry is a member of the nightshade family, which is known for some of the world's most important food plants as well as some of the most poisonous. At least one species in this genus has caused death to livestock.

SIMILAR AND RELATED SPECIES
In natural situations, the vegetation of sea blite (*Suaeda linearis*) might be confused with that of Christmasberry. However, sea blite is seldom encountered in the native plant trade.

Lyonia ferruginea

ly-O-nee-uh fe-roo-JI-nee-uh

Rusty Lyonia

Family: Ericaceae
Shrub or small tree
Height: 10 to 25 feet
Spread: 5 to 10 feet

LANDSCAPE USE

May be used as a hedge or patio tree. Also a worthy addition to a sunny shrub garden.

FORM

A large, evergreen shrub or small irregularly branched tree with arching branches.

NATIVE RANGE

Scrub, flatwoods, and sandy hammocks. South Carolina, southward to about Lake Okeechobee, and west to the central counties of the Florida panhandle.

CHARACTERISTICS

Flowers: White to pinkish, urn shaped like those of the blueberries, borne on wood of the previous season. Spring.

Leaves: Alternate, 1–3 inches long, dark green above and rusty-scaly below when mature, rusty or burnt orange on both surfaces and showy when new.

Fruit: A small, brownish capsule.

Bark: Brownish to rusty brown.

CULTURE

Soil: Rich, sandy, acid to slightly alkaline soils. Will tolerate poor soils, but achieves a smaller stature in them.

Exposure: Full sun to part shade.

Water: Moist to well-drained, dry situations.

Hardiness Zones: 8 to 10.

Life Span: Over 50 years.

BEST FEATURES

Rusty lyonia's overall hardiness and ease of care, evergreen habit, numerous bell-shaped flowers, and rusty orange new leaves are its main attractions.

COMPANION PLANTS

Inkberry and gallberry (*Ilex glabra* and *I. coriacea*), staggerbushes, fetterbushes, and dog-hobbles (*Lyonia* spp. and *Leucothoe* spp.), titi (*Cyrilla racemiflora*), loblolly bay (*Gordonia lasianthus*), sweetbay (*Magnolia virginiana*), summersweet (*Clethra alnifolia*), Virginia willow (*Itea virginica*), cinnamon fern (*Osmunda cinnamomea*), possum haw (*Viburnum nudum*), saw palmetto (*Serenoa repens*), scrub mints (*Conradina* spp.), Chapman and myrtle oaks (*Quercus chapmanii* and *Q. myrtifolia*), coontie (*Zamia pumila*).

ALLERGENIC AND TOXIC PROPERTIES

Caution is advised. The toxicity of *Lyonia ferruginea* is unknown. However, numerous members of the heath family are known to be toxic and produce a variety of symptoms including nausea, vomiting, altered heart rate, and dizziness.

SIMILAR AND RELATED SPECIES

Several species of *Lyonia* occur in Florida. Fetterbush (*L. lucida*) is also an excellent landscape plant, as is staggerbush (*L. fruticosa*). All occur in similar habitats.

Lyonia lucida

ly-O-nee-uh LOO-si-duh

Fetterbush

Family: Ericaceae
Small to large shrub
Height: 3 to 10 feet
Spread: 2 to 5 feet

J.C. Putnam H

LANDSCAPE USE
Appropriate for hedges, along foundations, in mixed shrub beds, or in naturalistic landscapes.

FORM
An erect, multistemmed, evergreen, colonial shrub with arching branches, shiny leaves, and showy flowers.

NATIVE RANGE
Flatwoods, bogs, and edges of swamps and cypress ponds. Virginia, south throughout Florida, and west to Louisiana.

CHARACTERISTICS
Flowers: Aromatic, bell shaped, pink to nearly white, about ½ inch long, but borne in numerous conspicuous fascicles along the stem. Spring.
Leaves: Shiny green, oval to elliptic, with a conspicuously thickened margin.
Fruit: A brown, rounded capsule. Summer.
Bark: Reddish brown; thin.

CULTURE
Soil: Prefers well-drained, acid soil high in organic content.
Exposure: Full sun to part shade.
Water: Irrigate until established. Otherwise, little care is required.
Hardiness Zones: 7 to 10.
Life Span: Colonies spread by underground stems and tend to maintain themselves for many years.

BEST FEATURES
Profuse and prolonged flowering during spring. Attractive, shiny green, evergreen foliage. May be pruned to form a hedge. Requires little care once established.

COMPANION PLANTS
Inkberry and gallberry (*Ilex glabra* and *I. coriacea*), staggerbushes and dog-hobbles (*Lyonia* spp. and *Leucothoe* spp.), titi (*Cyrilla racemiflora*), loblolly bay (*Gordonia lasianthus*), sweetbay (*Magnolia virginiana*), summersweet (*Clethra alnifolia*), Virginia willow (*Itea virginica*), cinnamon fern (*Osmunda cinnamomea*), possum haw (*Viburnum nudum*), saw palmetto (*Serenoa repens*).

DISADVANTAGES
Leaf spotting has been reported.

ALLERGENIC AND TOXIC PROPERTIES
Caution is advised. The toxicity of *Lyonia lucida* is unknown. However, numerous members of the heath family are known to be toxic and produce a variety of symptoms including nausea, vomiting, altered heart rate, dizziness, and staggering.

SIMILAR AND RELATED SPECIES
In the same family as blueberries (*Vaccinium* spp.) and rhododendrons (*Rhododendron* spp.). Several other species of staggerbushes and fetterbushes (*Lyonia* spp.) occur in Florida. The dog-hobbles (*Leucothoe racemosa* and *L. axillaris*) are similar.

Lysiloma latisiliquum

ly-si-LO-muh la-ti-SI-li-kwum

Wild Tamarind

Family: Fabaceae
Medium to large tree
Height: 25 to 60 feet
Spread: 30 to 50 feet

LANDSCAPE USE

Used for shade in both residential and recreational situations and for highway beautification.

FORM

A large, erect to slightly leaning, spreading, essentially evergreen tree with divided, fernlike foliage and very attractive light gray bark.

NATIVE RANGE

Coastal hammocks and pinelands. Southernmost Florida and the Keys, the West Indies, southern Mexico, and parts of Central America.

CHARACTERISTICS

Flowers: White to greenish white, borne in conspicuous, 1-inch-long, ball-like clusters. Spring.

Leaves: Bipinnately compound with numerous entire, light green, asymmetrical, ½-inch-long leaflets.

Fruit: A thin, flattened, 6-inch-long pod with several shiny, dark brown, ½-inch-long seeds.

Bark: Smooth and light gray; becoming dark brown and separating into large plates with age.

CULTURE

Soil: Thin, neutral to slightly alkaline soil over limestone.

Exposure: Full sun to part shade. Resistant to salt spray. Intolerant of cold, and should probably be planted no farther north than Broward County.

Water: Drought tolerant.

Hardiness Zones: 10 to 11.

Life Span: 50 to 100 years.

BEST FEATURES

Attractive, smooth, gray trunk. Shade value. Overall hardiness. Very fast growing.

COMPANION PLANTS

Marlberry (*Ardisia escallonioides*), spicewood (*Calyptranthes pallens*), gumbo limbo (*Bursera simaruba*), satinleaf (*Chrysophyllum oliviforme*), stoppers (*Eugenia* spp.), myrsine (*Rapanea punctata*), snowberry (*Chiococca alba*), wild coffee (*Psychotria nervosa*), white indigoberry (*Randia aculeata*), sword ferns (*Nephrolepis* spp.).

DISADVANTAGES

Fallen fruit pods may be untidy in well-kept landscapes.

SIMILAR AND RELATED SPECIES

No other native tropical tree of southern Florida has the combination of gray trunk, large size, and bipinnate foliage. Several non-native members of the legume family are sometimes planted in southern Florida but should be avoided due to their invasive nature.

Magnolia grandiflora

mag-NO-lee-uh gran-di-FLO-ruh

Magnolia or Southern Magnolia

Family: Magnoliaceae
Large tree
Height: 30 to 100 feet
Spread: 20 to 50 feet

LANDSCAPE USE
Excellent as a specimen and shade tree, in large commercial landscapes, or to border the edges of large urban lots where space is adequate.

FORM
A large, handsome, stately, evergreen tree with a broad, conical crown, stout branches, large, shiny green leaves, and arresting blossoms.

NATIVE RANGE
Well-drained woodlands, mesic hammocks, and slope forests. Coastal Plain; North Carolina, southward to central peninsular Florida, and west to east Texas.

CHARACTERISTICS
Flowers: Large, fragrant, to about 12 inches wide, with creamy white petals surrounding a conelike mass of numerous stamens and pistils. Spring and summer.
Leaves: Showy, large, 6–10 inches long, leathery, dark shiny green above, and rusty orange to brownish below.
Fruit: A conspicuous, fuzzy, conelike structure, 2–6 inches long, bearing numerous bright red seeds that dangle from thin red threadlike structures prior to falling. Fall.
Bark: Smooth, grayish, somewhat like that of a beech tree.

CULTURE
Soil: Prefers rich, moist, acid soil with pH 4.5–6.5. Salt tolerant.
Exposure: Full sun to part shade. Blooms best in sun.
Water: Well-drained, moist conditions are best. Supplemental irrigation typically not required after becoming established.
Hardiness Zones: 7 to 9, perhaps to zone 10.
Life Span: Relatively long-lived; 75 years or more.

BEST FEATURES
Large, showy, fragrant flowers and extended blooming period. Shiny, dark green leaves with a rusty orange undersurface. Conelike fruit and showy, bright red seeds dangling from thin red threads.

COMPANION PLANTS
American beech (*Fagus grandifolia*), parsley haw (*Crataegus marshallii*), American hophornbeam (*Ostrya virginiana*), blue beech (*Carpinus caroliniana*), sweetgum (*Liquidambar styraciflua*), several species of oaks (*Quercus* spp.), winged elm (*Ulmus alata*), hickories (*Carya* spp.), spruce pine (*Pinus glabra*), tulip poplar (*Liriodendron tulipifera*), red buckeye (*Aesculus pavia*), sweetshrub (*Calycanthus floridus*).

DISADVANTAGES
Scales and mealybugs are known pests. Fallen leaves and fruiting cones decompose slowly. Few plants will grow beneath *M. grandiflora*. Requires supplemental watering and maintenance in open sun along road shoulders.

CULTIVARS
More than 100 cultivars have been selected, few of which are available in Florida.

SIMILAR AND RELATED SPECIES
Sweetbay (*M. virginiana*) and Ashe magnolia (*M. macrophylla* var. *ashei*) are closely related, as is tulip poplar (*Liriodendron tulipifera*). All three are excellent landscape plants. Three other magnolias are also native to Florida.

Magnolia virginiana

mag-NO-lee-uh vir-ji-nee-AY-nuh

Sweetbay

Family: Magnoliaceae
Large tree
Height: 25 to 60 feet
Spread: 20 to 40 feet

LANDSCAPE USE
Excellent for wet, soggy situations, especially along retention ponds, drainage swales, canal banks, and wet roadsides.

FORM
An erect, evergreen tree with a narrow, conical crown and leaves that are silvery below and shiny green above. During breezy weather trees situated in the open are showy as they appear to change color from silvery to green due to their two-toned leaves.

NATIVE RANGE
Swamps, wetland depressions, stream banks, bayheads, and bogs. Coastal Plain and Piedmont, from Massachusetts southward to southern Florida, and west to eastern Texas.

CHARACTERISTICS
Flowers: Fragrant, showy, with creamy white petals surrounding a small, conelike mass of numerous stamens and pistils, 3–6 inches across.

Leaves: Alternate, long-elliptic in outline, 3–6 inches long, dull shiny green above, conspicuously silvery below.

Fruit: An ovoid, knobby, purplish red to purplish conelike structure bearing bright red seeds.

Bark: Gray, smooth, and thin.

CULTURE
Soil: Prefers wet, acid soils, but will adapt to well-drained soils if kept moist.

Exposure: Full sun when growing in wet soils. Also part shade.

Water: Should be kept very moist to wet.

Hardiness Zones: 5 to 10.

Life Span: Moderately long-lived; over 50 years.

BEST FEATURES
Wetland habit, showy flowers and leaves, and interesting and showy fruit. Seeds are eaten by wildlife. Valuable for wetland restoration.

COMPANION PLANTS
Inkberry and gallberry (*Ilex glabra* and *I. coriacea*), staggerbushes, fetterbushes, and dog-hobbles (*Lyonia* spp. and *Leucothoe* spp.), titi (*Cyrilla racemiflora*), loblolly bay (*Gordonia lasianthus*), swamp bay (*Persea palustris*), summersweet (*Clethra alnifolia*), Virginia willow (*Itea virginica*), chain ferns (*Woodwardia* spp.), red maple (*Acer rubrum*).

DISADVANTAGES
Fallen fruiting cones can be messy.

CULTIVARS
Several cultivars and varieties are known but are not readily available in Florida.

SIMILAR AND RELATED SPECIES
Loblolly bay (*Gordonia lasianthus*) is similar to and occurs in the same habitat as sweetbay. Magnolia (*M. grandiflora*) and Ashe magnolia (*M. macrophylla* var. *ashei*) are closely related, as is tulip poplar (*Liriodendron tulipifera*).

Malus angustifolia

MAY-lus an-gus-ti-FO-lee-uh

Southern Crabapple

Family: Rosaceae
Small tree
Height: 15 to 25 feet
Spread: 10 to 15 feet

Used as a small, prolifically flowering, freestanding tree, in naturalistic shrub borders or woodlands, or along fences.

FORM
A small, erect, short-trunked, deciduous tree with a broad, open crown of nearly horizontal branches.

NATIVE RANGE
Dry calcareous hammocks. Virginia and West Virginia, southward to panhandle of Florida, and west to Mississippi.

CHARACTERISTICS
Flowers: Bright pink to almost white, with 5 petals typical of the rose family. Showy and fragrant. Midspring.
Leaves: Alternate, simple, scalloped along the margins, oval to ovate in outline, to about 1½ inches long, soft to shiny green.
Fruit: A small, yellowish "apple," about 1 inch in diameter. Maturing in autumn.
Bark: Reddish brown and scaly. Very attractive.

CULTURE
Soil: Tolerant of most soil conditions.
Exposure: Full sun to part shade.
Water: Water regularly until established.
Hardiness Zones: 5 to 9.
Life Span: Short; probably less than 50 years.

BEST FEATURES
Showy, fragrant flowers. Edible fruit. Wildlife value. Small size.

COMPANION PLANTS
Hickories (*Carya* spp.), sweetgum (*Liquidambar styraciflua*), black gum (*Nyssa sylvatica* var. *sylvatica*), white oak (*Quercus alba*), redbud (*Cercis canadensis*), persimmon (*Diospyros virginiana*), beautyberry (*Callicarpa americana*), yaupon (*Ilex vomitoria*), Adam's needle (*Yucca filamentosa*), Carolina jessamine (*Gelsemium sempervirens*), coral honeysuckle (*Lonicera sempervirens*), haws (*Crataegus* spp.).

DISADVANTAGES
Subject to disease and insect damage, like many of the apple trees. Should be grown in open spaces with good air circulation. A long life should not be expected.

CULTIVARS
Hundreds of cultivars and selections are available for the apples in general, but none are known for *M. angustifolia*.

ALLERGENIC AND TOXIC PROPERTIES
The toxicity of *M. angustifolia* is unknown. Related species are known to cause poisoning in livestock when ingested in large amounts.

SIMILAR AND RELATED SPECIES
Potentially confused only with the several species of haws (*Crataegus* spp.), all of which have white flowers.

Mimosa strigillosa

mi-MO-suh stri-ji-LO-suh

Sunshine Mimosa

Family: Fabaceae
Ground cover
Height: To 6 inches
Spread: Spreading into a mat covering many square feet

Best used as a mat-forming ground cover
that withstands mowing.

FORM

A prostrate, spreading perennial with finely
divided leaves and ornate, globular heads of
pink flowers.

NATIVE RANGE

Open, disturbed sites. Georgia, southward to
south-central peninsular Florida. Absent
from Alabama and the western Florida
panhandle. A western form occurs in
Louisiana and eastern and southern Texas.

CHARACTERISTICS

Flowers: Pinkish to lavender; borne in 1-
inch-diameter, showy, globular heads. Spring
to fall.

Leaves: Finely divided into 6–15 pairs of leaflets.

Fruit: An oblong, mostly three-segmented, 1-
inch-long legume.

CULTURE

Soil: Sandy, open, moist to well-drained soils.

Exposure: Full sun.

Water: Adapts well to dry conditions but tolerates
moist sites.

Hardiness Zones: 8 to 10.

Life Span: Perennial.

BEST FEATURES

Mat-forming habit. Showy flower heads.
Extended flowering period. Very attractive, finely
divided foliage.

COMPANION PLANTS

Pawpaws (*Asimina* spp.), tarflower (*Bejaria racemosa*), St. John's–
worts (*Hypericum* spp.), staggerbush and fetterbush and rusty
lyonia (*Lyonia fruticosa, L. lucida,* and *L. ferruginea*), saw
palmetto (*Serenoa repens*), broomsedges (*Andropogon* spp.),
lopsided Indiangrass (*Sorghastrum secundum*), lowbush
blueberries (*Vaccinium* spp.), coontie (*Zamia pumila*), butterfly
weed (*Asclepias tuberosa*), Florida paintbrush (*Carphephorus
corymbosus*).

DISADVANTAGES

May be difficult to control in restricted spaces.

SIMILAR AND RELATED SPECIES

Sensitive briar (*M. quadrivalvis*) is very similar in foliage and
flower but is not much used in landscaping and gardening. Its
stems are armed with tiny prickles.

Morus rubra

MO-rus ROO-bruh

Red Mulberry

Family: Moraceae
Medium-sized tree
Height: 40 to 70 feet
Spread: 40 to 50 feet

LANDSCAPE USE

Serves well as a specimen or shade tree, along woodland edges, in a shady understory, or in naturalistic landscapes.

FORM

An erect, single-trunked, fast-growing, deciduous tree with a short trunk, spreading crown, and large, coarsely textured leaves.

NATIVE RANGE

Floodplains, hammocks, and mesic slopes. Southeastern United States, south to and nearly throughout Florida.

CHARACTERISTICS

Flowers: Small, greenish, mostly inconspicuous, borne in 2- to 3-inch-long spikes. Male and female flowers borne on separate plants. Spring and summer.

Leaves: Simple, alternate, 3–10 inches long and nearly as wide, ovate to nearly oval in outline and pinched to a point at the apex; margins toothed, sometimes deeply lobed, especially on vigorous shoots and root sprouts. Stalk exudes a milky latex when broken.

Fruit: A 1-inch-long aggregate fruit, red to dark purple when mature; juicy and relished by birds. Late summer and fall.

Bark: Gray brown to brown; furrowed, with flattened ridges.

CULTURE

Soil: Fertile, moist, acid to alkaline soils.

Exposure: Full sun to part shade.

Water: Prefers moist conditions. Irrigation generally not required when properly sited and after becoming established.

Hardiness Zones: 7 to 10.

Life Span: Relatively short; probably less than 100 years.

BEST FEATURES

Fall color. Fruit relished by birds and other wildlife. Fast growth. Spreading crown.

COMPANION PLANTS

Magnolia (*Magnolia grandiflora*), red buckeye (*Aesculus pavia*), sweetshrub (*Calycanthus floridus*), flowering dogwood (*Cornus florida*), beautyberry (*Callicarpa americana*), oakleaf hydrangea (*Hydrangea quercifolia*), Carolina jessamine (*Gelsemium sempervirens*), Virginia creeper (*Parthenocissus quinquefolia*), purple coneflower (*Echinacea purpurea*).

DISADVANTAGES

Fallen fruit can be messy, especially over paved surfaces.

ALLERGENIC AND TOXIC PROPERTIES

Reported to cause dermatitis, stomach upset, and hallucinations.

SIMILAR AND RELATED SPECIES

The leaves of basswood (*Tilia americana*) are very similar but their stalks lack milky sap. Two non-native mulberries are established in Florida, including white mulberry (*Morus alba*) and paper mulberry (*Broussonetia papyrifera*); both should be avoided in favor of this native species.

Muhlenbergia capillaris

mew-lun-BIR-gee-uh ka-puh-LA-ris

Muhly Grass

Family: Poaceae or Gramineae
Specimen grass or ground cover
Height: 1 to 5 feet
Spread: By self-sown seed as allowed

J.C. Putnam H

LANDSCAPE USE

Used in mixed flower gardens, massed in sunny beds adjacent to homes and buildings, or in meadows. Excellent for use along roads and powerline rights-of-way, in medians, as well as along retention ponds and drainage swales, and to stabilize canal banks.

FORM

A perennial bunchgrass with narrow, partly in-rolled leaves and delicate, pinkish to purplish masses of fall flowers and fruit.

NATIVE RANGE

Back dunes and sandy, alkaline sites. Eastern North America from about Massachusetts, south throughout Florida, and west along the Gulf Coast.

CHARACTERISTICS

Flowers: Tiny, borne in conspicuous, elevated, pinkish to purplish, finely delicate inflorescences on 1-foot-tall branches; large populations give the appearance of a pinkish haze just above ground level. Fall.

Leaves: Narrow, partly in-rolled, 1–3 feet long.

Fruit: A tiny grain.

CULTURE

Soil: Dry, sandy, slightly acid to alkaline soils. Will tolerate some drought and flooding. Salt tolerant.

Exposure: Full sun.

Water: Well-drained, moist conditions are best. More robust and taller when irrigated.

Hardiness Zones: 5 to 11.

Life Span: Perennial; self-sown seeds will maintain populations for many years.

BEST FEATURES

General hardiness; requires little care. Showy flowering and fruiting periods, producing a stunning display of pinkish to purplish inflorescences.

COMPANION PLANTS

Broomsedges and bluestems (*Andropogon* spp.), wiregrass (*Aristida stricta* var. *beyrichiana*), lopsided Indiangrass (*Sorghastrum secundum*), St. John's–worts (*Hypericum* spp.), lowbush and highbush blueberries (*Vaccinium* spp.), cocoplum (*Chrysobalanus icaco*), longleaf pine (*Pinus palustris*), dahoon (*Ilex cassine*), gopher apple (*Licania michauxii*).

SIMILAR AND RELATED SPECIES

Gulf muhly (*M. capillaris* var. *filipes*), which is also sometimes listed as a separate species rather than a variety, is nearly identical in appearance and use. Both Elliott and purple lovegrass (*Eragrostis elliottii, E. spectabilis*) are similar.

Myrcianthes fragrans

mir-see-AN-theez FRAY-granz

Simpson's Stopper

Family: Myrtaceae
Small to large shrub
Height: 5 to 20 feet
Spread: 3 to 15 feet

J.C. Putnam H

LANDSCAPE USE
Excellent as a specimen plant and for softening corners of houses and buildings. Works well in mixed shrub beds or as a small background shrub or tree. Especially suited for difficult locations like parking lots, medians, road and powerline rights-of-way, and the borders of retention ponds, drainage swales, and canal banks. Can be pruned to maintain a smaller, more compact form.

FORM
An erect, graceful shrub or very small tree with stiff branches, small leaves, and tiny flowers.

NATIVE RANGE
Coastal and tropical hammocks. Native to southern Florida but has adapted well to landscape settings in northern Florida and along the Atlantic coast to about Charleston, South Carolina.

CHARACTERISTICS
Flowers: Small, bright white, very fragrant, with long, graceful stamens. Borne at the ends of paired stalks. Showy during spring and early summer.
Leaves: Small, opposite, bright green, rounded to oval, to about 1 inch long.
Fruit: Small, ¼–½ inch in diameter, up to 1 inch long, red to orange, and showy.
Bark: Reddish and flaking. Distinctive and showy.

CULTURE
Soil: Prefers neutral to slightly alkaline soil, but will adapt to almost any well-drained, upland situation.
Exposure: Full sun to shade. Blooms best and maintains a more compact form in sun. Taller and more loosely branched in shade. Has survived 17 degrees F with very little tip burn.
Water: Performs best in well-drained sites.
Hardiness Zones: 8B to 11.
Life Span: To at least 50 years.

BEST FEATURES
Graceful and delicate form. Profusion of attractive and fragrant flowers. Reddish, somewhat flaking, very ornamental bark. Showy orange to bright red fruit that are highly attractive to birds.

COMPANION PLANTS
Cocoplum (*Chrysobalanus icaco*), varnish leaf (*Dodonaea viscosa*), Cherokee bean (*Erythrina herbacea*), necklace pod (*Sophora tomentosa*), muhly grass (*Muhlenbergia capillaris*), spider lily (*Hymenocallis latifolia*), marlberry (*Ardisia escallonioides*), stoppers (*Eugenia* spp.), yaupon (*Ilex vomitoria*), wax myrtle (*Myrica cerifera*), coontie (*Zamia pumila*).

SIMILAR AND RELATED SPECIES
Myrcianthes fragrans var. *simpsonii* is sometimes considered distinct.

Myrica cerifera

MI-ri-kuh se-RI-fuh-ruh (or MY-ri-kuh, mi-RY-kuh)

Wax Myrtle

Family: Myricaceae
Shrub or small tree
Height: 4 to 20 feet
Spread: 4 to 20 feet

J.C. Putnam H

LANDSCAPE USE

Especially useful in screening yards, roadsides, retention ponds, and drainage swales and canals. Works well in mixed shrub beds and borders, and in foundation plantings. May be pruned to form a small tree.

FORM

An erect to somewhat leaning, often multistemmed, densely foliated shrub or small tree with a compact to spreading crown.

NATIVE RANGE

Wide range of habitats including hammocks, swamps, flatwoods, upland woods, coastal swales and back dunes, and disturbed sites. New Jersey, south throughout Florida, into the West Indies, and west to Texas.

CHARACTERISTICS

Flowers: Small, brownish, inconspicuous. Spring.
Leaves: Alternate, narrow but slightly wider at the apex, 1–5 inches long, bluntly toothed near the apex, green above, slightly rusty below. Mildly aromatic.
Fruit: A bluish green, waxy drupe, about ⅛ inch in diameter.
Bark: Grayish, thin, smooth.

CULTURE

Soil: Prefers rich, moist, acid soils with pH 5.5–7.0, but adapts to most soil types. Salt tolerant.
Exposure: Full sun to part shade.
Water: Supplemental irrigation usually not required when situated in moist soil.
Hardiness Zones: 7 to 11.
Life Span: Not particularly long-lived; probably less than 50 years.

BEST FEATURES

General hardiness. Excellent cover and food for birds and other wildlife. Fruit used in colonial America to produce candles.

COMPANION PLANTS

Yaupon and inkberry (*Ilex vomitoria* and *I. glabra*), Florida privet (*Forestiera segregata*), Simpson's stopper (*Myrcianthes fragrans*), stoppers (*Eugenia* spp.), sparkleberry (*Vaccinium arboreum*), sand live oak (*Quercus geminata*), beautyberry (*Callicarpa americana*), wild olive (*Osmanthus americanus*).

DISADVANTAGES

Caterpillars and cankers are mild pests. Brittle and easily damaged by storms in exposed areas. May tend to form root sprouts.

CULTIVARS

Dwarf wax myrtle, *M. cerifera* 'Dwarf,' is a clonal form that has also been considered by some to be a naturally occurring variety (*M. cerifera* var. *pumila*) of wax myrtle and by others to be a distinct species (*M. pumila*). It has a horizontal stature, grows to a maximum height of about 3 feet, and has smaller leaves and fruit.

ALLERGENIC AND TOXIC PROPERTIES

Airborne pollen may contribute to respiratory problems and hay fever in some people.

SIMILAR AND RELATED SPECIES

Two other species of *Myrica* occur in Florida. Odorless bayberry (*M. inodora*) and northern bayberry (*M. heterophyla*) occur in swamps, bogs, and bayheads in the panhandle. Northern bayberry also occurs in the peninsula south to Highlands County.

Nephrolepis spp.

ne-FRAH-luh-pis (or ne-fruh-LE-pis)

Sword Ferns

Family: Nephrolepidaceae
Ground cover
Height: 1 to 5 feet
Spread: Spreading by underground rhizomes and forming large colonies

LANDSCAPE USE

Excellent for mixed or single-species fern beds, bordering walkways, in damp edges or depressions, or as potted patio plants. Two species are native to Florida, including the giant sword fern (*N. biserrata*), the larger of the two, and Boston fern (*N. exaltata*). The common name of the latter species is misleading, for the plant is native only to subtropical and tropical climes.

FORM

An erect, pinnately divided fern with long, narrow leaves and numerous leaflets.

NATIVE RANGE

Swamps and wet hammocks. South-central peninsular Florida and southward; widespread in the New and Old World tropics.

CHARACTERISTICS

Leaves: Long, erect, 1–6 feet tall, 5–10 inches wide, divided into numerous linear to narrowly triangular leaflets. Lower surfaces producing numerous kidney-shaped clusters of spore cases.

CULTURE

Soil: Rich, moist, acid soils of hammocks and swamps.
Exposure: Part sun to shade.
Water: Performs best in moist to wet situations.
Hardiness Zones: 9 to 11.
Life Span: Reproducing vegetatively by belowground rhizomes and persisting for many years.

BEST FEATURES

Rapid growth rate and colonizing habit. Tolerance of moist to wet soils. Evergreen habit. Lush growth.

COMPANION PLANTS

Red maple (*Acer rubrum*), pond apple (*Annona glabra*), sweetbay (*Magnolia virginiana*), swamp fern (*Blechnum serrulatum*), cabbage palm (*Sabal palmetto*), wild coffee (*Psychotria nervosa*), pignut hickory (*Carya glabra*), marlberry (*Ardisia escallonioides*), red mulberry (*Morus rubra*).

DISADVANTAGES

May spread beyond small gardens and be difficult to control.

CULTIVARS

Cultivars and hybrids are reported and are sometimes available in the nursery trade. Be careful to avoid the invasive, non-native species; see below.

SIMILAR AND RELATED SPECIES

Several species of non-native sword fern are established in Florida, two of which are very invasive, difficult to control, and included in Florida's list of noxious pest plants. Care should be taken to ensure that purchased plants come from native stock and are indeed native. The two non-native species are often mislabeled as one of the natives.

Nymphaea odorata

nim-FEE-uh o-duh-RAY-tuh

Fragrant Water Lily

Family: Nymphaeaceae
Aquatic
Height: Leaves float flat on the water surface
Spread: Leaves of individual plants can spread across 3–6 square feet of water surface

LANDSCAPE USE
Appropriate for water gardens, ponds, lakes, ditches, canals, and slow-moving streams.

FORM
A floating aquatic with showy white flowers and large, floating leaves.

NATIVE RANGE
Ponds, lakes, and slow-moving streams. Throughout Florida and the southeastern United States.

CHARACTERISTICS
Flowers: Bright white, with numerous petals and showy yellow stamens; floating on or slightly elevated above the water surface. Spring to fall.
Leaves: Large, dark shiny green, nearly rounded in outline, to about 18 inches wide.
Fruit: A 1- to 2-inch-diameter, globose capsule with oblong, grayish to orange seeds.

CULTURE
Soil: Typically rooted in saturated soils.
Exposure: Full sun.
Water: Floating aquatic.
Hardiness Zones: 8 to 10.
Life Span: Perennial.

BEST FEATURES
Showy, white, fragrant floating flowers. Large, orbicular, floating leaves. Tolerant of both cold and warm climates.

COMPANION PLANTS
American lotus (*Nelumbo lutea*), spatterdock (*Nuphar lutea*), yellow water lily (*Nymphaea mexicana*), swamp rose (*Rosa palustris*), climbing aster (*Symphyotrichum carolinianum*), blue flags (*Iris* spp.), yellow canna (*Canna flaccida*), pickerelweed (*Pontederia cordata*).

DISADVANTAGES
Able to completely fill small ponds and may be difficult to confine.

CULTIVARS
Numerous cultivars and selections, some with pink flowers, are reported.

SIMILAR AND RELATED SPECIES
Leaves are similar to several other floating aquatics, including spatterdock (*Nuphar lutea*) and several other species of water lilies.

Nyssa spp.

NI-suh

Tupelo

Family: Cornaceae
Large tree
Height: 50 to 100 feet
Spread: 30 to 50 feet

LANDSCAPE USE
Excellent for swamps, ponds, and similar wetlands, and to beautify retention ponds, drainage swales, and canal banks.

FORM
Erect, deciduous trees with large green leaves and a swollen, buttressed base that tapers into a slender trunk.

NATIVE RANGE
Floodplain forests, swamps, ponds, and lake margins. Southeastern Missouri and Illinois, southward to northern Florida (to about the lower Suwannee River), and west to east Texas.

CHARACTERISTICS
Flowers: Small, inconspicuous, borne in stalkless, compact, rounded clusters.
Leaves: Alternate, simple, 4–12 inches long, 4–7 inches wide, tapered to a pointed tip, often with one to several large teeth along the margins.
Fruit: A 1-inch-long, long-stalked, reddish purple to dark blue, fleshy drupe containing a single, ribbed seed.
Bark: Gray to dark gray and shallowly furrowed.

CULTURE
Soil: Rich, acid, hydric soils are preferred.
Exposure: Full sun to part shade.
Water: Prefers saturated to inundated situations, but will adapt to slightly drier sites.
Hardiness Zones: 6 to 9.
Life Span: Long-lived; at least 100 years.

BEST FEATURES
Tolerance of inundation. Buttressed trunk.

COMPANION PLANTS
Sweetbay (*Magnolia virginiana*), water hickory (*Carya aquatica*), swamp tupelo (*Nyssa sylvatica* var. *biflora*), red maple (*Acer rubrum*), swamp bay (*Persea palustris*), fevertree (*Pinckneya bracteata*), buttonbush (*Cephalanthus occidentalis*), black titi (*Cliftonia monophylla*), titi (*Cyrilla racemiflora*), Virginia willow (*Itea virginica*), string lily (*Crinum americanum*), spider lilies (*Hymenocallis* spp.).

SIMILAR AND RELATED SPECIES
Several species of *Nyssa* occur in Florida. Both water tupelo (*N. aquatica*) and ogeechee tupelo (*N. ogeche*) are excellent landscape plants. Bees produce a delicious honey from the flowers of ogeechee tupelo and its fruit is a large, reddish, single-seeded drupe.

Nyssa sylvatica

NI-suh sil-VA-ti-kuh

Black Gum

Family: Cornaceae
Large tree
Height: 40 to 120 feet
Spread: 20 to 40 feet

Jean C. Putnam H.

LANDSCAPE USE

Two varieties of black gum are available, both of which make good specimen or shade trees. Swamp tupelo (*N. sylvatica* var. *biflora*), in particular, is especially useful in road medians and rights-of-way, for beautifying retention ponds and drainage swales, and is essential for wetland restoration. *N. sylvatica* var. *sylvatica* is an upland species of rich woods. Its leaves turn bright red in early fall and are especially attractive in association with those of sourwood (*Oxydendrum arboreum*).

FORM

An erect, tall, straight-trunked tree with attractive, horizontal branches and a generally pyramidal shape.

NATIVE RANGE

Moist hammocks and well-drained woodlands. Southern Maine, southward to south-central peninsular Florida, and west to east Texas.

CHARACTERISTICS

Flowers: Small, mostly inconspicuous, greenish, often hidden by the new foliage. Spring.

Leaves: Alternate, 3–6 inches long, typically widest toward the apex, sometimes with a few large teeth along the margins nearer the tip, turning a showy, brilliant red in fall.

Fruit: A small, 1-inch-diameter, dark blue drupe with a hard seed. Fall.

Bark: Grayish; blocky, furrowed with interlacing ridges.

CULTURE

Soil: Prefers rich, moist, acid soils with pH 4.5–6.0, but will adapt to a variety of inland soils.

Exposure: Requires full sun for best fall color, but will tolerate part shade.

Water: Performs best on moist, well-drained sites.

Hardiness Zones: 4 to 9.

Life Span: Long-lived; well over 100 years.

BEST FEATURES

Fruit and flowers are superior wildlife foods. Excellent fall color. Fast growth rate.

COMPANION PLANTS

Upland oaks (*Quercus* spp.), red maple (*Acer rubrum*), magnolia (*Magnolia grandiflora*), sweetgum (*Liquidambar styraciflua*), hickories (*Carya* spp.), black cherry (*Prunus serotina*), spruce pine (*Pinus glabra*).

SIMILAR AND RELATED SPECIES

At least three other species of *Nyssa* occur in Florida. Swamp tupelo (*N. sylvatica* var. *biflora*), mentioned above, is considered by some authorities to be a distinct species. It occurs in swamps and bayheads of north-central and northern Florida. Water tupelo (*N. aquatica*) grows in floodplains and swamps, mostly in the panhandle and along the lower Suwannee River. Ogeechee tupelo (*N. ogeche*) occurs in swamps and floodplains across the northern part of the state.

Osmunda cinnamomea

ahz-MUN-duh si-nuh-MO-mee-uh

Cinnamon Fern

Family: Osmundaceae
Shrublike fern
Height: 2 to 4 feet
Spread: 2 to 3 feet

LANDSCAPE USE

An excellent addition to moist, shady gardens and mixed fern beds. A good choice for stream or pond edges and for beautifying retention ponds, swales, and canal banks.

FORM

An erect, robust, clump-forming, deciduous fern with large, divided sterile fronds and narrow, cinnamon-colored fertile fronds.

NATIVE RANGE

Swamps, wet flatwoods, swamp edges, marshes, and bogs. Virginia, Tennessee, and Kentucky, south nearly throughout Florida.

CHARACTERISTICS

Leaves: Sterile fronds large, erect, soft to dark green and divided into numerous scalloped leaflets. Fertile fronds showy, more or less linear, erect, and conspicuously covered with numerous cinnamon-colored spore cases.

CULTURE

Soil: Moist to wet, rich, acid soils.
Exposure: Shade to full shade.
Water: Should be kept moist.
Hardiness Zones: 5 to 11.
Life Span: Perennial.

BEST FEATURES

Large size. Clump-forming habit. Showy fertile fronds.

COMPANION PLANTS

Red maple and box elder (*Acer rubrum* and *A. negundo*), river birch (*Betula nigra*), sugarberry (*Celtis laevigata*), sweetgum (*Liquidambar styraciflua*), sweetbay (*Magnolia virginiana*), pipestem (*Agarista populifolia*), bluestem palmetto (*Sabal minor*), pinxter azalea (*Rhododendron canescens*), highbush blueberries (*Vaccinium* spp.), royal fern (*Osmunda regalis*), chain ferns (*Woodwardia* spp.), climbing aster (*Symphyotrichum carolinianum*), string lily (*Crinum americanum*).

CULTIVARS

At least one selection is reported, and it is perhaps induced by disturbances such as fire and mowing. Otherwise, no cultivars are available in Florida.

SIMILAR AND RELATED SPECIES

Similar in some respects to Virginia chain fern (*Woodwardia virginica*), but cinnamon fern forms clumps and has a pale midrib. Closely related, but not similar to royal fern (*O. regalis*).

Osmunda regalis

ahz-MUN-duh ree-GAY-lis (or ree-GA-lis)

Royal Fern

Family: Osmundaceae
Shrublike fern
Height: 2 to 5 feet
Spread: 3 to 4 feet

LANDSCAPE USE

An excellent background species for moist, shady fern gardens, shrub beds, or for accent. Also excellent for beautifying retention ponds, drainage swales, and canal banks.

FORM

A large, more or less erect, clump-forming, deciduous fern with twice-divided leaves and the general aspect of a shrub.

NATIVE RANGE

Swamps, wet flatwoods, swamp edges, marshes, and bogs. Virginia, Tennessee, and Kentucky, south nearly throughout Florida.

CHARACTERISTICS

Leaves: Large, erect, spreading, divided into branches with large leaflets. Fertile portion of the frond slender, brownish, and borne at the branch tips.

CULTURE

Soil: Rich, acid soils are preferred.
Exposure: Shade to full sun.
Water: Moist conditions are best, but will tolerate wet sites.
Hardiness Zones: 5 to 11.
Life Span: Perennial.

BEST FEATURES

Large size. Very attractive, twice-divided leaves. Tolerance of wet sites.

COMPANION PLANTS

Swamp fern (*Blechnum serrulatum*), blue flags (*Iris* spp.), string lily (*Crinum americanum*), spider lilies (*Hymenocallis* spp.), red maple (*Acer rubrum*), dahoon (*Ilex cassine*), cypresses (*Taxodium* spp.), sweetbay (*Magnolia virginiana*), scarlet hibiscus (*Hibiscus coccineus*), Virginia willow (*Itea virginica*), buttonbush (*Cephalanthus occidentalis*).

CULTIVARS

Several varieties are known, but few are available in or appropriate for Florida.

SIMILAR AND RELATED SPECIES

Few native ferns are similar in appearance to royal fern. Cinnamon fern (*O. cinnamomea*) is closely related.

Ostrya virginiana

ahs-TRY-uh vir-ji-nee-AY-nuh

American Hophornbeam

Family: Betulaceae
Medium-sized tree
Height: 20 to 50 feet
Spread: 20 to 50 feet

LANDSCAPE USE
Best used as a specimen or patio shade tree, or
to beautify parks, golf courses, and roadsides.
Often planted for its showy, hoplike fruit.

FORM
An erect, deciduous tree with somewhat
shaggy, brownish bark, interesting, hoplike
fruit, and soft green, toothed leaves.

NATIVE RANGE
Moist hammocks and dry uplands. Southeast-
ern United States, south to about Hernando
County, Florida.

CHARACTERISTICS
Flowers: Small, inconspicuous, borne in
slender, 2-inch-long catkins. Spring.
Leaves: Alternate, soft green, elliptical or ovate
in general outline, doubly toothed along the margins, and
pinched to a long-tapering point.
Fruit: An interesting, showy, 1- to 3-inch-long, hoplike
catkin of thin-papery sacs containing small brown
nutlets. Summer.
Bark: Thin, brown, often peeling and shredding in thin
strips.

CULTURE
Soil: Rich, moist to dry, well-drained soils are best.
Exposure: Shade to sun.
Water: Adaptable in moist to dry situations. Does not
tolerate flooding.
Hardiness Zones: 3 to 9.
Life Span: At least 100 years.

BEST FEATURES
Erect stature. Spreading crown. Attractive, shredding
bark. Showy summer to early fall fruit.

COMPANION PLANTS
Red buckeye (*Aesculus pavia*), fringetree (*Chionanthus
virginicus*), flowering dogwood (*Cornus florida*), redbud
(*Cercis canadensis*), sweetshrub (*Calycanthus floridus*),
Florida azalea (*Rhododendron austrinum*), Carolina
jessamine (*Gelsemium sempervirens*), Virginia creeper
(*Parthenocissus quinquefolia*), Florida sugar maple (*Acer saccharum* subsp. *floridanum*), pignut hickory (*Carya
glabra*), oaks (*Quercus* spp.), winged elm (*Ulmus alata*), magnolia (*Magnolia grandiflora*).

DISADVANTAGES
Deciduous.

SIMILAR AND RELATED SPECIES
Leaves are similar to the closely related blue beech (*Carpinus caroliniana*), also of the birch family. American
hophornbeam is easily distinguished by its loose, brownish bark.

Panicum spp.

Pa-ni-kum

Panic Grasses

Family: Poaceae or Gramineae
Ground cover
Height: 1 to 5 feet
Spread: Creating large colonies by underground stems

LANDSCAPE USE

Several species of panic grass are used in Florida landscaping. These include maidencane (*P. hemitomon*), a common wetland species throughout Florida; beach panic grass (*P. amarum*), an excellent grass for beaches and dunes; switchgrass (*P. virgatum*), a large, salt-tolerant bunchgrass of coastal marshes and inland ponds; and *P. anceps,* a low, spreading rhizomatous grass of wet areas and moist flatwoods. Several species are excellent for the margins of retention ponds and canal banks.

FORM

The several species of *Panicum* range in form from large bunchgrasses to relatively low, spreading, rhizomatous perennials.

NATIVE RANGE

Fresh and brackish marshes, wet savannas, riverbanks, ditches, and ponds. Most are widespread in Florida and across the southeast.

CHARACTERISTICS

Flowers: Tiny, individually inconspicuous, but borne in conspicuous, spreading to spikelike panicles.

Leaves: Narrow, long-tapering, spreading or ascending from a mostly erect stem.

Fruit: A small, inconspicuous grain.

CULTURE

Soil: Rich, acid to neutral soils, depending upon species.

Exposure: Full to part sun. Various species are tolerant of salt and inundation.

Water: The species included here prefer wet to moist conditions.

Hardiness Zones: 4 to 10.

Life Span: Perennial.

BEST FEATURES

Fast growing and spreads rapidly.

COMPANION PLANTS

Smartweeds (*Polygonum* spp.), swamp rose (*Rosa palustris*), climbing aster (*Symphyotrichum carolinianum*), jointgrasses and knotgrasses (*Paspalum* spp.), narrowleaf sunflower (*Helianthus angustifolius*), yellow canna (*Canna flaccida*), string lily (*Crinum americanum*), blue flags (*Iris* spp.), water lilies (*Nymphaea* spp.), spatter-dock (*Nuphar lutea*).

DISADVANTAGES

Some species of *Panicum* can be difficult to control and may be difficult to confine to small areas.

CULTIVARS

P. virgatum 'Squaw' is available from several growers. Other panic grass cultivars include *P. amarum* 'North PA' and *P. amarum* 'South PA.'

SIMILAR AND RELATED SPECIES

At least 13 species of *Panicum* are native to Florida. Many are very similar in overall form and are often difficult to identify except by experts.

Paspalum spp.

PAS-puh-lum (or pas-PAY-lum)

Jointgrasses and Knotgrasses

Family: Poaceae or Gramineae
Specimen grass or ground cover
Height: 2 to 3 feet
Spread: As allowed by creeping stems and rhizomes

LANDSCAPE USE

Three species of *Paspalum* are used in Florida landscaping: salt jointgrass (*P. distichum*), seashore paspalum (*P. vaginatum*), and Gulfdune paspalum (*P. monostachyum*). All make excellent ground covers. The first two, in particular, are well adapted to saline situations, including beaches and the edges of salt marshes. Seashore paspalum is excellent for seashore restoration and stabilization.

FORM

The three species of *Paspalum* presented here are perennial grasses, 24–36 inches tall, sometimes forming mats with spreading rhizomes or creeping stems.

NATIVE RANGE

Seashore paspalum occurs along seashores from North Carolina south to Florida and Texas, and south to Argentina. Salt jointgrass ranges from New Jersey south throughout Florida, and west to California. Gulfdune paspalum is confined to the southernmost peninsula of Florida but also occurs in Louisiana and Texas.

CHARACTERISTICS

Flowers: Tiny; borne in pairs along conspicuous spikes near the apex of the culm. Spring to fall.
Leaves: Narrow, 1–8 inches long.
Fruit: A small, hard grain enclosed within the spikelets. Midsummer through fall.

CULTURE

Soil: Prefers wet, sandy, or mucky soils in brackish or freshwater situations, but will adapt to drier sites. Salt tolerant.
Exposure: Full sun.
Water: Performs best in moist to wet situations.
Hardiness Zones: 5 to 11, depending upon species.
Life Span: Perennial.

BEST FEATURES

The mat-forming habit of seashore paspalum and salt jointgrass make them excellent for soil stabilization. Highly salt tolerant.

COMPANION PLANTS

Cocoplum (*Chrysobalanus icaco*), Cherokee bean (*Erythrina herbacea*), saw palmetto (*Serenoa repens*), gopher apple (*Licania michauxii*), sea oats (*Uniola paniculata*), cordgrasses (*Spartina* spp.), climbing aster (*Symphyotrichum carolinianum*), buttonbush (*Cephalanthus occidentalis*), muhly grass (*Muhlenbergia capillaris*), Christmasberry (*Lycium carolinianum*).

SIMILAR AND RELATED SPECIES

Nearly 30 species of *Paspalum* occur in Florida, a little more than half of which are native.

Passiflora spp.

pa-si-FLO-ruh

Passionflower

Family: Passifloraceae
Vine
Height: Prostrate or climbing over fences and low vegetation
Spread: 3 to 12 feet

LANDSCAPE USE

Two species of passion flower are used in Florida landscaping. *Passiflora incarnata*, pictured right, is the more common, widespread, and showy of the two. Corky stem passionflower (*P. suberosa*) has much smaller, greenish flowers and occurs naturally in the southern two-thirds of the peninsula. Well suited as a ground cover in sunny to moderately shaded situations, or as a climbing vine on trellises and fences.

FORM

A hardy, prostrate to climbing, spreading, perennial vine with showy, ornate flowers and conspicuous yellow fruit.

NATIVE RANGE

Open hammocks, roadsides, fencerows, and disturbed sites. *P. incarnata* ranges from Illinois and Virginia, south throughout the southeastern United States, and west to Texas; nearly throughout Florida.

CHARACTERISTICS

Flowers: Those of *P. incarnata* are lavender to whitish, about 3 inches wide, very intricate and showy, with 5 petals and sepals surmounted by finely divided inner and outer coronas that surround conspicuous, stalked ovaries and stamens. Late spring and summer.

Leaves: Deeply 3-lobed to entire with toothed margins, alternate, bright green, 3–6 inches long.

Fruit: A 2-inch-wide berry, turning from green to pale yellow with maturity. Summer.

CULTURE

Soil: Prefers rich, acid to basic soils.
Exposure: Full sun to part shade.
Water: Dry to moderately moist. Should not be overwatered.
Hardiness Zones: 7 to 10.
Life Span: Herbaceous perennial.

BEST FEATURES

Scrambling habit. Showy late-spring and summer flowers. Attractive to butterflies. *P. incarnata* is the larval plant of the Gulf fritillary butterfly, the larvae of which can completely defoliate the plant.

COMPANION PLANTS

Summer haw (*Crataegus flava*), turkey oak (*Quercus laevis*), persimmon (*Diospyros virginiana*), pawpaws (*Asimina* spp.), garberia (*Garberia heterophylla*), rusty lyonia (*Lyonia ferruginea*), saw palmetto (*Serenoa repens*), lopsided Indiangrass (*Sorghastrum secundum*), coral honeysuckle (*Lonicera sempervirens*), butterfly weed (*Asclepias tuberosa*), blazing stars (*Liatris* spp.).

DISADVANTAGES

Should be provided suitable space. May scramble and require pruning in small gardens. Sends out underground stems producing plants some distance from the parent plant.

CULTIVARS

At least one is reported, but it is not generally available in Florida.

SIMILAR AND RELATED SPECIES

The two passionflowers treated here, as well as yellow passionflower (*P. lutea*), are host plants of the zebra longwing, Florida's state butterfly.

Persea spp.

PIR-see-uh

Red Bays

Family: Lauraceae
Small to large trees or shrubs
Height: 6 to 60 feet, depending upon species
Spread: 3 to 20 feet, depending upon species

Jean C. Putnam H.

LANDSCAPE USE

Works well as a background shrub or tree in naturalistic settings. Also serves to conceal retention ponds, drainage swales, and canal banks.

FORM

Two closely related species and one variety are recognized in Florida. Red bay (*P. borbonia*) is a shrubby to erect, dark-trunked evergreen tree mostly of dry sandy hammocks and coastal dune-scrub, but it also occasionally occurs in mesic hammocks. Its leaves are shiny green above and somewhat grayish below. Swamp bay (*P. palustris*) is similar to red bay in form but generally occurs in swamps, bayheads, and wet flatwoods. Its leaves are duller above and not whitish below. Silk bay (*P. borbonia* var. *humilis*) is normally a shrub with coppery to brownish to grayish lower leaf surfaces and occurs in central and south Florida's sand pine–oak scrub region.

NATIVE RANGE

Red and swamp bays range from about Delaware, southward to southern peninsular Florida, and west to eastern Texas. Silk bay occurs in central peninsular Florida and has also been reported (though with some disagreement) for eastern Texas.

CHARACTERISTICS

Flowers: Tiny, inconspicuous, borne in greenish yellow clusters. Spring and early summer.

Leaves: Alternate, lance shaped, green above, paler below, depending upon species.

Fruit: A dark blue to blackish, ellipsoid drupe about ½ inch long.

Bark: Dark brown (to blackish in silk bay) and fissured.

CULTURE

Soil: Red and silk bays prefer well-drained, xeric soils. Swamp bay prefers moist to wet acid soils.

Exposure: Full sun to part shade.

Water: Supplemental irrigation not required for red and silk bays. Swamp bay performs best in moist to wet situations.

Hardiness Zones: 7 to 10.

Life Span: Tall, handsome red bays with 3-foot-diameter trunks and ages in excess of 100 years are sometimes encountered in mesic uplands. Under most conditions, plants in excess of 50 years are considered old.

BEST FEATURES

The evergreen habit and tolerance of harsh situations commend these species. Reportedly an excellent wildlife food. Fruits eaten by numerous songbirds as well as by turkey and quail. Fruit and leaves browsed by deer.

COMPANION PLANTS

Red bay: fringetree (*Chionanthus virginicus*), beautyberry (*Callicarpa americana*), sourwood (*Oxydendrum arboreum*), American hophornbeam (*Ostrya virginiana*), sweetshrub (*Calycanthus floridus*). Swamp bay: blue beech (*Carpinus caroliniana*), sweetbay (*Magnolia virginiana*), tupelos (*Nyssa* spp.), cypresses (*Taxodium* spp.), fevertree (*Pinckneya bracteata*), swamp dogwood (*Cornus foemina*), buttonbush (*Cephalanthus occidentalis*), summersweet (*Clethra alnifolia*), titi (*Cyrilla racemiflora*), fetterbushes and dog-hobbles (*Lyonia* spp. and *Leucothoe* spp.).

DISADVANTAGES

All species are subject to large, numerous, and conspicuous leaf galls.

SIMILAR AND RELATED SPECIES

Several other members of the laurel family occur in Florida, including sweetwood (*Licaria triandra*), spicebush (*Lindera benzoin*), pondspice (*Litsea aestivalis*), lancewood (*Ocotea coriacea*), and sassafras (*Sassafras albidum*).

Piloblephis rigida

py-lo-BLE-fis RI-ji-duh

Florida Pennyroyal

Family: Lamiaceae or Labiatae
Sprawling ground cover
Height: 1 to 2 feet
Spread: Sprawling to several feet

LANDSCAPE USE
Useful as a ground cover, specimen, or nectar plant in butterfly gardens.

FORM
A low, evergreen, aromatic shrub or sprawling perennial herb with needlelike leaves and large numbers of showy flower clusters.

NATIVE RANGE
Sandhills, dry flatwoods, and oak scrub. Southern peninsular Florida.

CHARACTERISTICS
Flowers: Lavender to purple with dark purple spots; 2-lipped, fragrant, borne in conspicuous, dense, showy clusters. Late winter to spring.

Leaves: Small, closely set, opposite, needlelike; very aromatic when crushed.

Fruit: A tiny, inconspicuous nutlet.

CULTURE
Soil: Prefers well-drained, sandy, slightly to moderately acid soils.

Exposure: Full sun. Moderately cold tolerant.

Water: Dry sites preferred. Drought tolerant, once established.

Hardiness Zones: 8 to 10.

Life Span: Perennial but relatively short-lived; probably less than 15 years.

BEST FEATURES
Showy flower heads. All parts of the plant are aromatic. Attractive to butterflies. Flowers during winter and early spring when many plants are dormant.

COMPANION PLANTS
Scrub hickory (*Carya floridana*), sand live oak (*Quercus geminata*), rusty lyonia and staggerbush (*Lyonia ferruginea* and *L. fruticosa*), myrtle oak (*Quercus myrtifolia*), tarflower (*Bejaria racemosa*), pawpaws (*Asimina* spp.), lowbush blueberries (*Vaccinium* spp.), gopher apple (*Licania michauxii*), garberia (*Garberia heterophylla*), saw palmetto (*Serenoa repens*), coontie (*Zamia pumila*), butterfly weed (*Asclepias tuberosa*).

DISADVANTAGES
Tends to die out after a few years.

SIMILAR AND RELATED SPECIES
Several species of the mint family, including the scrub mints (*Conradina* spp.) and savories (*Calamintha* spp.), have similar flowers and leaves and are similarly aromatic.

Pinus clausa

PY-nus KLAW-zuh

Sand Pine

Family: Pinaceae
Medium-sized tree
Height: 30 to 60 feet
Spread: 20 to 40 feet

LANDSCAPE USE
Essential for reforestation and restoration of Florida scrub communities. Also useful as a specimen or shade tree.

FORM
An erect, sometimes leaning pine tree with short needles, a mostly conical crown, and numerous small cones.

NATIVE RANGE
Dunes and scrub. Scrub of the central peninsula and along old dunes of the central panhandle. Also occurs in southwestern Alabama.

CHARACTERISTICS
Leaves: Relatively short, 2–3 inches long, needlelike, borne 2 (sometimes 3) to the cluster.
Fruit: Borne in small, 2- to 3-inch-long, mostly ovoid, dark brown cones.
Bark: Becoming thick and divided into brownish to grayish plates.

CULTURE
Soil: Deep, well-drained sands.
Exposure: Full sun.
Water: Drought tolerant, once established.
Hardiness Zones: 8 to 10.
Life Span: Moderate; 60 to 100 years.

BEST FEATURES
Short needles. Tolerance of infertile, well-drained, sandy soils. Attractive form.

COMPANION PLANTS
Scrub hickory (*Carya floridana*), sand live, Chapman, and myrtle oaks (*Quercus geminata, Q. chapmanii,* and *Q. myrtifolia*), rusty lyonia (*Lyonia ferruginea*), pawpaws (*Asimina* spp.), tarflower (*Bejaria racemosa*), saw palmetto (*Serenoa repens*), scrub palmetto (*Sabal etonia*), scrub mints (*Conradina* spp.), garberia (*Garberia heterophylla*), Florida pennyroyal (*Piloblephis rigida*), butterfly weed (*Asclepias tuberosa*), blazing stars (*Liatris* spp.).

DISADVANTAGES
Roots are sensitive to disturbance.

CULTIVARS
None—though "improved" selections for the purposes of tree farming may be available.

ALLERGENIC AND TOXIC PROPERTIES
Ingestion of the needles of some pine species is said to have caused death in calves. Airborne pollen may cause allergic reactions in some people.

SIMILAR AND RELATED SPECIES
Seven species of pine trees occur naturally in Florida. Sand pine is distinguished by its combination of short needles, small cones, and habitat of well-drained sands.

Pinus elliottii

PY-nus e-lee-AH-tee-eye

Slash Pine

Family: Pinaceae
Large tree
Height: 60 to 100 feet
Spread: 20 to 60 feet

J. C. Putnam H.

LANDSCAPE USE
Used either as a specimen tree or in groupings to form a grove. Also used in moist to moderately wet sites. When growth space is allowed, it forms a broad, spreading crown with relatively low branches; otherwise it produces high branches and a tighter crown. Especially good for roadside applications within its natural range.

FORM
A tall, single-trunked pine with an ovoid crown, dense, elongated clusters of medium-long needles, tapering branches, medium-sized cones, and reddish brown bark that is divided into irregular, scaly, flaking plates.

NATIVE RANGE
Inland and coastal flatwoods. South Carolina, south throughout Florida, and west to Louisiana.

CHARACTERISTICS
Leaves: Needlelike, 8–12 inches long, typically borne 2 or 3 per cluster.
Fruit: Winged seeds, borne in conspicuous, 3- to 6-inch-long, lustrous brown cones with prickly scales.
Bark: Reddish brown, with irregular, flaking, and scaly plates.

CULTURE
Soil: Prefers moist, slightly acid, well-drained soils with pH 5.0–7.0.
Exposure: Full sun.
Water: Moderate soil moisture is best. Supplemental irrigation typically not required after becoming established except on very dry sites.
Hardiness Zones: 8 to 10.
Life Span: Trees in excess of 200 years are known, but may not exceed 100 years of age in urban landscapes.

BEST FEATURES
Its fast growth rate and evergreen habit make this an excellent pine. Provides a high canopy, as well as food and cover for birds and small mammals.

COMPANION PLANTS
Saw palmetto (*Serenoa repens*), broomsedges and bluestems (*Andropogon* spp.), fetterbushes, staggerbushes, and dog-hobbles (*Lyonia* spp. and *Leucothoe* spp.), wax myrtle (*Myrica cerifera*), longleaf and loblolly pines (*Pinus palustris* and *P. taeda*), beautyberry (*Callicarpa americana*), possum haw (*Viburnum nudum*), lopsided Indiangrass (*Sorghastrum secundum*), lowbush and highbush blueberries (*Vaccinium* spp.).

DISADVANTAGES
Fusiform rust will weaken and may kill infected trees. Pine tip moths and colaspis beetles are known pests. Plants stressed due to drought, bark damage, root disturbance from construction traffic, or lightning strikes are more susceptible.

CULTIVARS
P. elliottii 'Improved' is a hardy cultivar.

ALLERGENIC AND TOXIC PROPERTIES
Pollen may be bothersome to some people. Ingestion of the needles of some pine species is said to have caused death in calves.

SIMILAR AND RELATED SPECIES
South Florida slash pine (*P. elliottii* var. *densa*) is a natural variety that is particularly suitable to the southern peninsula. It is fast growing, once established, and is also good for roadside applications. Seven species of pine trees occur naturally in Florida. In addition to slash pine and the two considered on the following pages, spruce pine (*P. glabra*), sand pine (*P. clausa*), and pond pine (*P. serotina*) are available in the trade. Shortleaf pine (*P. echinata*), which has very small cones and very short needles, has a limited natural distribution in Florida. Of these, spruce pine is an extremely attractive tree with small leaves, small cones, and narrowly furrowed and blocky bark; it makes an excellent specimen tree in north Florida.

Pinus palustris

PY-nus puh-LUS-tris

Longleaf Pine

Family: Pinaceae
Large tree
Height: 60 to 120 feet
Spread: 30 to 50 feet

Jean C. Putnam H.

An essential component in the restoration of native sandhill pinelands and wiregrass savannas. An excellent specimen tree. Excellent for roadside applications, especially in drier sites.

FORM

A tall, single-trunked pine with a spreading crown of stout branches that taper little toward their tips, dense globular clusters of long to very long needles, large, conspicuous cones, and reddish orange bark that is divided into thin, irregular plates. Terminal buds are silvery white, showy, and a distinguishing character of this species. Seedlings may remain in a grasslike stage for many years before producing aboveground trunks.

NATIVE RANGE

Longleaf pine forests once covered more than 90 million acres across the Southeastern Coastal Plain, of which only a small fraction is left. Virginia, southward to south-central Florida, and west to Mississippi.

CHARACTERISTICS

Leaves: Needlelike, 8–18 inches long, borne in large, globular clusters at the tips of stout branches that taper little toward their tips.

Fruit: A small, winged seed borne in a large, brown cone, 6–12 inches long.

Bark: Pale burnt orange to yellowish brown; divided into thin, irregular plates.

CULTURE

Soil: Prefers deep, sandy or clay-sand soils with little organic material and pH 6.0–7.0.

Exposure: Full sun.

Water: Supplemental irrigation typically not required.

Hardiness Zones: 7 to 10.

Life Span: Hardier and likely longer lived than our other pines. Life spans in excess of 200 years are known, though those situated in urban landscapes may not reach the species' full age potential.

BEST FEATURES

Large size, large cones, silvery white terminal buds, beautiful, globular clusters of very long needles, relatively open crown, importance to wildlife. Fast growing, once established. Unsurpassed for restoration of sand ridge pineland communities.

COMPANION PLANTS

Wiregrass (*Aristida stricta* var. *beyrichiana*), bluestems and broomsedges (*Andropogon* spp.), slash and loblolly pines (*Pinus elliottii* and *P. taeda*), turkey oak (*Quercus laevis*), summer haw (*Crataegus flava*), gopher apple (*Licania michauxii*), sand live oak (*Quercus geminata*), garberia (*Garberia heterophylla*), Chickasaw plum (*Prunus angustifolia*).

DISADVANTAGES

Does not perform well in heavy soils.

ALLERGENIC AND TOXIC PROPERTIES

Ingestion of the needles of some pine species is said to have caused death in calves. Airborne pollen is bothersome to some people.

SIMILAR AND RELATED SPECIES

See comments for slash pine.

Pinus taeda

PY-nus TEE-duh (or TAY-duh)

Loblolly Pine

Family: Pinaceae
Large tree
Height: 60 to 100 feet
Spread: 30 to 60 feet

LANDSCAPE USE

Specimen tree. Excellent for quickly reclaiming abandoned fields. May be used with or similarly to slash pine. Well suited for moist roadsides.

FORM

A tall, single-trunked pine with an open, somewhat rounded crown of short, thick, divided branches, dense clusters of relatively short to medium-length needles, small to medium-sized cones that often remain on the tree in great numbers, and reddish brown bark that is divided into narrow blocks by shallow furrows that often appear to follow a single vertical path along the trunk.

NATIVE RANGE

Old fields, disturbed sites, and well-drained wetlands. New Jersey southward to south-central Florida, and west to Texas.

CHARACTERISTICS

Leaves: Needlelike, borne mostly 3 (sometimes 2) per fascicle, and typically less than 9 inches long.
Fruit: A winged seed, borne in a brown, 2- to 6-inch-long cone. Cones often persist on the tree in large numbers year-round.
Bark: Reddish brown; often divided into narrow plates separated by conspicuous, vertical furrows.

CULTURE

Soil: Prefers well-drained soils with pH 4.5–7.0, but very adaptable.
Exposure: Full sun.
Water: Should be situated on well-drained sites. Supplemental irrigation usually not required.
Hardiness Zones: 6 to 9.
Life Span: Moderately long-lived in urban landscapes; probably less than 100 years. Life spans in excess of 100 years are known.

BEST FEATURES

Provides high shade. Allows for understory plantings. Fast growth. Evergreen.

COMPANION PLANTS

Live, laurel, southern red, and water oaks (*Quercus virginiana, Q. laurifolia, Q. falcata,* and *Q. nigra*), slash, longleaf, and pond pines (*Pinus elliottii, P. palustris,* and *P. serotina*), dahoon (*Ilex cassine*), tarflower (*Bejaria racemosa*), broomsedges (*Andropogon* spp.), saw palmetto (*Serenoa repens*), inkberry (*Ilex glabra*), red buckeye (*Aesculus pavia*), sweetshrub (*Calycanthus floridus*), yellow and Florida anises (*Illicium parviflorum* and *I. floridanum*). Also see those listed above for slash pine.

DISADVANTAGES

Extremely susceptible to fusiform rust. Pine tip moths and colaspis beetles are insect pests.

ALLERGENIC AND TOXIC PROPERTIES

Ingestion of the needles is said to have caused death in calves. Airborne pollen is bothersome to some people.

SIMILAR AND RELATED SPECIES

See comments for slash pine.

Platanus occidentalis

PLA-tuh-nus ahk-si-den-TAY-lis

Sycamore

Family: Platanaceae
Large tree
Height: 75 to 150 feet
Spread: 75 to 100 feet

LANDSCAPE USE

Street tree, especially for large boulevards and highways, as well as in parks and roadside rest areas. Specimen tree in very large yards. Erosion control along stream banks.

FORM

A large, tall, deciduous tree with a flaking, mottled trunk, a spreading crown, stout to very large branches, and an oval to pyramidal form.

NATIVE RANGE

Floodplain forests. Maine, southward to northern Florida, and west to Texas and Mexico.

CHARACTERISTICS

Flowers: Reddish; borne in spherical clusters. Spring.

Leaves: Large, coarse, shallowly 3- to 5-lobed, about 10 inches long and wide. Turn tan to pale yellow in fall.

Fruit: Seeds borne in dense, round, brownish, 1-inch-diameter clusters that dangle at the end of 3- to 6-inch-long stalks. Summer.

Bark: Smooth, mottled, peeling in large plates that expose varying shades of green, brownish, grayish, or tan to creamy white.

CULTURE

Soil: Occurs naturally in the moist, slightly acid, fertile soils of floodplains with pH 4.9–6.5. Adapts well to most soil types whether dry or wet, but is only mildly drought tolerant.

Exposure: Full sun.

Water: Adapts to almost any soil moisture, though growth tends to be restricted on very dry or very wet sites with poor soil. Performs best with moderate moisture.

Hardiness Zones: 4 to 9.

Life Span: Fast growing and moderately long-lived, potentially exceeding 75 years in urban landscapes.

BEST FEATURES

Fast growth rate. Interesting and attractive trunk. Fall color.

COMPANION PLANTS

Coastal Plain and black willows (*Salix caroliniana* and *S. nigra*), river birch (*Betula nigra*), red maple (*Acer rubrum*), water and ogeechee tupelos (*Nyssa aquatica* and *N. ogeche*), cottonwood (*Populus deltoides*), blue beech (*Carpinus caroliniana*), loblolly pine (*Pinus taeda*).

DISADVANTAGES

Susceptible to anthracnose, a fungus that can defoliate the tree in early spring. Large leaves and fruit fall in great numbers, decompose slowly, and may require cleanup.

ALLERGENIC AND TOXIC PROPERTIES

The fuzz on the leaves, fruits, and young twigs reportedly can cause allergic reactions if handled.

SIMILAR AND RELATED SPECIES

Few species, except perhaps the equally large tulip poplar (*Liriodendron tulipifera*), are similar in aspect to the sycamore.

Polygonum spp.

pah-LI-guh-num

Smartweeds

Family: Polygonaceae
Aquatic ground cover
Height: 1 to 5 feet
Spread: Spreading into large colonies by reclining stems that root at the nodes

LANDSCAPE USE

Most appropriate for the edges of ponds, marshes, swamps, and small, slow-moving streams, and for wetland restoration.

FORM

Annual or perennial herbs with alternate, mostly narrowly lance-shaped leaves, swollen leaf nodes, and numerous small, whitish to pinkish flowers.

NATIVE RANGE

Swamps, marshes, and floodplains. Throughout the southeastern United States and Florida.

CHARACTERISTICS

Flowers: Small, white to pinkish, without petals, borne in spikelike clusters at the stem tips.

Leaves: Alternate, narrowly lance shaped, entire, sheathing the stem.

Fruit: A tiny, inconspicuous, 2- to 3-sided achene.

CULTURE

Soil: Rich, saturated soils of floodplains, marshes, and swamps.

Exposure: Full sun to shade.

Water: Most species require wet to very moist situations.

Hardiness Zones: 6 to 10.

Life Span: Perennial.

BEST FEATURES

Wetland species. Fast growth. Tendency to form large colonies in saturated soils.

COMPANION PLANTS

Water hyssop (*Bacopa monnieri*), swamp fern (*Blechnum serrulatum*), cinnamon and royal ferns (*Osmunda cinnamomea* and *O. regalis*), climbing aster (*Symphyotrichum carolinianum*), string lily (*Crinum americanum*), Virginia willow (*Itea virginica*), buttonbush (*Cephalanthus occidentalis*), leather fern (*Acrostichum danaeifolium*), scarlet hibiscus (*Hibiscus coccineus*).

SIMILAR AND RELATED SPECIES

At least 11 native and a number of non-native species of smartweed occur in Florida. With very few exceptions, all are wetland species. Swamp smartweed (*P. hydropiperoides*), dotted smartweed (*P. punctatum*), and dense-flower smartweed (*P. densiflorum*) are among the more common and widespread.

Pontederia cordata

pahn-tuh-DE-ree-uh kor-DAY-tuh

Pickerelweed

Family: Pontederiaceae
Rooted aquatic
Height: 2 to 4 feet
Spread: Spreading into large colonies by underground stems

LANDSCAPE USE

An excellent species for water gardens, shallow ponds, bogs, retention ponds, drainage swales, and muddy canal banks. May be used in a container or rooted in mud.

FORM

A perennial aquatic with dark green leaves and showy flower stalks, potentially spreading into large colonies by underground stems.

NATIVE RANGE

Marshes, swamps, and ditches. Throughout the eastern United States, from New England, south throughout Florida, and west to Texas.

CHARACTERISTICS

Flowers: Tubular, petals blue to violet, often with yellow markings; borne in erect, showy spikes above the leaves. Spring to fall.

Leaves: Heart shaped to lance shaped, dark green, with long-tapering, bluntly pointed tips.

Fruit: A fleshy expansion of the flower tube; ridged, ellipsoid, with a red seed. Eaten by wildlife.

CULTURE

Soil: Saturated, acid to neutral soils.

Exposure: Full sun to part shade.

Water: Prefers inundation or very wet situations.

Hardiness Zones: 4 to 10.

Life Span: Perennial.

BEST FEATURES

Rapid growth. Spreading habit. Showy flower spikes. Aquatic habit. Fruits are eaten by wildlife.

COMPANION PLANTS

Water hyssop (*Bacopa monnieri*), yellow canna (*Canna flaccida*), cinnamon and royal ferns (*Osmunda cinnamomea* and *O. regalis*), blue flags (*Iris* spp.), smartweeds (*Polygonum* spp.), water lilies (*Nymphaea* spp.), American lotus (*Nelumbo lutea*), climbing aster (*Symphyotrichum carolinianum*), string lily (*Crinum americanum*), Virginia willow (*Itea virginica*), buttonbush (*Cephalanthus occidentalis*), leather fern (*Acrostichum danaeifolium*), scarlet hibiscus (*Hibiscus coccineus*).

CULTIVARS

A white-flowered form, *P. cordata* 'Alba,' is reported.

SIMILAR AND RELATED SPECIES

The leaves of several species of arrowheads (*Sagittaria* spp.) are similar but their flowers are white. Care should be taken to avoid the somewhat similar but non-native, weedy, and very invasive water hyacinth (*Eichhornia crassipes*).

Prunus angustifolia

PROO-nus an-gus-ti-FO-lee-uh

Chickasaw Plum

Family: Rosaceae
Large shrub or small tree
Height: 8 to 20 feet
Spread: 8 to 12 feet

Jean C. Putnam H.

Performs best in naturalistic settings or where large, dense shrubbery is required. Good for soil stabilization and for roadside beautification.

FORM
An erect, much-branched, deciduous, colonizing, usually multistemmed shrub or very small tree with a showy display of spring flowers. Often forming dense thickets due to suckering from shoots and underground stems.

NATIVE RANGE
Woodland edges, dry hammocks, disturbed roadsides, fencerows, and open fields. Delaware, southward to central Florida, and west to Texas.

CHARACTERISTICS
Flowers: White, small, 5-petaled, borne profusely and making a showy display. Spring.
Leaves: Alternate, lance shaped, 1–3 inches long, often reflexed upward from the midrib, shiny green above, with minute teeth along the margins.
Fruit: A round, ½- to 1¼-inch-long, red to yellow drupe with a whitish glaze.
Bark: Reddish brown; furrowed, somewhat scaly with age.

CULTURE
Soil: Occurs naturally in dry to moist, sandy soil with pH 5.0–7.5. Mildly salt tolerant.
Exposure: Full sun.
Water: Performs well in well-drained situations. Supplemental irrigation not required.
Hardiness Zones: 5 to 9.
Life Span: Moderately fast growing and short-lived; probably less than 50 years.

BEST FEATURES
Profuse and showy spring flowering season and attractive fruit. Good for wildlife cover and food. Suckering habit makes it useful for soil stabilization.

COMPANION PLANTS
Beautyberry (*Callicarpa americana*), pignut hickory (*Carya glabra*), redbud (*Cercis canadensis*), southern crabapple (*Malus angustifolia*), sweetgum (*Liquidambar styraciflua*), bluestems and broomsedges (*Andropogon* spp.), Cherokee bean (*Erythrina herbacea*), Adam's needle (*Yucca filamentosa*), wax myrtle (*Myrica cerifera*).

DISADVANTAGES
Suckering habit can sometimes be difficult to control. Webworms are attracted to this species.

ALLERGENIC AND TOXIC PROPERTIES
Caution is advised. Some species in this genus are known to cause cyanide poisoning and can be lethal in large quantities. Ingestion of smaller amounts may cause a variety of debilitating symptoms.

SIMILAR AND RELATED SPECIES
Several related species occur naturally in Florida. Hog or flatwoods plum (*P. umbellata*) is similar but has purplish fruit, has a single trunk, and does not form dense colonies. American plum (*P. americana*) is a tree with reddish brown to tan, shaggy bark, an upright stature, and slightly larger flowers.

Prunus caroliniana

PROO-nus ka-ro-li-nee-AY-nuh

Cherry Laurel

Family: Rosaceae
Large shrub or small tree
Height: 20 to 45 feet
Spread: 15 to 30 feet

Jean C. Putnam H.

LANDSCAPE USE

Often used as a hedge or for screening large yards and parks. Excellent for upland restoration projects. Also serves as a pruned patio or specimen plant.

FORM

An erect, evergreen tree or dense, spreading to upright shrub with dark green leaves and an oval to somewhat irregular outline.

NATIVE RANGE

Hammocks, disturbed sites, vacant lots, and woodland edges. Virginia, southward to south-central Florida, and west to Louisiana.

CHARACTERISTICS

Flowers: Tiny, white, borne in dense, conspicuous, showy clusters. Spring.
Leaves: Alternate, lustrous dark green, oblong to lance shaped, and 2–4 inches long.
Fruit: A shiny, dark black drupe to about ½ inch in diameter. Borne in abundance and relished by birds. Summer to fall.
Bark: Grayish to nearly black.

CULTURE

Soil: Occurs naturally in fertile, well-drained, acid to alkaline soils.
Exposure: Sun to part shade.
Water: Supplemental irrigation normally not required.
Hardiness Zones: 7 to 10.
Life Span: Probably not more than about 50 years.

BEST FEATURES

Forms an excellent hedge. Extended and prolific flowering period. Dense foliage and abundant fruit provides cover and food for birds and other wildlife.

COMPANION PLANTS

Pignut hickory (*Carya glabra*), American beech (*Fagus grandifolia*), white ash (*Fraxinus americana*), magnolia (*Magnolia grandiflora*), oaks (*Quercus* spp.), red buckeye (*Aesculus pavia*), beautyberry (*Callicarpa americana*), sweetshrub (*Calycanthus floridus*), flatwoods plum (*Prunus umbellata*).

DISADVANTAGES

Rapid growth may make it outgrow its space. Displays weedy tendencies. Susceptible to some leaf spotting and chewing insects, but not significantly so.

ALLERGENIC AND TOXIC PROPERTIES

Caution is advised. Some species in this genus are known to cause cyanide poisoning and can be lethal in large quantities. Ingestion of smaller amounts may cause a variety of debilitating symptoms. Known to have caused loss of livestock.

SIMILAR AND RELATED SPECIES

Black cherry (*P. serotina*) matures into a much larger tree, is deciduous with thin, elliptical leaves, and displays blocky, grayish bark at maturity.

Psychotria nervosa

sy-KAH-tree-uh nir-VO-suh (or sy-KO-tree-uh)

Wild Coffee

Family: Rubiaceae
Large shrub
Height: 5 to 15 feet
Spread: 3 to 6 feet

J. C. Putnam H.

LANDSCAPE USE
May be used in mixed or single-species shrub beds, as an open hedge, or as a specimen plant in shady understory gardens.

FORM
An upright, multistemmed evergreen shrub with attractive, dark green leaves and showy maroon to scarlet fruit.

NATIVE RANGE
Coastal and tropical hammocks. North-central peninsular Florida southward, including the West Indies.

CHARACTERISTICS
Flowers: Small, white, borne in obvious clusters. Spring and summer.
Leaves: Opposite, dark, shiny green, 3–6 inches long, with prominent venation that gives the upper surface a quilted appearance.
Fruit: A scarlet to maroon, 5/16-inch-diameter drupe. Showy; eaten by blue jays, cardinals, and catbirds. Summer and fall.
Bark: Brownish.

CULTURE
Soil: Moderately drained, neutral to slightly alkaline soils, with only small amounts of organic matter. Somewhat drought tolerant, but may wilt. Somewhat salt tolerant.
Exposure: Sun to shade. Will freeze back.
Water: Moist soil is best, but will adapt to dry situations if irrigated.
Hardiness Zones: 9 to 11.
Life Span: Probably less than 50 years.

BEST FEATURES
Fruit is showy and attracts wildlife. Leaves are interesting and attractive. Tolerant of shade.

COMPANION PLANTS
Rough-leaf velvetseed (*Guettarda scabra*), Simpson's stopper (*Myrcianthes fragrans*), myrsine (*Rapanea punctata*), white indigoberry (*Randia aculeata*), coontie (*Zamia pumila*), spicewood (*Calyptranthes pallens*), Jamaica caper (*Capparis cynophallophora*), gumbo limbo (*Bursera simaruba*), pigeon plum and seagrape (*Coccoloba diversifolia* and *C. uvifera*), stoppers (*Eugenia* spp.).

DISADVANTAGES
Chewing insects sometimes attack the leaves but are only a minor inconvenience.

SIMILAR AND RELATED SPECIES
Two other species of *Psychotria* occur naturally in Florida. Bahama coffee (*P. ligustrifolia*) is a rare component of pinelands and rocky hammocks at the state's southernmost tip, while softleaf wild coffee (*P. sulzneri*) is fairly common in the central and southern peninsula. Both are available in the native plant trade.

Quercus alba

KWIR-kus AL-buh

White Oak

Family: Fagaceae
Large tree
Height: 60 to 100 feet
Spread: 30 to 60 feet

LANDSCAPE USE
Best used in parks and other large landscapes that allow it to achieve its full proportions.

FORM
A large, single-trunked, deciduous tree with attractive, shaggy bark, a mostly pyramidal form, spreading branches, and deeply lobed leaves.

NATIVE RANGE
Moist hammocks and bluffs. Eastern North America, from New England, south to the Florida panhandle, and west to Texas.

CHARACTERISTICS
Flowers: Borne in solitary, greenish yellow, dangling catkins. Spring.
Leaves: Alternate, simple, 3–7 inches long, deeply cut into 7–9 narrow lobes.
Fruit: A ¾-inch-long, chestnut-brown acorn resting in a shallow, warty cup.
Bark: Light gray to whitish; shredding into narrow, flaking strips at maturity.

CULTURE
Soil: Fertile, acid, well-drained soils, with pH 5.5–6.5.
Exposure: Full sun to part shade.
Water: Prefers moist, well-drained situations.
Hardiness Zones: 4 to 8.
Life Span: More than 100 years.

BEST FEATURES
High-character trunk. Large acorn crop. Soft green, deeply lobed leaves.

COMPANION PLANTS
Florida sugar maple (*Acer saccharum* subsp. *floridanum*), pignut hickory (*Carya glabra*), sweetgum (*Liquidambar styraciflua*), laurel

oak (*Quercus hemisphaerica*), basswood (*Tilia americana*), winged elm (*Ulmus alata*), red buckeye (*Aesculus pavia*), red mulberry (*Morus rubra*), redbud (*Cercis canadensis*), American hophornbeam (*Ostrya virginiana*), Carolina jessamine (*Gelsemium sempervirens*), purple coneflower (*Echinacea purpurea*), wild petunia (*Ruellia caroliniensis*).

DISADVANTAGES
Heavy fruit crops can require cleaning in formal landscapes. Beset by a number of minor insects but long-lived in spite of them.

ALLERGENIC AND TOXIC PROPERTIES
Caution is advised. Humans should not consume large amounts of acorns due to their tannin content. Airborne pollen may be bothersome to some people.

SIMILAR AND RELATED SPECIES
Bluff oak (*Q. sinuata*) is most similar in form, bark, and leaves and is more widespread in Florida. Swamp chestnut oak (*Q. michauxii*). pictured above, also has a shaggy trunk, but its leaves are larger and coarsely toothed and its acorns are larger with larger cups. It is also a very good landscape tree for larger landscapes.

Quercus hemisphaerica

KWIR-kus he-mi-SFEE-ri-kuh

Laurel Oak

Family: Fagaceae
Medium-sized tree
Height: 40 to 60 feet
Spread: 30 to 40 feet

LANDSCAPE USE

The relatively small size of this tree in comparison to other oaks makes it appropriate for residential landscapes and roadsides.

FORM

An erect, slender, tardily deciduous, fast-growing tree with a mostly pyramidal to rounded crown.

NATIVE RANGE

Dry hammocks and well-drained woodlands. New Jersey, southward to south-central peninsular Florida, and west to Texas.

CHARACTERISTICS

Flowers: Borne in dangling catkins. Spring.

Leaves: Alternate, simple, narrowly elliptic to lance shaped, 1½–4 inches long. Often overwintering until February or later, then dropping all at once just before new leaf growth.

Fruit: An acorn borne in a sessile to short-stalked cup covering about half the kernel.

Bark: Thin and grayish; smooth on young trees, becoming increasingly furrowed with age.

CULTURE

Soil: Moist to dry, well-drained, fertile soils.

Exposure: Full sun to part shade.

Water: Tolerates relatively dry situations.

Hardiness Zones: 6 to 10.

Life Span: Relatively short-lived; probably less than 100 years in most cases.

BEST FEATURES

Fast growth rate. Moderate size. Tardily deciduous.

COMPANION PLANTS

Box elder and red maple (*Acer negundo* and *A. rubrum*), sugarberry (*Celtis laevigata*), magnolia (*Magnolia grandiflora*), loblolly pine (*Pinus taeda*), Florida sugar maple (*Acer saccharum* subsp. *floridanum*), pignut hickory (*Carya glabra*), sweetgum (*Liquidambar styraciflua*), redbud (*Cercis canadensis*), American hophornbeam (*Ostrya virginiana*), Carolina jessamine (*Gelsemium sempervirens*), purple coneflower (*Echinacea purpurea*), wild petunia (*Ruellia caroliniensis*).

CULTIVARS

Q. hemisphaerica 'Darlington' is a reported cultivar but is not universally accepted.

ALLERGENIC AND TOXIC PROPERTIES

Caution is advised. Humans should not consume large amounts of acorns due to their tannin. Airborne pollen may be bothersome to some people.

SIMILAR AND RELATED SPECIES

Very similar to and sometimes considered indistinct from *Q. laurifolia,* which is also called laurel oak and diamond-leaf oak; it occurs mostly in wet habitats, and its leaves are often diamond shaped in outline. Also very similar to willow oak (*Q. phellos*), an 80- to 100-foot-tall, moderately fast-growing oak with narrow leaves reminiscent of a willow. Willow oak tolerates wet to dry soils.

Quercus laevis

KWIR-kus LEE-vis (LAY-vis)

Turkey Oak

Family: Fagaceae
Small tree
Height: 30 to 40 feet
Spread: 10 to 15 feet

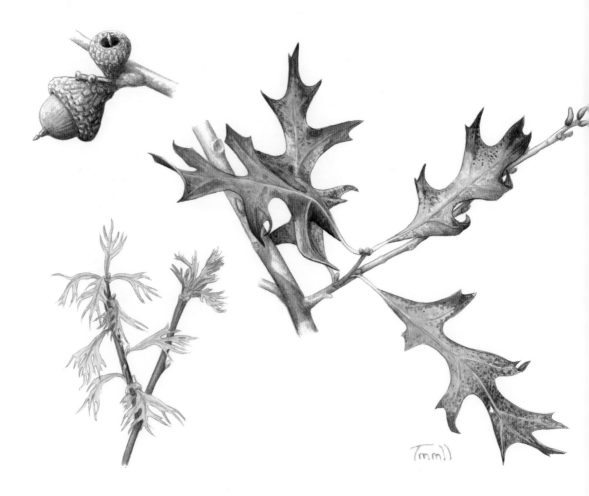

LANDSCAPE USE

Appropriate for use as a small tree in residential landscapes, as well as in the restoration of degraded sandhills and longleaf pinelands.

FORM

A small, erect, scrubby deciduous tree with relatively large leaves, grayish to blackish bark, and an open, irregular crown.

NATIVE RANGE

Sandhills. Virginia, south nearly throughout Florida, and west to Mississippi.

CHARACTERISTICS

Flowers: Borne in 3- to 5-inch-long, dangling, yellowish catkins. Spring.

Leaves: Alternate, simple, 4–14 inches long, deeply 3- to 7-lobed, dark, shiny green above, often oriented so that the edge of the blade is held perpendicular to the ground. Turning bright red and showy in fall.

Fruit: A brown acorn, about 1 inch long, borne in a relatively shallow cup that covers about one-third of the kernel.

Bark: Thick, deeply furrowed; dark gray to nearly black on older trees.

CULTURE

Soil: Well-drained, infertile, sandy, acid soils.

Exposure: Full sun.

Water: Drought tolerant.

Hardiness Zones: 8 to 10.

Life Span: To at least 100 years in natural situations, but perhaps not exceeding 75 years under cultivation.

BEST FEATURES

Small size. Large, interesting, shiny green leaves. Fast growth. Drought tolerance. Deeply furrowed, dark bark. Showy fall leaves.

COMPANION PLANTS

Longleaf pine (*Pinus palustris*), bluejack, blackjack, and myrtle oaks (*Quercus incana, Q. marilandica,* and *Q. myrtifolia*), summer haw (*Crataegus flava*), pawpaws (*Asimina* spp.), saw palmetto (*Serenoa repens*), highbush blueberries (*Vaccinium* spp.), sparkleberry (*Vaccinium arboreum*), shiny blueberry (*Vaccinium myrsinites*), muhly grass (*Muhlenbergia capillaris*), lopsided Indiangrass (*Sorghastrum secundum*), butterfly weed (*Asclepias tuberosa*), wild petunia (*Ruellia caroliniensis*), lovegrasses (*Eragrostis* spp.).

ALLERGENIC AND TOXIC PROPERTIES

Caution is advised. Humans should not consume large amounts of acorns due to their tannin content. Airborne pollen may be problematic for some people.

SIMILAR AND RELATED SPECIES

Several "scrub oaks" occur in natural communities with turkey oak, but none have deeply lobed leaves. Southern red oak (*Q. falcata*) has somewhat similar leaves but is a very large tree. Its leaves have a characteristic U-shaped base, unlike those of turkey oak.

Quercus laurifolia

KWIR-kus law-ri-FO-lee-uh

Laurel Oak

Family: Fagaceae
Large tree
Height: 30 to 100 feet
Spread: 30 to 80 feet

J. C. Putnam &.

LANDSCAPE USE

Often used as a street tree. Excellent for restoration projects. Also serves well as a specimen tree, especially in moist to wet areas.

FORM

A large, erect, deciduous, single-trunked, fast-growing, robust oak with an oval crown of horizontal to ascending branches, often producing a buttressed base.

NATIVE RANGE

Floodplain forests and moist calcareous hammocks. New Jersey, south nearly throughout Florida, and west to Texas.

CHARACTERISTICS

Flowers: Inconspicuous, yellowish, borne in drooping catkins (male) or small spikes (female) at the leaf base.
Leaves: Dark shiny green, 3–4 inches long, varying from lance shaped to diamond shaped.
Fruit: An acorn, about 1 inch long and nearly half covered by the cup.
Bark: Dark grayish to blackish and furrowed.

CULTURE

Soil: Occurs naturally in sites ranging from wet floodplain soils to dry hammocks, in soils with pH 4.0–6.0.
Exposure: Sun to part shade.
Water: Irrigate to keep soil moist for best performance.
Hardiness Zones: 6 to 10.
Life Span: Probably to at least 100 years.

BEST FEATURES

Buttressed base, large size, attractive leaves, fast growth rate, tolerance of wet conditions, soil versatility.

COMPANION PLANTS

American elm (*Ulmus americana*), red maple (*Acer rubrum*), Simpson's stopper (*Myrcianthes fragrans*), wild coffees (*Psychotria* spp.), royal palm (*Roystonea regia*), eastern gamagrass (*Tripsacum dactyloides*), firebush (*Hamelia patens*), oaks (*Quercus* spp.), sugarberry (*Celtis laevigata*), basswood (*Tilia americana*), red buckeye (*Aesculus pavia*), blue beech (*Carpinus caroliniana*), sweetgum (*Liquidambar styraciflua*), loblolly pine (*Pinus taeda*), winged elm (*Ulmus alata*).

DISADVANTAGES

Susceptible to the same insect pests as most oaks, but not seriously so.

ALLERGENIC AND TOXIC PROPERTIES

Caution is advised. Humans should not consume large amounts of acorns due to their tannin content. Airborne pollen may be problematic for some people.

SIMILAR AND RELATED SPECIES

At least 25 oak species and natural hybrids occur in Florida, all of which are native. Laurel oak is most similar to *Q. hemisphaerica*, a tree that some experts do not consider a distinct species. Also called laurel oak or Darlington oak, *Q.*

hemisphaerica is a short-lived tree confined mostly to well-drained uplands and is sometimes considered a "weed tree" due to its relative abundance on disturbed sites. Chestnut oak (*Q. michauxii*) occurs in similar places and is a good companion for laurel oak.

Quercus myrtifolia

KWIR-kus mir-ti-FO-lee-uh

Myrtle Oak

Family: Fagaceae
Small tree or shrub
Height: 6 to 30 feet
Spread: 3 to 20 feet

J. C. Hancock

LANDSCAPE USE

Massed to produce shrub beds on sandy, somewhat shifting soils. Excellent for dune stabilization.

FORM

An erect, densely foliated, evergreen shrub or small tree with a short, straight trunk. Rounded to oval shape when young. Crown becoming more spreading at maturity.

NATIVE RANGE

Back dunes, dry, sandy hammocks, oak scrub, and sandhills. South Carolina, south throughout Florida, and west to Mississippi.

CHARACTERISTICS

Flowers: Tiny, inconspicuous, borne in catkins.
Leaves: Shiny medium green, oval to nearly rounded, and often folding under along the margins. Very attractive.
Fruit: An acorn. Small, less than ½ inch long, about one-third covered by a shallow cup.
Bark: Smooth; grayish to brown.

CULTURE

Soil: Well-drained, sandy soils of oak and oak–pine scrub. Drought and salt tolerant.
Exposure: Full sun.
Water: Prefers dry, sandy, well-drained situations. Irrigation not required.
Hardiness Zones: 8 to 10.
Life Span: Forms thickets that may persist for many years even though individual plants may die out.

BEST FEATURES

Dense, attractive foliage. Evergreen habit. Tolerance of salt air, drought, sandy soils, and generally poor growing conditions. Heavily used by the threatened Florida scrub jay.

COMPANION PLANTS

Scrub holly (*Ilex arenicola*), scrub hickory (*Carya floridana*), sand pine (*Pinus clausa*), rusty lyonia and staggerbush (*Lyonia ferruginea* and *L. fruticosa*), Chapman and scrub oaks (*Quercus chapmanii* and *Q. inopina*), tarflower (*Bejaria racemosa*), gopher apple (*Licania michauxii*), coontie (*Zamia pumila*), garberia (*Garberia heterophylla*), pawpaws (*Asimina* spp.).

ALLERGENIC AND TOXIC PROPERTIES

Caution is advised. Humans should not consume large amounts of acorns due to their tannin content. Airborne pollen may cause allergic reactions.

SIMILAR AND RELATED SPECIES

Scrub oak (*Q. inopina*), a shrubby oak of the south-central peninsular Florida scrub, is very similar in appearance and habit to myrtle oak. Chapman oak (*Q. chapmanii*) is also somewhat similar and occurs in similar situations. Its leaves ordinarily have undulating margins.

Quercus nigra

KWIR-kus NY-gruh

Water Oak

Family: Fagaceae
Medium-sized tree
Height: 50 to 80 feet
Spread: 20 to 50 feet

LANDSCAPE USE
Often used as a medium-sized street tree and for shade in parks and residential landscapes.

FORM
An erect, moderately sized, fast-growing deciduous oak with spreading to ascending branches.

NATIVE RANGE
Moist to dry hammocks and disturbed sites. New Jersey, south nearly throughout Florida, and west to Texas.

CHARACTERISTICS
Flowers: Borne in a yellowish brown, dangling catkin. Spring.

Leaves: Alternate, simple, variable in shape and lobing but with at least some leaves having an abruptly broadened apex reminiscent of a spatula. Tardily deciduous; usually falling gradually over winter rather than in fall.

Fruit: An acorn, about ½ inch wide and deep, borne in a shallow cup.

Bark: Thin, grayish, smooth to very slightly rippled.

CULTURE
Soil: Occurs naturally in moist floodplain soils, but adapts to almost any moist to well-drained soil.

Exposure: Full sun to part shade.

Water: Adaptable to relatively dry or moist conditions.

Hardiness Zones: 6 to 10.

Life Span: Moderate; probably 80 to 100 years.

BEST FEATURES
Tolerance of a wide range of soil conditions. Often remains mostly green over much of the winter.

COMPANION PLANTS
Laurel, swamp chestnut, Shumard, and live oaks (*Quercus hemisphaerica, Q. michauxii, Q. shumardii,* and *Q. virginiana*), blue beech (*Carpinus caroliniana*), red cedar (*Juniperus virginiana*), redbud (*Cercis canadensis*), yaupon (*Ilex vomitoria*), needle palm (*Rhapidophyllum hystrix*), pinxter azalea (*Rhododendron canescens*), coral honeysuckle (*Lonicera sempervirens*).

DISADVANTAGES
Often considered a "weed tree" due to its tendency to invade old fields and other disturbed sites. Sometimes attacked and seriously damaged by boring insects.

ALLERGENIC AND TOXIC PROPERTIES
Caution is advised. Humans should not consume large amounts of acorns due to their tannin content. Airborne pollen may produce allergic reactions.

SIMILAR AND RELATED SPECIES
Often seen in residential landscapes with laurel oak (*Q. hemisphaerica*), but not especially similar to it. Water oak differs from laurel oak by having at least some spatula-shaped leaves.

Quercus shumardii

KWIR-kus shoo-MAR-dee-eye

Shumard Oak

Family: Fagaceae
Medium-sized to large tree
Height: 60 to 110 feet
Spread: 40 to 60 feet

J. C. Putnam H.

LANDSCAPE USE

Specimen tree. Often used to provide shade and ornamentation in parking lots, along medians and roadsides, and in commercial landscapes. Very good shade tree.

FORM

A potentially large, erect, straight-trunked, deciduous tree. Crown oval when young, becoming spreading with age.

NATIVE RANGE

Floodplain forests and wet hammocks. North Carolina, southward to central Florida, and west to Michigan and Texas.

CHARACTERISTICS

Flowers: Small, inconspicuous, borne in catkins.

Leaves: Alternate, simple, 4–8 inches long, deeply 7-lobed, with each lobe tipped with a tiny point. Turning deep purplish red to red in autumn.

Fruit: An acorn, nearly 1 inch in diameter, in a shallow cup that covers less than one-fourth of the nut.

Bark: Grayish to grayish brown; slightly furrowed.

CULTURE

Soil: Moist, well-drained to bottomland soils with pH 5.8–8.0. Drought tolerant.

Exposure: Full sun. Intolerant of shade.

Water: Performs best in moist, well-drained situations, but adapts to dry sites.

Hardiness Zones: 5 to 10.

Life Span: Moderately fast growing and relatively long-lived, likely exceeding 100 years.

BEST FEATURES

Large size. Shade. Drought tolerance. Distinctive and attractive leaves with good fall color.

COMPANION PLANTS

Pignut hickory (*Carya glabra*), white ash (*Fraxinus americana*), magnolia (*Magnolia grandiflora*), basswood (*Tilia americana*), flowering dogwood (*Cornus florida*), American holly (*Ilex opaca*), redbud (*Cercis canadensis*), cherry laurel (*Prunus caroliniana*), witch hazel (*Hamamelis virginiana*), needle palm (*Rhapidophyllum hystrix*), pinxter and Florida azaleas (*Rhododendron canescens* and *R. austrinum*).

DISADVANTAGES

Mildly susceptible to typical oak diseases and insects.

ALLERGENIC AND TOXIC PROPERTIES

Caution is advised. Humans should not consume large amounts of acorns due to their tannin content. Airborne pollen may cause allergic reactions.

SIMILAR AND RELATED SPECIES

Similar or associated native oaks include southern red oak (*Q. falcata*), white oak (*Q. alba*), overcup oak (*Q. lyrata*), post oak (*Q. stellata*), and cherrybark oak (*Q. pagoda*).

Quercus virginiana

KWIR-kus vir-ji-nee-AY-nuh

Live Oak

Family: Fagaceae
Large tree
Height: 40 to 80 feet
Spread: 60 to 130 feet

J. C. Putnam H.

LANDSCAPE USE

A longtime favorite in southern landscapes. Excellent shade or specimen tree for large spaces such as parks, golf courses, and school campuses. Popular as a street and parking lot tree.

FORM

A massive, hardy, long-lived, evergreen oak, typically with a short, thick trunk and large, spreading branches ascending into the crown. Branches sometimes sagging under their own weight and, in very old specimens, drooping to, or almost to, the ground.

NATIVE RANGE

Moist to wet hammocks, often near the coast. Virginia, south throughout Florida, and west to eastern Texas and Mexico.

CHARACTERISTICS

Flowers: Borne in drooping, conspicuous, yellow-green catkins. Spring.
Leaves: Alternate, dark green above, paler and grayish below, leathery, 1–5 inches long.
Fruit: An acorn, about one-third enclosed by the cup. Often borne in clusters of 2 to 5.
Bark: Dark gray when old; lighter when young. Deeply divided into narrow furrows but becoming blocky with age.

CULTURE

Soil: Performs best in moist, fertile soils with pH 4.5–6.5, but adapts to a wide range of soil types. Salt tolerant.
Exposure: Full sun.
Water: Locate in well-drained situations. Performs well in all but the wettest soils.
Hardiness Zones: 8 to 11.
Life Span: Long; specimens with ages in excess of 300 years are known.

BEST FEATURES

Long-lived and salt tolerant. Broad, spreading crown. Moderately fast growth rate when young, slowing with age. Overall hardiness. Excellent for shade.

COMPANION PLANTS

Magnolia (*Magnolia grandiflora*), wild olive (*Osmanthus americanus*), cabbage palm (*Sabal palmetto*), red bay (*Persea borbonia*), lancewood (*Ocotea coriacea*), pigeon plum (*Coccoloba diversifolia*), gumbo limbo (*Bursera simaruba*), sugarberry (*Celtis laevigata*), basswood (*Tilia americana*), blue beech (*Carpinus caroliniana*), flowering dogwood (*Cornus florida*), redbud (*Cercis canadensis*), American holly (*Ilex opaca*), American hophornbeam (*Ostrya virginiana*), witch hazel (*Hamamelis virginiana*), needle palm (*Rhapidophyllum hystrix*), bluestem palmetto (*Sabal minor*), other oaks (*Quercus* spp.).

CULTIVARS

A few selections have been made, but none are available or often used in Florida. As a group the oaks have produced many hybrids, at least 15 of which have been reported for Florida. Hence, morphological variation in Florida's oaks is common.

ALLERGENIC AND TOXIC PROPERTIES

Caution is advised. Humans should not consume large amounts of acorns due to their tannin content. Airborne pollen may cause allergic reactions.

SIMILAR AND RELATED SPECIES

Sand live oak (*Q. geminata*), considered by some to be a variety of live oak rather than a distinct species, is very attractive and occurs in sandhills, scrub, and dry coastal hammocks. Its leaves are strongly rolled under along the margins, and the veins of the upper surfaces are deeply impressed. Dwarf live oak (*Q. minima*), also considered by some to be a variety of live oak, is a low-growing, clonal shrub normally 2–6 feet in height.

Randia aculeata

RAN-dee-uh uh-kew-lee-AY-tuh

White Indigoberry

Family: Rubiaceae
Large shrub
Height: 3 to 10 feet
Spread: 3 to 6 feet

LANDSCAPE USE

An attractive, evergreen, specimen shrub that may also be used in mixed shrub beds, as a foundation plant, or as a semiopen hedge. Excellent for difficult situations and recommended for highway and powerline rights-of-way, medians, parking lots, and other sites with little irrigation.

FORM

A small, multistemmed, mostly densely foliated, often spiny shrub, with a distinctive pattern of successive, short, opposite branches, each pair of which subtends and appears to constitute a single unit with the shoot extension. Sometimes becomes treelike and more openly branched.

NATIVE RANGE

Pinelands, dune thickets, and edges of tropical hammocks. Central and southern peninsular Florida, and throughout the Caribbean from the Bahamas to northern South America.

CHARACTERISTICS

Flowers: Small but showy, about ½ inch long, fragrant, tubular, with 5 bright white, spreading petals.
Leaves: Opposite, relatively small, usually less than about 2 inches long, oval to rounded in shape.
Fruit: A round, ½-inch-diameter, whitish (green when unripe) berry with a dark purple to black pulp. Year-round.
Bark: Grayish.

CULTURE

Soil: Dry, thin, well-drained soils.
Exposure: Full sun to part shade.
Water: Supplemental irrigation not required.
Hardiness Zones: 10 to 11.
Life Span: Probably less than 50 years.

BEST FEATURES

Adaptability to difficult areas. Interesting branching pattern and whitish fruit. Small, attractive white flowers.

COMPANION PLANTS

Wild coffee (*Psychotria nervosa*), snowberry (*Chiococca alba*), myrsine (*Rapanea punctata*), stoppers (*Eugenia*

spp.), satinleaf (*Chrysophyllum oliviforme*), beautyberry (*Callicarpa americana*), lancewood (*Ocotea coriacea*), gumbo limbo (*Bursera simaruba*), paradise tree (*Simarouba glauca*), marlberry (*Ardisia escallonioides*), blolly (*Guapira discolor*), sword ferns (*Nephrolepis biserrata* and *N. exaltata*).

DISADVANTAGES

Often produces sharp pairs of thorns in the leaf axils.

SIMILAR AND RELATED SPECIES

White indigoberry is in the same family as numerous other important native Florida landscape plants, including the wild coffees (*Psychotria* spp.), buttonbush (*Cephalanthus occidentalis*), fevertree (*Pinckneya bracteata*), black torch (*Erithalis fruticosa*), firebush (*Hamelia patens*), and velvetseeds (*Guettarda* spp.). None of these are closely similar to *Randia*.

Rapanea punctata

ruh-PA-nee-uh punk-TAY-tuh

Myrsine

Family: Myrsinaceae
Large shrub
Height: 8 to 20 feet
Spread: 3 to 5 feet

LANDSCAPE USE

Serves equally well as a specimen plant or as part of a hedge or mixed shrub bed. Appropriate for difficult areas, such as parking lots, or as a narrow tree in areas where lateral space is restricted.

FORM

A versatile, upright, single- to multistemmed, little-branched, evergreen, potentially thicket-forming shrub, with an often-contorted trunk, typically columnar form, open crown, and flowers and fruits conspicuously positioned on the bare portions of the branches just below the leaves. Vegetatively similar to marlberry (*Ardisia escallonioides*).

NATIVE RANGE

Tropical and coastal temperate hammocks and moist pinelands. Mostly central and southern peninsular Florida and throughout the West Indies into southern Mexico and South America, but also reported as far north as Levy County, Florida.

CHARACTERISTICS

Flowers: Small, greenish white, borne in conspicuous clusters along bare portions of the stem; male and female flowers borne mostly on separate plants. Mainly winter, but possible year-round.

Leaves: Alternate, mostly clustered toward the tips of the branches, elliptical, medium to dark green, 2–5 inches long.

Fruit: Small, rounded, dark blue to blackish drupes, less than ¼ inch in diameter, conspicuous along bare portions of the branches. Year-round.

Bark: Thin; grayish to brownish.

CULTURE

Soil: Dry or moist, acid to mildly alkaline soils. Very adaptable. Salt tolerant.

Exposure: Full sun to part shade.

Water: Supplemental irrigation not required.

Hardiness Zones: 10 to 11.

Life Span: Probably less than 50 years.

BEST FEATURES

Overall hardiness. Tolerance of difficult situations. Interestingly disposed flowers and fruits. Columnar form.

COMPANION PLANTS

Wild coffee (*Psychotria nervosa*), stoppers (*Eugenia* spp.), beautyberry (*Callicarpa americana*), marlberry (*Ardisia escallonioides*), Jamaica caper (*Capparis cynophallophora*), Florida privet (*Forestiera segregata*), tough buckthorn (*Sideroxylon tenax*), coontie (*Zamia pumila*), red bay (*Persea borbonia*).

SIMILAR AND RELATED SPECIES

Myrsine can sometimes have vegetative characters that are very similar to marlberry (*Ardisia escallonioides*), leading to nonflowering and nonfruiting plants sometimes being misidentified in the wild. They are easily distinguished by the striking differences between the way they bear both flowers and fruits. Myrsine is more cold hardy than marlberry.

Rhapidophyllum hystrix

ra-pi-do-FI-lum HIS-triks

Needle Palm

Family: Arecaceae or Palmae
Shrub
Height: 3 to 8 feet
Spread: 4 to 8 feet

J.C.Putnam H.

LANDSCAPE USE

Useful for accent, as a specimen shrub, in a spaced planting of several individuals, or along the base of elevated decks. Reportedly used with success in parking-lot plantings.

FORM

A mostly single-stemmed, shrublike, evergreen palm with conspicuous, fanlike blades and a short, erect trunk that is covered with numerous sharp-pointed, 8- to 10-inch-long needles.

NATIVE RANGE

Mesic hammocks, ravine bottoms, and edges of floodplain woods. South Carolina, southward to south-central Florida, and west to Mississippi.

CHARACTERISTICS

Flowers: Tiny, inconspicuous, borne among the needles and fibers that encircle the stem. Spring.
Leaves: Fan shaped, 2–3 feet both long and broad, borne on a long stalk.
Fruit: Tiny, reddish brown to purplish brown, borne among the needles and fibers of the stem. Fall.
Bark: The 1- to 3-foot-tall stem bears masses of 8- to 10-inch-long, stiff, sharp-pointed needles that are piercing to the touch.

CULTURE

Soil: Rich, moist to very moist, poorly drained soils.
Exposure: Shade to part shade produces best results, but will tolerate full sun.
Water: Prefers moist conditions, but has been used successfully in parking lots.
Hardiness Zones: 8 to 10.
Life Span: Slow growing and at least moderately long-lived; likely exceeding 50 years.

BEST FEATURES

Evergreen habit and long life span.

COMPANION PLANTS

Yaupon (*Ilex vomitoria*), blue-stem palmetto (*Sabal minor*), witch hazel (*Hamamelis virginiana*), devil's walking stick (*Aralia spinosa*), American holly (*Ilex opaca*), Florida sugar maple (*Acer saccharum* subsp. *floridanum*), flowering dogwood (*Cornus florida*), American hophornbeam (*Ostrya virginiana*), fringetree (*Chionanthus virginicus*), red buckeye (*Aesculus pavia*), blue beech (*Carpinus caroliniana*).

DISADVANTAGES

The needles that cover the stem are stiff and very sharp.

SIMILAR AND RELATED SPECIES

Blue-stem palmetto (*Sabal minor*) is vegetatively very similar but lacks

needles and produces flowers and fruit in long stalks that extend well above the longest leaves. Saw palmetto (*Serenoa repens*) has sawlike teeth along the leaf stalk, lacks the needles along the stem, and produces large, conspicuous fruit.

Rhizophora mangle

ry-ZAH-fuh-ruh MAN-gluh

Red Mangrove

Family: Rhizophoraceae
Large saltwater shrub or tree
Height: 15 to 50 feet
Spread: 15 to 40 feet

LANDSCAPE USE

Red mangrove is one of three true mangroves native to
Florida. It and the white and black mangroves (*Laguncularia
racemosa* and *Avicennia germinans*) are extremely valuable for
protecting south Florida's shoreline. All three, especially when
used together, are excellent for controlling and reducing
coastal erosion and related damage from hurricanes, winter
storms, and high tides. All three are also essential for coastal
and inland waterway restoration projects.

FORM

An erect, multi- to single-stemmed
tree of coastal saline waters, character-
istically producing a tangle of aerial
"prop" roots that emanate from the
lower portions of the trunk.

NATIVE RANGE

Shallow saline waters of bays
throughout tropical portions of the
world, including southern Florida.

CHARACTERISTICS

Flowers: Small, about 1 inch wide, pale
yellow, with 4 petals. Year-round.
Leaves: Opposite, dark, lustrous green,
lance shaped, 2–7 inches long.
Fruit: Brown, conical, fleshy, germinat-
ing and giving rise to a new plant
while still attached to the branch,
resulting in a narrow, 12-inch-long or
longer shoot. Year-round.
Bark: Smooth and reddish brown.

CULTURE

Soil: Occurs naturally in saline soils, but adapts to freshwater.
Extremely salt tolerant.
Exposure: Full sun.
Water: Does best in coastal saline waters.
Hardiness Zones: 10 to 11.
Life Span: Slow growing and at least moderately long-lived; at
least 50 years.

BEST FEATURES

Capacity to reduce and control coastal erosion, especially that
inflicted by tropical and winter storms. Provides habitat, food
sources, and nursery areas for a wide array of fish, crabs, and
other saltwater inhabitants.

COMPANION PLANTS

White mangrove (*Laguncularia racemosa*), black mangrove
(*Avicennia germinans*), buttonwood (*Conocarpus erectus*),
leather fern (*Acrostichum danaeifolium*), string lily (*Crinum
americanum*), sea oxeyes (*Borrichia* spp.), saltwort (*Batis
maritima*).

SIMILAR AND RELATED SPECIES

The several mangrove species mentioned above are all in
separate families and are easily distinguished from one
another with a little practice.

Rhododendron austrinum

ro-do-DEN-drawn aws-TRY-num

Florida Azalea

Family: Ericaceae
Shrub
Height: 3 to 10 feet
Spread: 3 to 8 feet

LANDSCAPE USE
Appropriate as a specimen plant, in mixed or single-species shrub beds, or in naturalistic landscapes.

FORM
An open, irregular, upright to leggy, multistemmed, deciduous shrub, producing showy clusters of yellowish to orange flowers in late spring.

NATIVE RANGE
Slopes, bluffs, and wooded stream banks at the bottom of steep-sided ravines. South-central Alabama, southwest Georgia, and Florida panhandle.

CHARACTERISTICS
Flowers: Tubular, yellow to orange, sweetly fragrant, borne in showy clusters near the tips of branches. Spring.
Leaves: Alternate, simple, entire, 1–4 inches long, widest near the tip.
Fruit: A narrow, light brown, 1-inch-long capsule.
Bark: Brownish to gray; thin.

CULTURE
Soil: Prefers rich, acid, well-drained, sandy loams.
Exposure: Full sun to shade.
Water: Moist to wet conditions are preferred.
Hardiness Zone: 8.
Life Span: Probably less than 50 years.

BEST FEATURES
Showy, fragrant orange flowers.

COMPANION PLANTS
American hophornbeam (*Ostrya virginiana*), witch hazel (*Hamamelis virginiana*), flowering dogwood (*Cornus florida*), black gum (*Nyssa sylvatica*), sourwood (*Oxydendrum arboreum*), sweetshrub (*Calycanthus floridus*), mountain laurel (*Kalmia latifolia*), needle palm (*Rhapidophyllum hystrix*), oakleaf hydrangea (*Hydrangea quercifolia*), highbush blueberries (*Vaccinium* spp.), Carolina jessamine (*Gelsemium sempervirens*), columbine (*Aquilegia canadensis*).

DISADVANTAGES
Deciduous.

CULTIVARS
At least a dozen cultivars are reported, of which 'Lisa's Gold' is available in Florida.

ALLERGENIC AND TOXIC PROPERTIES
Caution is advised. The toxicity of *Rhododendron austrinum* is unknown. However, numerous members of the heath family, especially the genus *Rhododendron,* are known to be toxic and if eaten produce a variety of symptoms including nausea, vomiting, altered heart rate, and dizziness.

SIMILAR AND RELATED SPECIES
Alabama azalea (*R. alabamense*) and pinxter azalea (*R. canescens*) are vegetatively indistinguishable from Florida azalea. The former has white flowers with a yellow petal spot; the latter has pinkish flowers.

Rhododendron canescens

ro-do-DEN-drawn kay-NE-senz (or kuh-NE-senz)

Pinxter Azalea

Family: Ericaceae
Shrub
Height: 10 to 15 feet
Spread: 10 to 15 feet

LANDSCAPE USE

Excellent along woodland edges, in naturalistic landscapes, in mixed shrub gardens with Florida azalea (*R. austrinum*) and Alabama azalea (*R. alabamense*), or as a single specimen. Prized for its beautiful pinkish flowers.

FORM

A multistemmed, sometimes leggy, deciduous shrub with clustered leaves and showy, fragrant, tubular flowers.

NATIVE RANGE

Bay swamps, flatwoods, moist to wet hammocks, hammock streams, and floodplains. North Carolina, southward to central Florida, and west to Texas.

CHARACTERISTICS

Flowers: Tubular, whitish to more often pinkish, very fragrant, borne in early spring at the tips of mostly leafless branches.

Leaves: Alternate, simple, entire, borne in whorl-like clusters near the branch tips.

Fruit: A hard, elongated, reddish brown capsule.

Bark: Thin and brownish.

CULTURE

Soil: Rich, acid soils are best.

Exposure: Flowers best in full sun, but will tolerate shade.

Water: Moist, well-drained situations are preferred.

Hardiness Zones: 6 to 9.

Life Span: To 50 years.

BEST FEATURES

Showy, fragrant flowers.

COMPANION PLANTS

Alabama and Florida azaleas (*Rhododendron alabamense* and *R. austrinum*), pipestem (*Agarista populifolia*), fetterbush (*Lyonia lucida*), highbush blueberries (*Vaccinium* spp.), sugarberry (*Celtis laevigata*), loblolly bay (*Gordonia lasianthus*), Walter's viburnum (*Viburnum obovatum*), cross vine (*Bignonia capreolata*), blue-stem palmetto (*Sabal minor*).

DISADVANTAGES

Deciduous.

CULTIVARS

Several selections are reported; these differ mainly in flower color. Few are available in Florida.

ALLERGENIC AND TOXIC PROPERTIES

Caution is advised. The toxicity of *R. canescens* is unknown. However, numerous members of the heath family, especially the genus *Rhododendron,* are known to be toxic and if eaten produce a variety of symptoms including nausea, vomiting, altered heart rate, and dizziness.

SIMILAR AND RELATED SPECIES

Vegetatively indistinguishable from Florida azalea (*R. austrinum*) and Alabama azalea (*R. alabamense*), both of which make good companions in naturalistic shrub beds.

Rhus copallinum

ROOS ko-puh-LI-num

Winged Sumac

Family: Anacardiaceae
Large shrub
Height: 10 to 25 feet
Spread: 5 to 15 feet

LANDSCAPE USE

Appropriate for large, naturalistic settings and woodland edges where its aggressive nature will not pose a control problem. May also be used in urban landscapes as a background or in large shrub beds.

FORM

A deciduous, multistemmed, irregular, sometimes arborescent shrub with open, crooked, ascending branches, shiny compound leaves, large, showy clusters of whitish green flowers, and dense clusters of dull red fruit.

NATIVE RANGE

Hammocks, sandhills, flatwoods, and disturbed sites. Maine, south nearly throughout Florida, and west to Texas.

CHARACTERISTICS

Flowers: Individually small, greenish white, borne in showy, 8-inch-long panicles at the tips of the branches. Spring to early summer.

Leaves: Alternate, compound, with 9–21 ovate to lance-shaped, shiny, toothed leaflets borne along a winged rachis. Those of some plants turning bright red and showy in fall, especially with an early cold front following a dry summer.

Fruit: Small, hairy, dull red, borne in summer and fall in conspicuous, showy clusters.

Bark: Thin, smooth, and brown to brownish gray.

CULTURE

Soil: Sandy, acid soils are best.

Exposure: Requires full sun for best flowering and fruiting.

Water: Performs best in dry situations.

Hardiness Zones: 5 to 10.

Life Span: Fast growing; likely less than 50 years.

BEST FEATURES

Fall color. Showy flower and fruit clusters. Shiny compound leaves. Tolerance of dry situations.

COMPANION PLANTS

Longleaf pine (*Pinus palustris*), bluejack, turkey, and blackjack oaks (*Quercus incana, Q. laevis,* and *Q. marilandica*), summer haw (*Crataegus flava*), pawpaws (*Asimina* spp.), sweetgum (*Liquidambar styraciflua*), saw palmetto (*Serenoa repens*), muhly grass (*Muhlenbergia capillaris*), lopsided Indiangrass (*Sorghastrum secundum*), butterfly weed (*Asclepias tuberosa*), wild petunia (*Ruellia caroliniensis*), blazing stars (*Liatris* spp.), black-eyed Susan (*Rudbeckia hirta*).

DISADVANTAGES

Deciduous. Can be aggressive and difficult to control. May be shaded out by maturing hardwoods.

ALLERGENIC AND TOXIC PROPERTIES

Many members of the family, such as poison sumac and poison ivy, can cause skin irritations, but this is not true for winged sumac.

SIMILAR AND RELATED SPECIES

The leaves of smooth sumac (*R. glabra*), which occurs sparingly in north Florida, lack the winged rachis.

Roystonea regia

roy-STO-nee-uh REE-jee-uh

Royal Palm

Family: Arecaceae or Palmae
Large tree
Height: 60 to 100 feet
Spread: 20 to 30 feet

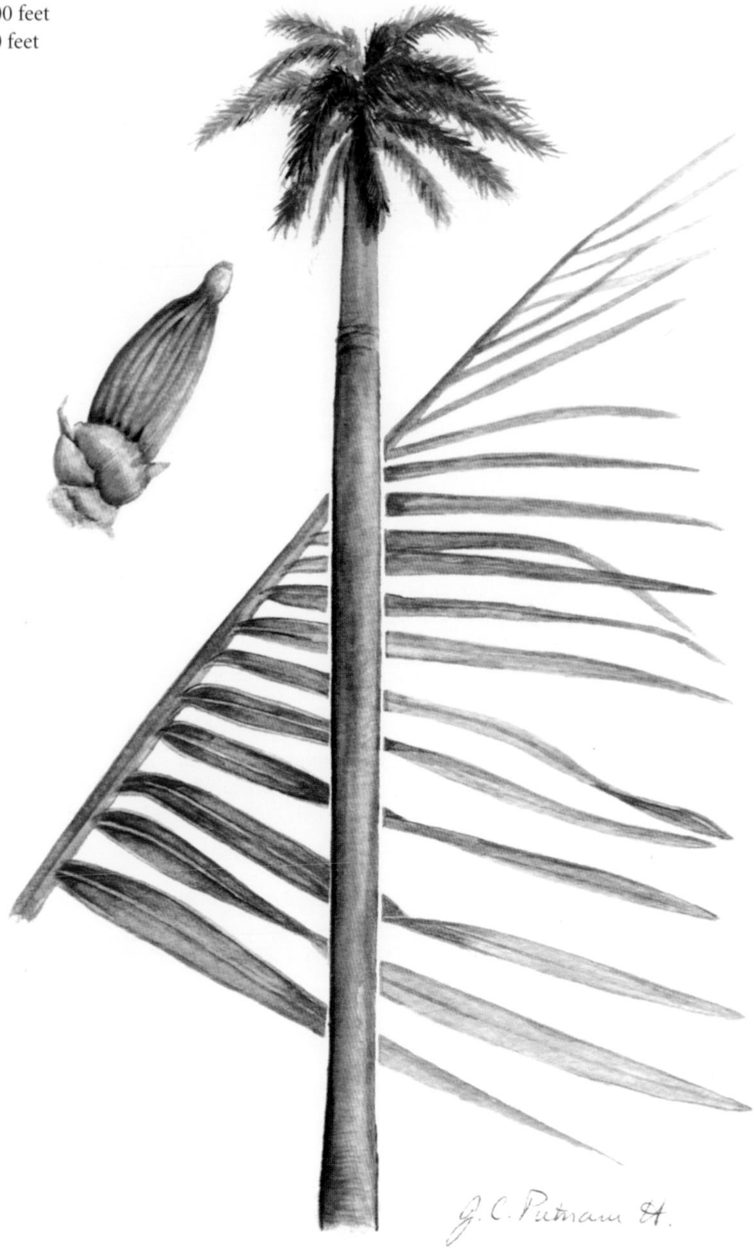

LANDSCAPE USE

South Florida's most popular and widely used native palm. Most often employed as a street or accent tree or along pools, walkways, and the edges of yards. No longer common in the wild but often used in commercial and residential landscaping for framing buildings or in single- or mixed-species palm groups. Care should be taken in placement of this tree to ensure that the large, heavy fronds do not fall on people or property.

FORM

A tall, majestic palm with silvery gray trunk and large, dark green, graceful fronds that emanate from a shiny green, smooth crownshaft. Trunk more often straighter and thicker than the typically bulging Cuban royal palm.

NATIVE RANGE

Hammocks and edges of swamps. Southernmost Florida.

CHARACTERISTICS

Flowers: Tiny, white, borne in conspicuous, elegant, 2-foot-long clusters.
Leaves: Large, divided like a feather, to about 15 feet long and 6 feet wide, dark green, graceful, very attractive. Drooping with age and eventually falling at maturity. Large leaves can weigh in excess of 50 pounds.
Fruit: A rounded, purplish drupe, about ½ inch in diameter, borne in large, branching clusters.
Bark: Trunk is silvery gray.

CULTURE

Soil: Moist to very moist, fertile soils. Moderately salt tolerant.
Exposure: Full sun to broken shade. Not tolerant of frost.
Water: Prefers moist to wet conditions, but adapts to less than optimum soils and moisture regimes.
Hardiness Zones: 10 to 11.
Life Span: Long-lived; in excess of 100 years.

BEST FEATURES

Graceful countenance, large size, adaptability to roadside plantings and large commercial landscapes.

COMPANION PLANTS

Cypresses (*Taxodium* spp.), red maple (*Acer rubrum*), cabbage palm (*Sabal palmetto*), dahoon (*Ilex cassine*), myrsine (*Rapanea punctata*), pop ash (*Fraxinus caroliniana*), leather fern (*Acrostichum danaeifolium*), swamp fern (*Blechnum serrulatum*), royal fern (*Osmunda regalis*).

DISADVANTAGES

Royal palm bug, scales, and leaf spot fungi are minor annoyances.

CULTIVARS

Some growers recognize *R. regia* 'Florida population' as a different and more purely Florida-based genetic strain.

SIMILAR AND RELATED SPECIES

Of the numerous native palms that occur in Florida, none are as majestic as royal palm, nor could be confused with it.

Rudbeckia hirta

rood-BE-kee-uh HIR-tuh

Black-Eyed Susan

Family: Asteraceae or Compositae
Wildflower
Height: 1 to 3 feet
Spread: 1 to 2 feet, spreading from year to year by self-sown seed

LANDSCAPE USE

Excellent for mixed wildflower gardens, roadside rights-of-way, powerline easements, and highway medians.

FORM

An erect, short-lived perennial or biennial wildflower with showy flower heads of yellow ray flowers and dark purplish disk flowers.

NATIVE RANGE

Disturbed sites, flatwoods, roadsides, and sandhills. Southern Canada, south nearly throughout Florida, and west to Texas.

CHARACTERISTICS

Flowers: Showy, daisylike, 2–3 inches broad, with numerous bright yellow ray flowers encircling a head of purplish to brownish disk flowers.

Leaves: Alternate, toothed, with roughened surfaces.

Fruit: A tiny, black, inconspicuous achene.

CULTURE

Soil: Rich, well-drained soils preferred, but adaptable to most conditions.

Exposure: Full sun to part shade.

Water: Flowers best with regular watering, but tolerant of drier conditions.

Hardiness Zones: 2 to 9.

Life Span: Annual to short-lived perennial.

BEST FEATURES

Fast growth rate. Showy, bright yellow flowers. Produces copious seeds and readily reseeds in most gardens.

COMPANION PLANTS

Butterfly weed (*Asclepias tuberosa*), tickseeds (*Coreopsis* spp.), narrowleaf sunflower (*Helianthus angustifolius*), blazing stars (*Liatris* spp.), Stokes' aster (*Stokesia laevis*), broomsedges (*Andropogon* spp.), lopsided Indiangrass (*Sorghastrum secundum*), tropical sage (*Salvia coccinea*), passionflower (*Passiflora incarnata*), wild petunia (*Ruellia caroliniensis*).

DISADVANTAGES

Prolific reseeding tends to make this species expand beyond small gardens.

SIMILAR AND RELATED SPECIES

At least eight species of *Rudbeckia* are native to Florida, several of which make excellent additions to mixed wildflower gardens.

Ruellia caroliniensis

roo-E-lee-uh ka-ro-li-nee-EN-sis

Wild Petunia

Family: Acanthaceae
Wildflower
Height: 1 to 2 feet
Spread: Individually narrow, but spreads by seed

LANDSCAPE USE

A hardy addition to mixed wildflower gardens. A good replacement for impatiens along the edges of walkways and patios.

FORM

A mostly erect, perennial wildflower with tubular lavender flowers and dark green leaves.

NATIVE RANGE

Roadsides, disturbed sites, hammocks, and sandhills. North Carolina, south nearly throughout Florida, and west to Texas.

CHARACTERISTICS

Flowers: Tubular, lavender, borne in clusters near the top of the stem. Spring to fall.

Leaves: Opposite, ovate to elliptic, to about 4 inches long.

Fruit: A ½-inch-long capsule with brown seeds.

CULTURE

Soil: Tolerant of a wide range of soil conditions.

Exposure: Full sun for best flowering, but will tolerate light shade.

Water: Moist, well-drained sites are preferred.

Hardiness Zones: 8 to 11.

Life Span: Perennial.

BEST FEATURES

Showy flowers. Reproduces by self-sown seeds. Hardy and easy to grow.

COMPANION PLANTS

Butterfly weed (*Asclepias tuberosa*), lanceleaf coreopsis and tickseed (*Coreopsis lanceolata* and *C. leavenworthii*), narrowleaf sunflower (*Helianthus angustifolius*), blazing stars (*Liatris* spp.), Stokes' aster (*Stokesia laevis*), broomsedges (*Andropogon* spp.), lopsided Indiangrass (*Sorghastrum secundum*), tropical sage (*Salvia coccinea*), passionflower (*Passiflora incarnata*), black-eyed Susan (*Rudbeckia hirta*).

DISADVANTAGES

Easily spreads into nearby areas by self-sown seed.

SIMILAR AND RELATED SPECIES

At least five species of *Ruellia* are native to Florida; some are used in landscaping, but few besides the present species are available in the nursery trade. A variety of non-native ruellias are sold in Florida but should be avoided.

Sabal etonia

SAY-bawl ee-TO-nee-uh (or e-tuh-NY-uh)

Scrub Palmetto

Family: Arecaceae or Palmae
Shrub
Height: 4 to 6 feet
Spread: 4 to 6 feet

Use as a low shrub in sunny, sandy, well-drained situations.

FORM
A low, evergreen, shrublike palm with fan-shaped fronds and a subterranean trunk.

NATIVE RANGE
Endemic to central Florida's sand scrub.

CHARACTERISTICS
Flowers: Borne along a many-flowered stalk that can be up to 3 feet long. Spring to summer.
Leaves: Fan shaped, blades to about 3 feet wide, with stems to about 3 feet long.
Fruit: Small, shiny, bluish black berries. Mostly summer to fall.

CULTURE
Soil: Well-drained sands of the central Florida scrub.
Exposure: Full sun.
Water: Drought tolerant.
Hardiness Zones: 9 to 11.
Life Span: Long-lived; likely well over 100 years.

BEST FEATURES
Tolerant of heat, drought, and sun.

COMPANION PLANTS
Saw palmetto (*Serenoa repens*), tarflower (*Bejaria racemosa*), fetterbush and stagger-bush (*Lyonia lucida* and *L. fruticosa*), garberia (*Garberia heterophylla*), pawpaws (*Asimina* spp.), butterfly weed (*Asclepias tuberosa*), blazing stars (*Liatris* spp.), gopher apple (*Licania michauxii*), scrub mints (*Conradina* spp.), coontie (*Zamia pumila*), Florida pennyroyal (*Piloblephis rigida*).

SIMILAR AND RELATED SPECIES
Very similar to and nearly indistinguishable from young cabbage palms (*Sabal palmetto*). Distinguished from saw palmetto (*Serenoa repens*) by lacking sawlike teeth along the leaf stalk.

Sabal minor

SAY-bawl MY-nir

Blue-Stem Palmetto

Family: Arecaceae or Palmae
Shrub
Height: 4 to 9 feet
Spread: 4 to 8 feet

LANDSCAPE USE

Used as a shrubby specimen palm or as part of a planted shrub understory. Particularly suited for retention ponds, drainage swales, canal banks, parking lots, and other difficult areas.

FORM

A trunkless fan palm with several leaves and a long flowering stalk rising well above the leaf blades.

NATIVE RANGE

Moist woods, bottoms of rich slopes, and edges of floodplains. Wide-ranging across the southern United States from North Carolina, southward to central Florida, and west to east Texas.

CHARACTERISTICS

Flowers: Tiny, white, borne in somewhat showy clusters on 3- to 5-foot-long, branching stalks. Spring and summer.

Leaves: Fan shaped, deeply divided, bluish green to dark green, 2–4 feet broad and long, borne on long stalks that lack the sharp marginal teeth of the saw palmetto.

Fruit: Small, rounded, shiny black, conspicuous. Fall.

CULTURE

Soil: Often occurs naturally in rich, moist soil with pH 5.5–6.5, but will adapt to a variety of soil types and dry situations. Slightly salt tolerant.

Exposure: Part sun to shade. Very cold tolerant.

Water: Performs best in moist situations, but tolerant of drier sites after becoming established.

Hardiness Zones: 7 to 10.

Life Span: Moderately long-lived; exceeding 50 years.

BEST FEATURES

Excellent specimen where a palmlike shrub is desired, or for use in naturalistic settings. Adaptable to a variety of soils, very hardy, and useful for landscaping in difficult situations as described above. Fall-ripening fruit is consumed by an array of wildlife.

COMPANION PLANTS

Box elder and red maple (*Acer negundo* and *A. rubrum*), sweetbay (*Magnolia virginiana*), red bay and swamp bay (*Persea borbonia* and *P. palustris*), needle palm (*Rhapidophyllum hystrix*), highbush blueberries (*Vaccinium corymbosum* and *V. elliottii*), possumhaw holly (*Ilex decidua*), tupelos (*Nyssa* spp.).

SIMILAR AND RELATED SPECIES

Vegetatively similar to needle palm (*Rhapidophyllum hystrix*), but lacking the needle palm's spiny trunk. Distinguished from saw palmetto (*Serenoa repens*) by the lack of sawlike teeth along the leaf stalk.

Sabal palmetto

SAY-bawl pawl-ME-to

Cabbage Palm

Family: Arecaceae or Palmae
Medium-sized to large tree
Height: 20 to 60 feet
Spread: 10 feet

LANDSCAPE USE

Often planted in small groups to accent homes or buildings. Regularly and often planted in city, county, and state parks and recreation areas as well as along the shoulders and in the medians of state and interstate highways. The cabbage palm's overall hardiness and durability also make it an excellent choice for difficult situations, including retention ponds, drainage swales, canal banks, and commercial parking lots.

FORM

An erect fan palm with a grayish trunk that is sometimes smooth and other times covered with "boots" (the remaining bases of fallen leaves).

NATIVE RANGE

Pinelands, inland and coastal hammocks, and edges of marshes and prairies, often near limestone. South Carolina, south throughout Florida, and west to Texas. This is Florida's state tree and its most common and widespread palm—the signature tree of the Florida skyline.

CHARACTERISTICS

Flowers: Small, white, borne just below the leaves in conspicuous, 3-foot-long, pendent clusters. Summer.
Leaves: Semi-fan shaped, 3–5 feet wide, slightly longer, reflexed upward from the central axis, giving the leaf a V-shaped appearance. Blade divisions have threadlike fibers along their edges.
Fruit: Round, shiny black, about ½ inch in diameter.
Bark: Grayish and smooth to slightly roughened on mature trees. Younger trees often retain the attractive bases of fallen leaves.

CULTURE

Soil: Performs best in moist, fertile, somewhat sandy soil with the presence of limestone, but highly adaptable to almost any situation.
Exposure: Full sun. Intolerant of shade.
Water: Moist conditions are best, but very adaptable to almost any situation, except regular flooding.
Hardiness Zones: 8 to 11.
Life Span: Slow growing and at least moderately long-lived, probably reaching well over 100 years.

BEST FEATURES

Cabbage palm is versatile, hardy, and easy to grow. Its fruit is eaten by wildlife and its dense crown provides excellent cover for nesting birds. These features, coupled with its wide adaptability to numerous difficult situations, make it an exceptional Florida native landscape plant. At its best when planted in clusters.

COMPANION PLANTS

Live oak (*Quercus virginiana*), beautyberry (*Callicarpa americana*), red bay (*Persea borbonia*), sugarberry (*Celtis laevigata*), flatwoods plum (*Prunus umbellata*), red maple (*Acer rubrum*), oaks (*Quercus* spp.), sweetbay and magnolia (*Magnolia virginiana* and *M. grandiflora*), loblolly bay (*Gordonia lasianthus*), coontie (*Zamia pumila*).

DISADVANTAGES

A number of epiphytic plants get their start on this tree in southern Florida. The most troublesome is strangler fig (*Ficus aurea*), which can eventually destroy a cabbage palm if not removed.

SIMILAR AND RELATED SPECIES

Several other tree-sized palms are native to Florida. The brittle and Florida thatch palms (*Thrinax morrisii* and *T. radiata*), paurotis palm (*Acoelorrhaphe wrightii*), Sargent's cherry palm (*Pseudophoenix sargentii*), and royal palm (*Roystonea regia*) are all available in the native plant trade and are excellent substitutes for any of the multitude of non-native palms that are sometimes planted in the state.

Sagittaria spp.

sa-ji-TE-ree-uh

Arrowheads, Duck Potatoes

Family: Alismataceae
Rooted aquatics
Height: 1 to 5 feet
Spread: 1 to 3 feet, but some species spread by underground stems

LANDSCAPE USE

Most appropriate for water gardens, shallow ponds, bogs, retention ponds, drainage swales, and wet canal banks. May be used in a container or rooted in mud. Four species are regularly used in Florida, including grass-leaved sagittaria (*S. graminea*), arrowhead (*S. lancifolia*), duck potato (*S. latifolia*), and dwarf arrowhead (*S. subulata*).

FORM

Rooted aquatics with narrow to broadly lance-shaped leaves and white, 3-petaled flowers borne on long stalks. Often forming large colonies in ditches and marshes.

NATIVE RANGE

Marshes, ditches, spring runs, stream banks, and lake edges. Virginia, south nearly throughout Florida, and west to at least Mississippi.

CHARACTERISTICS

Flowers: White, 3-petaled, typically borne along an elongated, narrow flowering stalk. Spring to fall.
Leaves: Dark green, luxuriant, ranging in form from narrow and grasslike to broadly ovate or lance shaped.
Fruit: Flattened achenes borne in conspicuous, rounded clusters.

CULTURE

Soil: Rich, saturated soils.
Exposure: Full sun.
Water: Prefers inundation most of the year.
Hardiness Zones: 8 to 10.
Life Span: Perennial.

BEST FEATURES

Tolerant of continuous inundation. Attractive flowers and flowering stalks. Extended flowering period. Luxuriant leaves. Fruit eaten by wildlife.

COMPANION PLANTS

Pickerelweed (*Pontederia cordata*), water hyssop (*Bacopa monnieri*), yellow canna (*Canna flaccida*), cinnamon and royal ferns (*Osmunda cinnamomea* and *O. regalis*), blue flags (*Iris* spp.), smartweeds (*Polygonum* spp.), water lilies (*Nymphaea* spp.), spatterdock (*Nuphar lutea*), climbing aster (*Symphyotrichum carolinianum*), string lily (*Crinum americanum*), Virginia willow (*Itea virginica*), buttonbush (*Cephalanthus occidentalis*), leather fern (*Acrostichum danaeifolium*), scarlet hibiscus (*Hibiscus coccineus*).

SIMILAR AND RELATED SPECIES

At least ten species of *Sagittaria* are native to Florida. Many are similar to each other, but they can be distinguished with a little practice.

Salix spp.

SAY-liks

Willows

Family: Salicaceae
Trees
Height: 25 to 60 feet
Spread: 20 to 40 feet

LANDSCAPE USE

Two willows are used in Florida landscaping: the Coastal Plain willow (*S. caroliniana*) and the black willow (*S. nigra*). Both are excellent along retention ponds and drainage canals but also are used in naturalistic wetland edges and along the borders of small ponds.

FORM

Erect to leaning, deciduous trees with drooping leaves, furrowed bark, and interesting flowering catkins.

NATIVE RANGE

Wetlands, riverbanks, wet disturbed sites, and pond edges. Black willow occurs mostly from the eastern panhandle westward and northward throughout much of the eastern United States. Coastal Plain willow occurs from the eastern panhandle eastward and southward nearly throughout Florida.

CHARACTERISTICS

Flowers: Borne in dense, conspicuous catkins as the leaves emerge. Male and female flowers borne on separate trees. Spring.
Leaves: Alternate, lance shaped, 3–5 inches long, finely toothed along the margins. Those of Coastal Plain willow are whitish below; those of black willow are green below.
Fruit: Tiny, 2-parted capsules, borne in the remains of the flowering catkins, opening to reveal many small seeds with long cottony hairs.
Bark: Brown; attractively ridged and furrowed in maturity.

CULTURE

Soil: Acid soils of floodplains and riverbanks.
Exposure: Full sun.
Water: Occurs naturally in moist to wet areas, but tolerant of a wide range of moisture regimes.
Hardiness Zones: 4 to 10.
Life Span: Relatively short-lived; probably less than 100 years.

BEST FEATURES

Fast growth. Tolerant of inundation. Ornamental bark. Attractive to butterflies.

COMPANION PLANTS

Buttonbush (*Cephalanthus occidentalis*), swamp dogwood (*Cornus foemina*), red maple (*Acer rubrum*), green ash (*Fraxinus pennsylvanica*), sweetbay (*Magnolia virginiana*), string lily (*Crinum americanum*), cardinal flower (*Lobelia cardinalis*), cypresses (*Taxodium* spp.), Virginia willow (*Itea virginica*).

SIMILAR AND RELATED SPECIES

Three other willows are native to Florida, including the prairie or small pussy willow (*S. humilis*), a shrubby plant to about 9 feet tall that is sometimes used in landscaping. The other two species, Florida willow (*S. floridana*) and heart-leaved willow (*S. eriocephala*), are small trees.

Salvia coccinea

SAL-vee-uh kahk-SI-nee-uh

Tropical Sage

Family: Lamiaceae
Wildflower
Height: 2 to 6 feet
Spread: Individually narrow but forming patches from self-sown seed

LANDSCAPE USE
May be used as a specimen plant, but sought after mostly for butterfly, hummingbird, and wildflower gardens.

FORM
An erect wildflower, sometimes reaching 6 feet in height, with toothed leaves and a showy spike of bright red, 2-lipped flowers.

NATIVE RANGE
Hammocks, disturbed sites, and sandy woodlands. South Carolina, south nearly throughout Florida, and west to Mississippi.

CHARACTERISTICS
Flowers: Bright red, about 1 inch long, and borne in erect, conspicuous, showy spikes. Summer and fall in the north; all year farther south.
Leaves: Opposite, oval in outline, toothed along the margins, aromatic when crushed.
Fruit: A dark brown, ellipsoid capsule.

CULTURE
Soil: Poor, neutral to slightly alkaline soils.
Exposure: Full sun to dappled shade.
Water: Drought tolerant, but adaptable to a wide range of conditions.
Hardiness Zones: 8 to 10.
Life Span: A short-lived perennial, but readily reseeding in most gardens.

BEST FEATURES
Showy red flowers. Extended flowering period. Attractive to hummingbirds and butterflies. Self-seeding.

COMPANION PLANTS
Cherokee bean (*Erythrina herbacea*), Simpson's stopper (*Myrcianthes fragrans*), necklace pod (*Sophora tomentosa*), muhly grass (*Muhlenbergia capillaris*), railroad vine (*Ipomoea pes-caprae*), blanket flower (*Gaillardia pulchella*), beach sunflower (*Helianthus debilis*), wild petunia (*Ruellia caroliniensis*), black-eyed Susan (*Rudbeckia hirta*), Stokes' aster (*Stokesia laevis*).

DISADVANTAGES
Tends to spread into adjacent areas by self-sown seeds.

CULTIVARS
A variety of selections with varying flower colors are available.

SIMILAR AND RELATED SPECIES
Lyre-leaved sage (*S. lyrata*), common in hammocks and disturbed sites throughout Florida, has purplish blue, 2-lipped flowers and is also widely used in landscaping.

Sassafras albidum

SA-suh-fras AL-bi-dum

Sassafras

Family: Lauraceae
Medium-sized tree
Height: 30 to 60 feet
Spread: 20 to 40 feet

LANDSCAPE USE

Excellent as a small to medium-sized tree for residential yards and roadsides, to provide shade over sidewalks, or for naturalistic landscapes.

FORM

An irregular, moderately fast-growing, deciduous tree with a pyramidal form. Sometimes forming dense thickets.

NATIVE RANGE

Hammocks, woodlands, and disturbed sites. Maine, southward to central peninsular Florida, and west to Texas.

CHARACTERISTICS

Flowers: Yellow, borne in conspicuous terminal, rounded racemes prior to new leaf growth. Early spring.

Leaves: Alternate, simple, 3–7 inches long, varying from unlobed to 2- to 5-lobed, with some leaves on any given plant appearing mitten shaped. Turning yellow or golden in fall.

Fruit: A ½-inch-diameter, dark blue drupe borne on a colorful red stalk in late summer and early fall.

Bark: Grayish to reddish brown; furrowed, ridged, and very attractive.

CULTURE

Soil: Typically found on poor, dry, acid, sandy upland soils.

Exposure: Full sun to part shade.

Water: Supplemental irrigation usually not required.

Hardiness Zones: 4 to 9.

Life Span: Perhaps less than 100 years in cultivation, but potentially longer.

BEST FEATURES

Fast growth. Moderate size. Early spring flowers. Fruit eaten by birds and other wildlife. Fall color.

COMPANION PLANTS

Redbud (*Cercis canadensis*), Chickasaw plum (*Prunus angustifolia*), magnolia (*Magnolia grandiflora*), laurel and live oaks (*Quercus hemisphaerica* and *Q. virginiana*), winged elm (*Ulmus alata*), red buckeye (*Aesculus pavia*), devil's walking stick (*Aralia spinosa*), flowering dogwood (*Cornus florida*), witch hazel (*Hamamelis virginiana*), oakleaf hydrangea (*Hydrangea quercifolia*), Carolina jessamine (*Gelsemium sempervirens*), purple coneflower (*Echinacea purpurea*), wild petunia (*Ruellia caroliniensis*).

DISADVANTAGES

Insect pests can be a minor nuisance; otherwise hardy and mostly free of problems.

ALLERGENIC AND TOXIC PROPERTIES

Previously used medicinally and to produce sassafras tea. Now known to contain carcinogenic compounds.

SIMILAR AND RELATED SPECIES

Closely related to the bays of the genus *Persea* but not similar to them.

Saururus cernuus

saw-ROO-rus SIR-new-us

Lizard's Tail

Family: Saururaceae
Wildflower
Height: 2 to 3 feet
Spread: Forming large colonies by underground runners

LANDSCAPE USE

Best along wet pond edges or depressions but may also be used in upland wildflower gardens if kept wet. Also used to beautify the edges of retention ponds, canals, and drainage swales.

FORM

An herbaceous, colony-forming, perennial, mostly aquatic wildflower with zigzag stems, conspicuous, heart-shaped leaves, and showy racemes of white flowers.

NATIVE RANGE

Stream and lake edges, ditches, swamps, and wetland depressions. Throughout the southeastern United States, including most of Florida.

CHARACTERISTICS

Flowers: White, borne on long, showy, recurved and nodding racemes that stand above the leaves. Early spring to summer.

Leaves: Alternate, to about 8 inches long, heart shaped, with pointed tips and entire margins.

Fruit: A tiny, 1-seeded nutlet.

CULTURE

Soil: Rich, mildly to very acid, saturated soils of wetland edges.

Exposure: Part shade to shade.

Water: Prefers saturated, freshwater conditions, including standing water to about 6 inches deep. Must be kept moist.

Hardiness Zones: 4 to 10.

Life Span: Perennial.

BEST FEATURES

Colony-forming habit. Showy, curving racemes of tiny white flowers. Shade tolerance.

COMPANION PLANTS

Coastal Plain willow (*Salix caroliniana*), cypresses (*Taxodium* spp.), pond apple (*Annona glabra*), scarlet hibiscus (*Hibiscus coccineus*), Virginia willow (*Itea virginica*), swamp fern (*Blechnum serrulatum*), royal fern (*Osmunda regalis*), smartweeds (*Polygonum* spp.), climbing aster (*Symphyotrichum carolinianum*), string lily (*Crinum americanum*), water hyssop (*Bacopa monnieri*), dahoon (*Ilex cassine*).

DISADVANTAGES

Can be aggressive in desirable habitats.

SIMILAR AND RELATED SPECIES

No other wetland species has this plant's recurved flowering raceme.

Scirpus spp.

SKIR-pus

Bulrushes

Family: Cyperaceae
Aquatic rushes
Height: 3 to 9 feet
Spread: Spreading as allowed by underground stems

LANDSCAPE USE

Numerous *Scirpus* species occur in Florida, four of which are available in the native plant trade. Two of these, three-square rush (*S. americanus*) and salt-marsh bulrush (*S. robustus*), occur in saline environments and are excellent aquatics for use in brackish marshes. The other two, giant bulrush (*S. californicus*) and soft-stem bulrush (*S. tabernaemontani*), reach heights approaching 10 feet, are more typical of freshwater environments, and are more appropriate for freshwater marshes and gardens.

FORM

Erect, herbaceous perennials with dark green leaves and soft, three-angled stems.

NATIVE RANGE

Brackish and freshwater marshes. Nova Scotia, south to Florida and the West Indies, and west to the Pacific and South America, depending upon species.

CHARACTERISTICS

Flowers: Tiny; concealed by minute scales that are borne in conspicuous, brownish spikelets that in some species are knotlike and borne close to the stem and in others borne in spreading, stalked clusters.

Leaves: Dark green; those treated here mostly short, sometimes barely or not even exceeding the sheath around the stem.

Fruit: A tiny, hard, inconspicuous seed concealed within the spikelet.

CULTURE

Soil: Wet soils, often in places with standing water. *S. americanus* and *S. robustus* are salt tolerant, whereas the two larger bulrushes (*S. californicus* and *S. tabernaemontani*) prefer freshwater.

Exposure: Full sun.

Water: Requires an aquatic environment.

Hardiness Zones: Throughout North America and Florida.

Life Span: Perennial.

BEST FEATURES

As a group the bulrushes are quite useful for screening the edges of ponds, lakes, and brackish sloughs and bayous. Valued for their dark green color, graceful form, and overall hardiness in all zones.

COMPANION PLANTS

Coastal Plain willow (*Salix caroliniana*), buttonbush (*Cephalanthus occidentalis*), yellow canna (*Canna flaccida*), sawgrass (*Cladium jamaicense*), pickerelweed (*Pontederia cordata*), prairie blue flag (*Iris hexagona*), string lily (*Crinum americanum*), spider lily (*Hymenocallis latifolia*), scarlet hibiscus (*Hibiscus coccineus*), salt bush (*Baccharis halimifolia*).

SIMILAR AND RELATED SPECIES

About 13 species of *Scirpus*, all of which are wetland plants, occur in Florida. Only those treated here are regularly used in landscaping.

Serenoa repens

se-ruh-NO-uh REE-penz

Saw Palmetto

Family: Arecaceae or Palmae
Shrub
Height: 3 to 20 feet, depending upon form
Spread: 3 to 8 feet

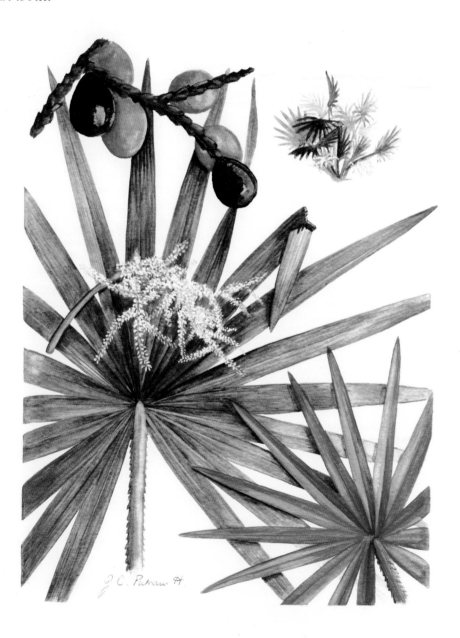

LANDSCAPE USE

A major component in the restoration of native pine flatwoods. Used in mass plantings, along foundations, or to conceal the open space under decks and raised patios. Also used for erosion control as well as in road and powerline rights-of-way, highway medians, and to soften and beautify parking lots.

FORM

A reclining to upright, thicket-forming palm, often with a creeping, prostrate trunk but sometimes trained into a slender tree.

NATIVE RANGE

A variety of habitats including well- to poorly drained flatwoods, sand pine–oak scrub, coastal dunes, cabbage palm hammocks, and scrub oak ridges. North Carolina, south throughout Florida, and west to Louisiana.

CHARACTERISTICS

Flowers: Tiny, white, borne in conspicuous clusters on elongated, branched inflorescences. Spring and summer.

Leaves: Fan shaped, medium to dark green, 3–4 feet long and wide, borne at the apex of a long leaf stalk that is armed along its margins with sawlike teeth.

Fruit: A conspicuous, elliptical, 1-inch-long drupe, orange when fresh, turning blue-black to black at maturity. Summer and fall.

Bark: Trunks covered with brownish, fibrous scales.

CULTURE

Soil: Well- to poorly drained, acid to neutral soils. Adaptable to several soil profiles. The coastal form, called silver saw palmetto, is very salt tolerant.

Exposure: Full sun to part shade.

Water: Supplemental irrigation ordinarily not required.

Hardiness Zones: 8 to 11.

Life Span: Saw palmetto is very long-lived. Those in well-established natural communities have been estimated to be several hundred years old.

BEST FEATURES

Long life. Thicket-forming habit. Tolerance of difficult situations such as parking lots and highway medians. Fruit is relished by a variety of wildlife, including deer, bears, and turkeys. Requires low maintenance once established and no irrigation.

COMPANION PLANTS

Slash and longleaf pines (*Pinus elliottii* and *P. palustris*), turkey, sand live, and bluejack oaks (*Quercus laevis, Q. geminata,* and *Q. incana*), summer haw (*Crataegus flava*), Chickasaw plum (*Prunus angustifolia*), gopher apple (*Licania michauxii*), Adam's needle (*Yucca filamentosa*), wiregrass (*Aristida stricta* var. *beyrichiana*), lowbush and highbush blueberries (*Vaccinium* spp.), tarflower (*Bejaria racemosa*), wild rosemary (*Conradina canescens*).

DISADVANTAGES

May require annual removal of old leaves to maintain a neat appearance.

CULTIVARS

Silver saw palmetto (*S. repens* 'Silver') occurs naturally along the Florida east coast, is very salt and drought tolerant, and is highly prized for the ornamental value of its attractive foliage.

SIMILAR AND RELATED SPECIES

Blue-stem palmetto (*Sabal minor*) and needle palm (*Rhapidophyllum hystrix*) are similar but lack the saw-toothed stem of saw palmetto.

Sesuvium portulacastrum

se-SOO-vee-um por-tew-luh-KAS-trum

Sea Purslane

Family: Aizoaceae
Ground cover
Height: 6 to 12 inches
Spread: Spreading by above- and belowground stems and runners

LANDSCAPE USE

Best used as a ground cover in sandy, dry to moist coastal situations.

FORM

A perennial, evergreen, mat-forming wildflower of coastal sand barrens and brackish marshes.

NATIVE RANGE

Mud and salt flats, saline and alkaline marsh edges, dunes, and creek bottoms. Missouri, southward to peninsular Florida, and west along the coast to California; also West Indies and Central America.

CHARACTERISTICS

Flowers: Pink to lavender, 5-petaled, borne in the leaf axils. Year-round.

Leaves: Opposite, fleshy, narrow below, slightly wider near the tip, borne along a greenish to purplish red stem.

Fruit: A small, multiseeded capsule.

CULTURE

Soil: Sandy, alkaline soils are preferred.

Exposure: Full sun. Salt tolerant.

Water: Moist to dry.

Hardiness Zones: 6 to 10.

Life Span: Perennial.

BEST FEATURES

Mat-forming habit. Attractive flowers. Fleshy foliage. Salt tolerance.

COMPANION PLANTS

Water hyssop (*Bacopa monnieri*), Christmasberry (*Lycium carolinianum*), seashore paspalum (*Paspalum vaginatum*), cordgrasses (*Spartina* spp.), seashore dropseed (*Sporobolus virginicus*), seaside goldenrod (*Solidago sempervirens*), coontie (*Zamia pumila*), blanket flower (*Gaillardia pulchella*).

SIMILAR AND RELATED SPECIES

Slender sea purslane (*S. maritimum*) occurs from the western panhandle to the central peninsula, but it is not often used in landscaping.

Sideroxylon foetidissimum

sy-duh-RAHK-si-lawn fee-ti-DI-si-mum (fe-ti-DI-si-mum)

Mastic

Family: Sapotaceae
Large tree
Height: 50 to 80 feet
Spread: 30 to 50 feet

Specimen or shade tree.

FORM
A large, upright, single-trunked, widely branched tree with an irregular crown and large, yellowish, wavy leaves.

NATIVE RANGE
Tropical hammocks. Southern Florida and the West Indies.

CHARACTERISTICS
Flowers: Small, yellow, borne in conspicuous clusters. Year-round.
Leaves: Large, 7–8 inches long, yellow green, with wavy margins.
Fruit: Attractive, conspicuous, oval, deep yellow to somewhat orange, 1-inch-long drupes with sticky juice. Spring.
Bark: Medium to dark brown; rough to the touch.

CULTURE
Soil: Occurs naturally in fertile hammock soils. Salt tolerant.
Exposure: Full sun.
Water: Supplemental irrigation generally not required.
Hardiness Zones: 10 to 11.
Life Span: Slow growing and probably long-lived; to at least 100 years. Precise life spans of tropical trees are difficult to discern since their trunks do not often produce annual growth rings.

BEST FEATURES
Larger than most other tropical trees. Becomes a shade tree. Salt tolerance.

COMPANION PLANTS
Gumbo limbo (*Bursera simaruba*), satinleaf (*Chrysophyllum oliviforme*), pigeon plum and seagrape (*Coccoloba diversifolia* and *C. uvifera*), blolly (*Guapira discolor*), cabbage palm (*Sabal palmetto*), marlberry (*Ardisia escallonioides*), spicewood (*Calyptranthes pallens*), Jamaica and limber capers (*Capparis cynophallophora* and *C. flexuosa*), cocoplum (*Chrysobalanus icaco*), Simpson's stopper (*Myrcianthes fragrans*), myrsine (*Rapanea punctata*), Florida privet (*Forestiera segregata*), wild coffee (*Psychotria nervosa*), white indigoberry (*Randia aculeata*), coontie (*Zamia pumila*).

DISADVANTAGES
Psyllids, scales, and tar spots are minor problems.

SIMILAR AND RELATED SPECIES
Eight species of *Sideroxylon* occur in Florida, all of which are native. Willow bustic (*S. salicifolium*) is an attractive and often-used native landscape plant in the southern peninsula. Other species available in the native plant trade include *S. tenax* and *S. reclinatum*.

Sideroxylon salicifolium

sy-duh-RAHK-si-lawn suh-li-si-FO-lee-um (or say-li-si-FO-lee-um)

Willow Bustic

Family: Sapotaceae
Small tree
Height: 20 to 30 feet
Spread: 10 to 20 feet

LANDSCAPE USE
Equally appropriate for small yards, city streets, or shade over a small patio.

FORM
A slender, erect, evergreen tree with a narrow crown of shiny green, lance-shaped leaves.

NATIVE RANGE
Pinelands and hammocks. Southernmost peninsular Florida, the West Indies, Mexico, and Central America.

CHARACTERISTICS
Flowers: Small, white, borne in conspicuous clusters along the stem and in the leaf axils. Year-round.

Leaves: Alternate, stalked, shiny green above, mostly lance shaped, 3–6 inches long.

Fruit: Tiny, blackish berries borne in dense, conspicuous clusters along the stem.

Bark: Grayish to light brown; scaly.

CULTURE
Soil: Poor soils, including thin, sandy, alkaline soils.

Exposure: Full sun to part shade.

Water: Tolerates moist to nearly dry situations.

Hardiness Zones: 10 to 11.

Life Span: Moderately long-lived; likely to 100 years.

BEST FEATURES
Evergreen. Small to medium size makes it appropriate for small landscapes. Interesting flowers and fruit arrangement along nearly naked stems.

COMPANION PLANTS
White indigoberry (*Randia aculeata*), broomsedges (*Andropogon* spp.), coontie (*Zamia pumila*), cocoplum (*Chrysobalanus icaco*), Geiger tree (*Cordia sebestena*), necklace pod (*Sophora tomentosa*), spicewood (*Calyptranthes pallens*), Simpson's stopper (*Myrcianthes fragrans*), saw palmetto (*Serenoa repens*).

SIMILAR AND RELATED SPECIES
Eight species of *Sideroxylon* occur in Florida, at least four of which are used in Florida landscaping.

Sideroxylon tenax

sy-duh-RAHK-si-lawn TE-naks

Tough Buckthorn

Family: Sapotaceae
Shrub or small tree
Height: 3 to 20 feet
Spread: 2 to 10 feet

LANDSCAPE USE
Excellent for poor soils and difficult situations such as powerline and highway rights-of-way and medians. Also useful to provide screening or to deter foot traffic.

FORM
An irregularly and densely branched, often thorny, evergreen tree or shrub with small, dark green leaves.

NATIVE RANGE
Scrub, sandhills, old dunes, and coastal hammocks. Central and southern peninsular Florida.

CHARACTERISTICS
Flowers: Tiny, white, borne in clusters in the leaf axils. Spring.
Leaves: Alternate, small, 1–3 inches long, dark green above, often densely hairy and copper colored below.
Fruit: A small, rounded, ½-inch-diameter, blackish berry. Fall.
Bark: Reddish brown; often armed with stout thorns.

CULTURE
Soil: Well-drained, poor, sandy soils.
Exposure: Full sun to part shade. Salt tolerant.
Water: Drought tolerant.
Hardiness Zones: 8 to 10.
Life Span: Relatively long-lived shrub; probably over 50 years.

BEST FEATURES
Drought and salt tolerance. Dense branching. Attractive green and copper-colored leaves.

COMPANION PLANTS
Fetterbush (*Lyonia lucida*), Chapman, turkey, and myrtle oaks (*Quercus chapmanii, Q. laevis,* and *Q. myrtifolia*), tarflower (*Bejaria racemosa*), wax myrtle (*Myrica cerifera*), shiny blueberry (*Vaccinium myrsinites*), scrub mints (*Conradina* spp.), gopher apple (*Licania michauxii*), coontie (*Zamia pumila*), butterfly weed (*Asclepias tuberosa*), Florida pennyroyal (*Piloblephis rigida*), blazing stars (*Liatris* spp.).

DISADVANTAGES
The potentially thorny stems may make this inappropriate for areas used by children.

SIMILAR AND RELATED SPECIES
Eight species of *Sideroxylon* occur in Florida, at least four of which are used in Florida landscaping.

Solidago spp.

sah-li-DAY-go

Goldenrods

Family: Asteraceae or Compositae
Wildflowers
Height: 2 to 6 feet, depending on species
Spread: Individually narrow, to about 2 feet; some species spreading into large colonies

LANDSCAPE USE

May be used in mixed or single-species wildflower beds, along roadsides or sunny woodland edges, or in sunny meadows.

FORM

At least four species of goldenrod are used in Florida landscaping, all of which are herbaceous, perennial, mostly erect, fall-flowering wildflowers. Those most likely to be found in native plant nurseries include *S. fistulosa, S. odora, S. sempervirens,* and *S. stricta.*

NATIVE RANGE

Sandhills, roadsides, disturbed areas, dunes, tidal marshes, flatwoods, and bogs, depending upon species. Goldenrods are native throughout the eastern United States and Florida.

CHARACTERISTICS

Flowers: Yellow; typically borne in showy, spikelike racemes at the tip, and sometimes along only one side of the stem. Summer and fall.

Leaves: Alternate, linear to lance shaped, toothed or entire, somewhat fleshy in some species.

Fruit: Tiny, inconspicuous achenes.

CULTURE

Soil: Sandy, acid to mildly alkaline.

Exposure: Full sun to part shade.

Water: Moist to dry.

Hardiness Zones: 6 to 10.

Life Span: Perennial.

BEST FEATURES

Bright yellow flowers. Profuse flower production.

COMPANION PLANTS

Wild petunias (*Ruellia* spp.), yellow canna (*Canna flaccida*), sea oxeyes (*Borrichia* spp.), saltgrass (*Distichlis spicata*), marsh and seaside elders (*Iva frutescens* and *I. imbricata*), sea purslane (*Sesuvium portulacastrum*), jointgrasses and knot-grasses (*Paspalum* spp.), salt bush (*Baccharis halimifolia*), royal fern (*Osmunda regalis*), blazing stars (*Liatris* spp.), black-eyed Susan (*Rudbeckia hirta*).

ALLERGENIC AND TOXIC PROPERTIES

Goldenrod is often blamed for hay fever and other fall allergies, but its role as an allergen is likely overstated.

SIMILAR AND RELATED SPECIES

Nineteen native species of goldenrod occur in Florida, all of which are summer and fall-flowering species that produce conspicuous clusters of bright yellow flowers.

Sophora tomentosa

so-FO-ruh to-men-TO-suh

Necklace Pod

Family: Fabaceae or Leguminosae
Large shrub
Height: 4 to 15 feet
Spread: 4 to 8 feet

J.C. Putnam H.

LANDSCAPE USE

A background or specimen shrub for beach plantings and other dry or salty sites. Also performs well in inland situations. Particularly suited for parking lots and other difficult sites. Very tolerant of the typically high lime content along roadways.

FORM

An erect, irregularly branched, often leggy and sprawling shrub with attractive, bright yellow flowers and interesting fruit.

NATIVE RANGE

Hammocks and coastal strands. Central and southern peninsular Florida, the West Indies, and South America.

CHARACTERISTICS

Flowers: Irregular, pealike, bright yellow, borne in showy 6- to 15-inch-long spikes.

Leaves: Alternate, about 12 inches long, compound and composed of up to twenty-one 2-inch-long, oval, pale green to sometimes grayish leaflets.

Fruit: A long-stalked bean, up to 6 inches long, with several conspicuous, beadlike bean compartments divided by severe constrictions. Seeds yellowish brown and round.

Bark: Yellowish brown; rough, with raised, whitish, corky lenticels.

CULTURE

Soil: Well-drained, neutral to slightly alkaline soils composed of coarse sands with little organic matter.

Exposure: Full sun. Only mildly tolerant of frost. Very tolerant of salt spray, drought, and wind.

Water: Drought tolerant.

Hardiness Zones: 10 to 11.

Life Span: Moderately long-lived.

BEST FEATURES

The bright yellow, showy flowers attract hummingbirds, warblers, bees, and butterflies. The flowers, interesting and distinctive pods, drought- and salt-tolerant habit, and overall hardiness make this an often-used ornamental in the southern peninsula.

COMPANION PLANTS

Saw palmetto (*Serenoa repens*), varnish leaf (*Dodonaea viscosa*), bay cedar (*Suriana maritima*), white indigoberry (*Randia aculeata*), silver palm (*Coccothrinax argentata*), cocoplum (*Chrysobalanus icaco*), muhly grass (*Muhlenbergia capillaris*), gopher apple (*Licania michauxii*), sea oats (*Uniola paniculata*), salt cordgrass (*Spartina patens*), coontie (*Zamia pumila*), salt jointgrass (*Paspalum distichum*), beach bean (*Canavalia rosea*).

DISADVANTAGES

Caterpillars are mildly problematic; otherwise insect free.

ALLERGENIC AND TOXIC PROPERTIES

The seeds contain the alkaloid cytisine and are dangerously emetic.

SIMILAR AND RELATED SPECIES

Few plants of the southern peninsula resemble necklace pod.

Sorghastrum secundum

sor-GAS-trum se-KUN-dum

Lopsided Indiangrass

Family: Poaceae or Gramineae
Ground cover, grass
Height: 3 to 6 feet
Spread: 2 to 4 feet, spreads slowly by underground stems

J. C. Putnam H.

LANDSCAPE USE

Serves as an accent plant in wildflower beds or as a ground cover in meadows or under pines. Excellent for naturalistic landscapes. Especially well suited for road and powerline rights-of-way and highway medians.

FORM

A tall, wispy grass with attractive, drooping, one-sided inflorescences emanating from clumps of relatively short, flat, narrow leaves.

NATIVE RANGE

Flatwoods, sandhills, and pine barrens. South Carolina, south throughout Florida, and west to Texas.

CHARACTERISTICS

Flowers: Tiny; borne in distinctive, one-sided inflorescences of hairy, tan spikelets with conspicuously long awns and yellow anthers. Fall.
Leaves: Narrow, green, about 12 inches long, borne in loose basal clusters.
Fruit: A tiny grain borne within hairy, tan spikelets.

CULTURE

Soil: Acid, well-drained soils of pinelands and sandhills.
Exposure: Full sun.
Water: Prefers moist, well-drained conditions, but tolerates dry conditions.
Hardiness Zones: 7 to 10.
Life Span: Perennial.

BEST FEATURES

Most appreciated for its graceful habit, naturalistic appeal, and beautiful and delicate one-sided inflorescence, especially when used along medians and roadsides.

COMPANION PLANTS

Broomsedges and bluestems (*Andropogon* spp.), slash and longleaf pines (*Pinus elliottii* and *P. palustris*), cabbage palm (*Sabal palmetto*), tarflower (*Bejaria racemosa*), inkberry (*Ilex glabra*), lowbush blueberries (*Vaccinium* spp.), gopher apple (*Licania michauxii*), wiregrass (*Aristida stricta* var. *beyrichiana*).

SIMILAR AND RELATED SPECIES

Four species of *Sorghastrum* occur naturally in Florida. Yellow Indiangrass (*S. nutans*), an extremely attractive grass that is wide-spread across the southeastern United States and southward to central Florida, is excellent as a forage grass for livestock as well as for erosion control and ornamental use.

Spartina alterniflora

spar-TY-nuh awl-tir-ni-FLO-ruh

Smooth Cordgrass

Family: Poaceae or Gramineae
Large grass
Height: 2 to 6 feet
Spread: Forming large colonies by underground stems

LANDSCAPE USE

Often used to reduce erosion along low-energy, salty shores with regular tidal washing.

FORM

An erect, perennial grass of saltwater shores; spreading by underground stems.

NATIVE RANGE

Low-energy, saltwater shores, tidal marshes, and salt barrens. Along the Atlantic and Gulf coasts from Newfoundland, south nearly throughout Florida, and west to Texas.

CHARACTERISTICS

Flowers: Small; borne in conspicuous clusters of ½-inch-long spikelets.
Leaves: About 1 inch wide and 2 feet long; narrow, flat, tapering to a long-pointed tip.
Fruit: A tiny, inconspicuous grain.

CULTURE

Soil: Saline coastal soils.
Exposure: Full sun.
Water: Tolerant of daily dousings of salt water.
Hardiness Zones: 5 to 10.
Life Span: Perennial.

BEST FEATURES

Tolerance of saline soils and saltwater inundation. Fast growing. Spreading habit.

COMPANION PLANTS

Seashore paspalum (*Paspalum vaginatum*), sea oxeyes (*Borrichia* spp.), leather fern (*Acrostichum danaeifolium*), broomsedges and bluestems (*Andropogon* spp.), muhly grass (*Muhlenbergia capillaris*), wax myrtle (*Myrica cerifera*), seaside goldenrod (*Solidago sempervirens*), saltgrass (*Distichlis spicata*), marsh elder (*Iva frutescens*), saltmeadow cordgrass (*Spartina patens*).

SIMILAR AND RELATED SPECIES

Five species of *Spartina* are native to Florida, at least four of which are used in landscaping.

Spartina bakeri

spar-TY-nuh BAY-kih-ry

Sand Cordgrass

Family: Poaceae or Gramineae
Large bunchgrass
Height: 3 to 5 feet
Spread: 3 to 5 feet

J. C. Putnam H.

An excellent bunchgrass that can be used as a background plant, for accent in large, single-species grassy beds and borders, or in naturalistic settings. Particularly suited for large commercial landscapes, such as parks and golf courses, as well as for beautifying and softening parking lots, powerline and roadside rights-of-way, and highway medians. The related saltmeadow cordgrass (*S. patens*) is especially suited for embellishing retention ponds, drainage swales, and canal banks.

FORM

A robust bunchgrass forming large, leafy clumps and spreading by basal offshoots or short subterranean stems.

NATIVE RANGE

Wet prairies, wet pinelands, edges of lakes, and brackish and freshwater marshes. South Carolina, southeastern Georgia, throughout Florida, and west to Texas.

CHARACTERISTICS

Flowers: Borne in crowded, but mostly inconspicuous, 2½-inch-long spikes. Mostly spring.

Leaves: Flat to rolled inward, less than ¼ inch wide, pale green, and rough to the touch.

Fruit: A tiny achene, concealed within the tiny spikelets.

CULTURE

Soil: Moist, sandy soils with pH 5.5–6.5. Salt tolerant.

Exposure: Full sun.

Water: Performs best in moist, freshwater sites, but adapts to dry situations.

Hardiness Zones: 7 to 10.

Life Span: Perennial.

BEST FEATURES

General hardiness. Tolerance of salt and other difficult situations. Large, attractive form. An excellent replacement for the non-native pampas grass.

COMPANION PLANTS

Seashore paspalum (*Paspalum vaginatum*), sea oxeyes (*Borrichia* spp.), leather fern (*Acrostichum danaeifolium*), broomsedges and bluestems (*Andropogon* spp.), wiregrass (*Aristida stricta* var. *beyrichiana*), muhly grass (*Muhlenbergia capillaris*), lopsided Indiangrass (*Sorghastrum secundum*), wax myrtle (*Myrica cerifera*).

SIMILAR AND RELATED SPECIES

Five species of *Spartina* occur naturally in Florida, four of which are available in the native plant trade. Saltmeadow cordgrass (*S. patens*) is a popular and widely available, somewhat smaller, meadow-forming grass that occurs on dunes and at the edges of salt marshes throughout the state. Smooth cordgrass (*S. alterniflora*) is a robust, salt-loving species that is found on the tide-flooded edges of shallow saltwater bays. Gulf cordgrass (*S. spartinae*) is a less often used bunchgrass with a form similar to that of *S. bakeri*.

Spartina patens

spar-TY-nuh PAY-tenz

Saltmeadow Cordgrass

Family: Poaceae or Gramineae
Ground cover
Height: 2 to 3 feet
Spread: Forms colonies by seed and underground stems

LANDSCAPE USE

Most appropriate as a ground cover in saline situations. Useful for beautifying retention ponds, drainage swales, and canal banks. Essential for salt marsh restoration.

FORM

A tufted to running perennial grass, forming large colonies of erect plants typically less than 3 feet tall.

NATIVE RANGE

Brackish marshes and flats, edges of tidal pools, and low, moist dunes. Southern Canada, southward to southern Florida, and west to Texas.

CHARACTERISTICS

Flowers: Individually small; borne in mostly one-sided, 2- to 3-inch-long, short-stalked, ascending spikes. Spring to fall.

Leaves: Slender, mostly linear, somewhat flattish near the base, but in-rolled and rounded in cross-section toward the tip, to about 1½ feet long.

Fruit: A tiny, inconspicuous grain.

CULTURE

Soil: Sandy, salt-rich soils.

Exposure: Full sun. Salt tolerant.

Water: Occurs mostly in wet situations, but will tolerate some drying.

Hardiness Zones: 4 to 10.

Life Span: Perennial.

BEST FEATURES

Salt tolerance. Fast growth. Spreads easily.

COMPANION PLANTS

Seashore paspalum (*Paspalum vaginatum*), sea oxeyes (*Borrichia* spp.), salt bush (*Baccharis halimifolia*), scarlet hibiscus (*Hibiscus coccineus*), saltwort (*Batis maritima*), broomsedges and bluestems (*Andropogon* spp.), muhly grass (*Muhlenbergia capillaris*), wax myrtle (*Myrica cerifera*), seaside goldenrod (*Solidago sempervirens*), saltgrass (*Distichlis spicata*), marsh elder (*Iva frutescens*).

SIMILAR AND RELATED SPECIES

Five species of *Spartina* are native to Florida, at least four of which are used in landscaping.

Sporobolus virginicus

spo-RAH-bo-lus vir-JI-ni-kus

Seashore Dropseed

Family: Poaceae or Gramineae
Ground cover
Height: To about 1 foot
Spread: Forms colonies by underground stems

LANDSCAPE USE

Most appropriate as a ground cover in coastal landscapes, especially along the edges of salt marshes and dunes.

FORM

An erect, colony-forming perennial grass to about 1 foot tall. Produces extensive underground stems.

NATIVE RANGE

Salt marshes, dunes, and edges of saline flats. Virginia, southward to southern Florida, and west to Texas.

CHARACTERISTICS

Flowers: Individually tiny; borne in narrow, erect, 1- to 4-inch-long, congested spikes of numerous ascending, short-stalked spikelets. Year-round.

Leaves: Alternate, linear, to about 5 inches long, sheathing the stem, slightly ascending along opposite sides of the stem in the form of a feather, the uppermost leaves much shorter than those below.

Fruit: A tiny, inconspicuous grain.

CULTURE

Soil: Sandy, salt-rich soils.

Exposure: Full sun.

Water: Prefers moist sites, but tolerates drier, well-drained dunes.

Hardiness Zones: 8 to 10.

Life Span: Perennial.

BEST FEATURES

Salt tolerance. Fast growth. Colony-forming habit.

COMPANION PLANTS

Cordgrasses (*Spartina* spp.), seashore paspalum (*Paspalum vaginatum*), seaside oxeyes (*Borrichia* spp.), salt bush (*Baccharis halimifolia*), scarlet hibiscus (*Hibiscus coccineus*), saltwort (*Batis maritima*), broomsedges and bluestems (*Andropogon* spp.), muhly grass (*Muhlenbergia capillaris*), wax myrtle (*Myrica cerifera*), seaside goldenrod (*Solidago sempervirens*), saltgrass (*Distichlis spicata*), marsh elder (*Iva frutescens*).

SIMILAR AND RELATED SPECIES

At least ten species of *Sporobolus* occur in a variety of habitats in Florida, eight of which are native. Seashore dropseed is most similar vegetatively to saltgrass (*Distichlis spicata*), with which it often occurs. The two may be distinguished from one another by their flower spikes.

Stokesia laevis

sto-KEE-zee-uh LEE-vis (or STOK-see-uh)

Stokes' Aster

Family: Asteraceae or Compositae
Wildflower
Height: 1 to 2 feet
Spread: 1 to 2 feet

LANDSCAPE USE

An excellent addition to mixed-species wildflower and butterfly gardens.

FORM

A perennial, herbaceous wildflower with a rosette of basal leaves and conspicuous, showy heads of mostly lavender to bluish flowers.

NATIVE RANGE

Savannas, pitcher-plant bogs, flatwoods, and low pinelands. South Carolina, southward to northernmost Florida and the Florida panhandle, and west to Mississippi, but used in landscaping southward to at least central Florida.

CHARACTERISTICS

Flowers: Lavender to bluish or whitish, showy, borne in dense, 2- to 4-inch-wide heads of disk and ray flowers at the tip of the stem. Spring and summer. Removing spent heads will ensure a longer flowering period.

Leaves: Alternate, borne mostly in 1- to 2-foot-broad clusters at the base of the plant.

Fruit: A tiny achene.

CULTURE

Soil: Rich, acid soils best simulate natural conditions.

Exposure: Part shade to full sun.

Water: Moist sites are preferred.

Hardiness Zones: 8 to 9.

Life Span: Perennial.

BEST FEATURES

Showy flowers. Extended flowering period. Attractive to butterflies.

COMPANION PLANTS

Florida paintbrush and related species (*Carphephorus* spp.), tickseeds (*Coreopsis* spp.), narrowleaf and rayless sunflowers (*Helianthus angustifolius* and *H. radula*), St. John's–worts (*Hypericum* spp.), blazing stars (*Liatris* spp.), black-eyed Susan (*Rudbeckia hirta*).

DISADVANTAGES

Will colonize an area and may require thinning after 2–3 seasons.

CULTIVARS

Forms with varying flower color are reported.

SIMILAR AND RELATED SPECIES

Numerous lavender-flowered members of the aster family occur in Florida, but none have the appearance of Stokes' aster.

Styrax americanus

STY-raks uh-me-ri-KAY-nus

Snowbell

Family: Styracaceae
Shrub or small tree
Height: 6 to 10 feet
Spread: 6 to 10 feet

LANDSCAPE USE

Perhaps best used in shady, moist, naturalistic landscapes, but also appropriate as a flowering shrub or small, delicate tree in shady or sunny suburban yards.

FORM

A slender, sometimes multistemmed, mostly loosely branched shrub or very small tree with a rounded crown of ascending to spreading, slightly zigzag branches.

NATIVE RANGE

Swamps, wet pond margins, and wet woodlands, typically in standing water. Virginia and Tennessee, southward to central peninsular Florida, and west to Texas and Oklahoma.

CHARACTERISTICS

Flowers: With 5 white petals; bell shaped, but with petals often curved backward so as to completely expose the pistils and bright yellow anthers. Spring.

Leaves: Alternate, simple, dull green, elliptic to obovate, 1–3 inches long, margins sometimes minutely toothed.

Fruit: A dry, rounded to obovoid, grayish green capsule. Summer.

Bark: Brownish to grayish, becoming fissured with age.

CULTURE

Soil: Fertile, acid, hydric soils.

Exposure: Shade to part sun.

Water: Occurs naturally in very wet situations, including standing water, but will adapt to suburban landscapes if kept reasonably moist and partially shaded.

Hardiness Zones: 8 to 10.

Life Span: Little is known about the life span of this species, but it probably lives more than 50 years.

BEST FEATURES

Showy, recurved flowers. Profuse flowering. Tolerates standing water.

COMPANION PLANTS

Red maple (*Acer rubrum*), sweetbay (*Magnolia virginiana*), swamp bay (*Persea palustris*), swamp tupelo (*Nyssa sylvatica* var. *biflora*), buttonbush (*Cephalanthus occidentalis*), summersweet (*Clethra alnifolia*), fetterbush (*Lyonia lucida*), titi (*Cyrilla racemiflora*), blue-stem palmetto (*Sabal minor*), highbush blueberries (*Vaccinium* spp.), lizard's tail (*Saururus cernuus*), string lily (*Crinum americanum*), flowering dogwood (*Cornus florida*).

SIMILAR AND RELATED SPECIES

Bigleaf snowbell (*S. grandifolia*) occurs sparingly in the central part of the Florida panhandle but is not generally used in landscaping in Florida. Two-winged silverbell (*Halesia diptera*) is also closely related.

Suriana maritima

suh-ree-AY-nuh muh-RI-ti-muh (or suh-ree-AH-nuh)

Bay Cedar

Family: Surianaceae
Large shrub
Height: 3 to 16 feet
Spread: 3 to 12 feet

G C. Putnam H.

LANDSCAPE USE
Most useful as a hardy shrub in dry, sandy, open areas that are subject to bright sun, salt winds, and brief saltwater flooding.

FORM
An evergreen shrub or small tree with a dense, conical to rounded crown, sturdy trunk, and masses of slim, erect to ascending branchlets, and succulent green leaves. Typically shrublike in open sun, becoming more arborescent in shady, sheltered situations.

NATIVE RANGE
Coastal beaches and dunes. Coastal central Florida, south through the Florida peninsula, the West Indies, and South America.

CHARACTERISTICS
Flowers: Yellow, 5-petaled, and about ½ inch wide. Predominately fall to summer, but essentially year-round.

Leaves: Succulent and fleshy, 1–1½ inches long, grayish green, alternate, but clustered on short, upturned twigs along and near the tips of branchlets.

Fruit: Dry, hard, brown, rounded, inconspicuous. Year-round.

Bark: Brown, rough to the touch, and flaky.

CULTURE
Soil: Dry, sandy, exceptionally well-drained coastal soils.

Exposure: Full sun to part shade.

Water: Drought and salt tolerant. Supplemental irrigation not required.

Hardiness Zones: 10 to 11.

Life Span: Slow growing and moderately long-lived.

BEST FEATURES
Very hardy and tolerant of salt spray, temporary saltwater inundation, and drought. Works well for erosion control on beaches and dunes.

COMPANION PLANTS
White indigoberry (*Randia aculeata*), varnish leaf (*Dodonaea viscosa*), cocoplum (*Chrysobalanus icaco*), necklace pod (*Sophora tomentosa*), black torch (*Erithalis fruticosa*), muhly grass (*Muhlenbergia capillaris*), gopher apple (*Licania michauxii*), seagrape (*Coccoloba uvifera*), silver palm (*Coccothrinax argentata*), inkberry (*Scaevola plumieri*).

SIMILAR AND RELATED SPECIES
Bay cedar is somewhat similar to sea rosemary (*Argusia gnaphalodes*), a rare native of southernmost Florida that is not readily available in the native plant trade.

Swietenia mahagoni

swee-TE-nee-uh muh-HAH-guh-nee

Mahogany

Family: Meliaceae
Large tree
Height: 30 to 70 feet
Spread: 20 to 60 feet

J.C. Putnam H.

LANDSCAPE USE

One of south Florida's most popular street, median, and yard trees. Also used to beautify retention ponds, drainage swales, and canal banks.

FORM

Erect, low-branching tree with a rounded to elliptical crown, attractive compound, delicate leaves, and attractive bark.

NATIVE RANGE

Tropical and coastal hammocks. Southern Florida and the West Indies.

CHARACTERISTICS

Flowers: Small, greenish, inconspicuous, borne in slender clusters in the leaf axils.

Leaves: Dark green, compound, 6–8 inches long, with 4–8 opposite, slightly curving, 1- to 4-inch-long leaflets.

Fruit: A large, conspicuous, brownish, egg-shaped capsule, 3–5 inches long, splitting from the base to expose numerous dark brown, winged seeds.

Bark: Reddish brown; roughened by broad, thick scales.

CULTURE

Soil: Occurs naturally in thin hammock soils, but adapts to a variety of situations from coral rock to sand.

Exposure: Full sun.

Water: Supplemental irrigation not required.

Hardiness Zones: 10 to 11.

Life Span: Long-lived; more than 100 years.

BEST FEATURES

Hardy in difficult situations such as roadsides, medians, and parks. Interesting fruit. Attractive, pleasing shape.

COMPANION PLANTS

Gumbo limbo (*Bursera simaruba*), satinleaf (*Chrysophyllum oliviforme*), pigeon plum (*Coccoloba diversifolia*), willow bustic (*Sideroxylon salicifolium*), paradise tree (*Simaruba glauca*), marlberry (*Ardisia escallonioides*), spicewood (*Calyptranthes pallens*), stoppers (*Eugenia* spp.), blolly (*Guapira discolor*), myrsine (*Rapanea punctata*), white indigoberry (*Randia aculeata*), wild coffee (*Psychotria nervosa*), snowberry (*Chiococca alba*).

DISADVANTAGES

Susceptible to webworms, Cuban May beetle, scales, and tar spot. Somewhat brittle and may suffer wind damage.

SIMILAR AND RELATED SPECIES

Few south Florida trees are similar in appearance. No other member of this family is native to Florida.

Symphyotrichum carolinianum

sim-fy-AH-tri-kum ka-ro-li-nee-AY-num

Climbing Aster

Family: Asteraceae or Compositae
Viney shrub or "subshrub"
Height: To about 10 feet
Spread: To about 10 feet

LANDSCAPE USE

Excellent for wet areas along streams or ponds. Also works well in drier woodland settings and along raised patios or decks. Sprawling habit makes it best for informal gardens. Climbing aster should be pruned periodically to ensure profuse flowering and healthy growth.

FORM

A sprawling, sometimes vinelike, semiwoody shrub.

NATIVE RANGE

Swamp, stream, and spring edges. South Carolina, south to southern Florida, and west along the Gulf Coast.

CHARACTERISTICS

Flowers: A 2-inch-wide head with numerous lavender to bluish ray flowers and yellow disk flowers. Typically fall, but may bloom any time of year.

Leaves: Alternate, grayish green, oval in outline.

Fruit: A small, dry, hard achene.

Bark: Thin; brownish.

CULTURE

Soil: Prefers moist, organic soil, but will also perform well in normal garden soils.

Exposure: Full sun but tolerates part shade.

Water: Prefers moist conditions and moderate watering.

Hardiness Zones: 8 to 11.

Life Span: Moderate.

BEST FEATURES

Adaptable to sun or part shade. Attractive blue flowers. A superior addition to naturalistic landscapes. Though a wetland species in nature, adapts well to typical garden conditions. A very good choice for butterfly gardens. Prolific bloomer.

COMPANION PLANTS

String lily (*Crinum americanum*), yellow canna (*Canna flaccida*), blue flag (*Iris virginica*), swamp rose (*Rosa palustris*), buttonbush (*Cephalanthus occidentalis*), Coastal Plain willow (*Salix caroliniana*), cypresses (*Taxodium* spp.), dahoon (*Ilex cassine*), red maple (*Acer rubrum*).

DISADVANTAGES

Sprawling, clambering habit may create an untidy appearance and may require effort to control.

SIMILAR AND RELATED SPECIES

Elliott's aster (*S. elliottii*) occurs in similar habitats and is similar in appearance. Several other asters, including *S. adnatus, S. concolor,* and *S. dumosus,* have lavender to sometimes whitish ray flowers.

Taxodium distichum

tak-SO-dee-um DIS-ti-kum

Bald Cypress

Family: Cupressaceae
Large tree
Height: 50 to 80 feet
Spread: 20 to 30 feet

J. C. Putnam H.

LANDSCAPE USE

An excellent specimen tree for medium to large sites, or planted in groups along the edges of ponds and small streams. Especially useful for beautifying retention ponds, drainage swales, and canal banks. Also useful as a street tree, especially along wet roadsides. Sometimes used in parking lots. Essential for wetland restoration projects.

FORM

A tall, stately, slender, deciduous conifer with a swollen base, conical crown (when grown in the open), stout branches, and reddish brown bark. Pond cypress (*T. ascendens*) is closely related to bald cypress and similar in appearance, habit, form, and landscape value. They are two of only a few deciduous conifers.

NATIVE RANGE

Pond margins, stream banks, floodplains, and swamps. Southern Delaware and southern Illinois, south throughout Florida, and west to Texas and Oklahoma.

CHARACTERISTICS

Leaves: Short, green, linear, flattened, ½–1 inch long, sometimes pressed to the branchlet, more often spreading from the branchlet in the form of a feather.

Fruit: Spherical cones, changing from green to brown at maturity, about 1 inch in diameter. Summer and fall. Mature in about one year.

Bark: Reddish brown; shallowly and narrowly furrowed to somewhat smooth. Sometimes exfoliating in narrow strips.

CULTURE

Soil: Wet to saturated, acid soils, high in organic matter and with pH 4.5–6.0. Exceptionally tolerant of oxygen-poor soils.

Exposure: Full sun, but will tolerate part shade.

Water: Performs best in moist to wet conditions, but will adapt to drier sites with normal rainfall if irrigated until well established.

Hardiness Zones: 6 to 11.

Life Span: Very long-lived; some specimens may reach life spans of 1,000 years.

BEST FEATURES

Fast growth rate for the first 10 years. Long life. Excellent fall color, coppery to rusty orange in good years. Winter, leafless stature is very stately and attractive. Very hardy and virtually carefree once established.

COMPANION PLANTS

Ogeechee, water, and swamp tupelos (*Nyssa ogeche, N. aquatica,* and *N. sylvatica* var. *biflora*), red maple (*Acer rubrum*), sweetbay (*Magnolia virginiana*), loblolly bay (*Gordonia lasianthus*), Virginia willow (*Itea virginica*), swamp bay (*Persea palustris*), pond apple (*Annona glabra*), swamp dogwood (*Cornus foemina*), pop ash (*Fraxinus caroliniana*).

DISADVANTAGES

Sheds its deciduous twigs with leaves still attached, which can be messy and require cleanup when planted in parking lots or formal landscapes. Not well suited to alkaline soils.

CULTIVARS

Several cultivars have been selected, but these are generally not available in—nor are they appropriate for—Florida.

SIMILAR AND RELATED SPECIES

Atlantic white cedar (*Chamaecyparis thyoides*) is an evergreen conifer of northern and north-central peninsular Florida. It also occurs in swamps and along pond and stream margins. Red cedar (*Juniperus virginiana*) is also an evergreen conifer, but it typically occurs in drier sites.

Thalia geniculata

THA-lee-uh je-ni-kew-LAY-tuh (or TAH-lee-uh)

Alligator Flag

Family: Marantaceae
Herbaceous shrub
Height: 6 to 9 feet
Spread: 5 to 10 feet

LANDSCAPE USE

Most useful in continually wet marshes, to beautify artificial holding ponds, or for wetland restoration.

FORM

A tall, robust, shrublike, herbaceous perennial with large green leaves, thick, underground runners, and tall flowering stalks held well above the leaves.

NATIVE RANGE

Marshes, cypress sloughs, ditches, and wetland depressions, mostly where water stands much of the time. Florida and the West Indies.

CHARACTERISTICS

Flowers: Purplish to lavender, with 3 petals and 3 sepals, borne in pairs on drooping racemes at the tip of a long stalk. Summer and fall.

Leaves: Large, green to yellowish green, to about 3 feet long, borne from near the base of the plant on long leaf stalks.

Fruit: Small, bluish purple, rounded, thin-walled, bladderlike, one-seeded.

CULTURE

Soil: Rich, acid soils are preferred.
Exposure: Full sun to part shade.
Water: Performs best in wet situations, especially in standing water.
Hardiness Zones: 9 to 11.
Life Span: Perennial.

BEST FEATURES

Large size. Tolerant of continuous inundation.

COMPANION PLANTS

Coastal Plain willow (*Salix caroliniana*), buttonbush (*Cephalanthus occidentalis*), scarlet hibiscus (*Hibiscus coccineus*), sand cordgrass (*Spartina bakeri*), water hyssop (*Bacopa monnieri*), yellow canna (*Canna flaccida*), horsetails (*Equisetum* spp.), cinnamon and royal ferns (*Osmunda cinnamomea* and *O. regalis*), smartweeds (*Polygonum* spp.), pickerelweed (*Pontederia cordata*), arrowheads (*Sagittaria* spp.), string lily (*Crinum americanum*), blue flags (*Iris* spp.).

DISADVANTAGES

Dies back to the ground in winter.

SIMILAR AND RELATED SPECIES

The only member of its family likely to be encountered in Florida. Not easily confused with any of Florida's other wetland plants.

Thrinax morrisii

THRY-naks mo-RI-see-eye

Brittle Thatch Palm

Family: Arecaceae or Palmae
Low palm tree
Height: 6 to 15 feet
Spread: 5 to 10 feet

Best used as a specimen or accent tree in coastal sites in full sun.

FORM
A stout, slow-growing, evergreen fan palm with gray-green leaves.

NATIVE RANGE
Hammocks. Miami-Dade and Monroe Counties (especially the Florida Keys), and the West Indies.

CHARACTERISTICS
Flowers: White, fragrant, borne in stiff to arching panicles.
Leaves: Fan shaped, about 3 feet wide, green above whitish below, borne on a 3- to 4-foot-long stalk.
Fruit: Small, rounded, white, ¼-inch-diameter berries.
Bark: Brownish; trunk thickened at the base.

CULTURE
Soil: Well-drained, coastal soils.
Exposure: Full sun to part shade. Tolerates salt, wind, and light frost.
Water: Drought tolerant.
Hardiness Zones: 10 to 11.
Life Span: Slow growing and long-lived.

BEST FEATURES
Slow growth rate. Low height. Fragrant flowers. Tolerance of salt and wind.

COMPANION PLANTS
Florida thatch palm (*Thrinax radiata*), pigeon plum and seagrape (*Coccoloba diversifolia* and *C. uvifera*), buttonwood (*Conocarpus erectus*), strangler fig (*Ficus aurea*), myrtle-of-the-river and spicewood (*Calyptranthes zuzygium* and *C. pallens*), fiddlewood (*Citharexylum spinosum*), Geiger tree (*Cordia sebestena*), stoppers (*Eugenia* spp.), lignum vitae (*Guaiacum sanctum*), black ironwood (*Krugiodendron ferreum*), wild lime (*Zanthoxylum fagara*), marlberry (*Ardisia escallonioides*), coontie (*Zamia pumila*).

SIMILAR AND RELATED SPECIES
More than ten native palms are used in Florida landscaping. Florida thatch palm (*T. radiata*) is most similar, but it lacks the whitish lower surfaces of the leaves that distinguish brittle thatch palm.

Thrinax radiata

THRY-naks ray-dee-AY-tuh

Florida Thatch Palm

Family: Arecaceae or Palmae
Low palm tree
Height: 15 to 30 feet
Spread: 5 to 15 feet

LANDSCAPE USE

Used as an accent or specimen tree in the home landscape, but well suited for use along roadsides, in medians, as well as to beautify powerline rights-of-way and parking lots.

FORM

A small, moderately slow-growing fan palm with shiny green leaves.

NATIVE RANGE

Coastal thickets and limestone woodlands. Florida Keys and West Indies.

CHARACTERISTICS

Flowers: Small, white, fragrant, borne in conspicuous, showy clusters.

Leaves: Fan shaped, about 3 feet wide, divided into numerous segments that are green on both sides, though paler below.

Fruit: Small, rounded, white, ¼-inch-diameter berries.

Bark: Grayish brown.

CULTURE

Soil: Well-drained, coastal soils.

Exposure: Full sun to light shade.

Water: Dry situations are best. Tolerant of salt spray and wind. Intolerant of frost.

Hardiness Zone: 11.

Life Span: Slow to moderately slow growing and long-lived.

BEST FEATURES

Growth rate. Low to medium height. Fragrant flowers. Tolerance of salt and wind.

COMPANION PLANTS

Brittle thatch palm (*Thrinax morrisii*), pigeon plum and seagrape (*Coccoloba diversifolia* and *C. uvifera*), buttonwood (*Conocarpus erectus*), strangler fig (*Ficus aurea*), myrtle-of-the-river and spicewood (*Calyptranthes zuzygium* and *C. pallens*), fiddlewood (*Citharexylum spinosum*), Geiger tree (*Cordia sebestena*), stoppers (*Eugenia* spp.), lignum vitae (*Guaiacum sanctum*), black ironwood (*Krugiodendron ferreum*), wild lime (*Zanthoxylum fagara*), marlberry (*Ardisia escallonioides*), coontie (*Zamia pumila*).

SIMILAR AND RELATED SPECIES

More than ten native palms are used in Florida landscaping. Florida thatch palm is most similar to brittle thatch palm (*T. morrisii*), which can be distinguished by the whitish lower surfaces of its leaves.

Tripsacum dactyloides

TRIP-suh-kum dak-ti-LOY-deez

Eastern Gamagrass

Family: Poaceae or Gramineae
Large, shrublike grass
Height: 4 to 8 feet
Spread: 2 to 3 feet

G. C. Putnam H.

LANDSCAPE USE

An excellent choice for moist borders or damp areas where a large, shrublike aspect is desired. Very useful for slope stabilization as well as for concealing drainage swales, retention ponds, and canal banks. Often used agriculturally for the production of palatable, nutritious hay. An excellent substitute for the often used but non-native pampas grass (*Cortaderia selloana*).

FORM

A robust bunchgrass that spreads primarily by thick, knotty, underground stems.

NATIVE RANGE

Hammocks, swamps, wet ditches and disturbed sites, riverbanks. Wide-ranging across the eastern United States from New York and Massachusetts, west to Iowa, south to Texas, and throughout Florida.

CHARACTERISTICS

Flowers: Borne in two or three conspicuous, stout, brownish spikes at the tip of the culm. Spring to fall.
Leaves: Flat, dark green, about 1 inch wide, 2–3 feet long, and arching outwards from a 2- to 3-foot-diameter clump.
Fruit: A grain, concealed within the developing spikelets.

CULTURE

Soil: Moderately well-drained to poorly drained soils with pH 5.7–7.5.
Exposure: Full sun to part shade. Intolerant of heavy shade.
Water: Performs best in moist conditions and with at least minimum irrigation, though it will adapt to dry, though not droughty sites.
Hardiness Zones: 4 to 11.
Life Span: Perennial.

BEST FEATURES

Attractive, dark green leaves. Robust habit makes it useful as a shrub. Interesting flower and fruit spikes. Tolerant of a variety of soil conditions.

COMPANION PLANTS

Fetterbushes and staggerbushes (*Lyonia* spp.), wax myrtle (*Myrica cerifera*), sand cordgrass (*Spartina bakeri*), lopsided Indiangrass (*Sorghastrum secundum*), dahoon (*Ilex cassine*), cabbage palm (*Sabal palmetto*), slash pine (*Pinus elliottii*), blue beech (*Carpinus caroliniana*), pipestem (*Agarista populifolia*), Simpson's stopper (*Myrcianthes fragrans*), myrsine (*Rapanea punctata*), blue-stem palmetto (*Sabal minor*), cinnamon and royal ferns (*Osmunda cinnamomea* and *O. regalis*).

DISADVANTAGES

May turn brown and die back in very cold winters with extended periods of below-freezing temperatures. Annual trimming may be required. Spider mites may pose a problem.

CULTIVARS

None known for Florida, though at least one agricultural selection has been produced from midwestern populations.

SIMILAR AND RELATED SPECIES

Florida gamagrass (*T. floridanum*) is shorter and finer in aspect than eastern gamagrass and is not as wide-ranging. It occurs naturally in the United States only in the rocky pinelands of southernmost Florida. Its leaves are narrow and rolled under rather than flat, and it seldom exceeds about 3 feet in height. Sand cordgrass (*Spartina bakeri*) is similar in form to eastern gamagrass.

Ulmus alata

UL-mus uh-LAY-tuh

Winged Elm

Family: Ulmaceae
Medium-sized tree
Height: 40 to 70 feet
Spread: 30 to 60 feet

J.C.Putnam H.

LANDSCAPE USE

A neat, clean, erect tree useful along streets and roadsides, or for shade in yards, parking lots, and along sidewalks.

FORM

A tough, drought-resistant, medium-sized tree with a rounded crown and spreading branches that are often lined with corky wings.

NATIVE RANGE

Moist to wet hammocks, rich woods, and bluffs. Virginia southward to about central Florida, and west to Texas.

CHARACTERISTICS

Flowers: Tiny, inconspicuous, reddish. Early spring.
Leaves: Alternate, lance shaped, small, 1–2½ inches long, doubly toothed along the margins, typically asymmetrical near the base.
Fruit: Rounded, winged, hairy, flat and waferlike.
Bark: Grayish, shallowly furrowed, very attractive.

CULTURE

Soil: Prefers moist, fertile soils with pH 5.0–7.0, but adapts to or tolerates many soil conditions.
Exposure: Full sun to part shade.
Water: Thrives best and grows larger in moist situations, but very adaptable to drier situations including poor, sandy sites.
Hardiness Zones: 6 to 9.
Life Span: Relatively fast growing but short-lived. Less than 100 years.

BEST FEATURES

Fast growth rate. Clean appearance. Leaves sometimes turn a beautiful, soft yellow in fall. Tolerant of a variety of conditions. Excellent tree for a small space. Relatively free of pests and insects.

COMPANION PLANTS

Basswood (*Tilia americana*), upland oaks (*Quercus* spp.), pignut hickory (*Carya glabra*), American holly (*Ilex opaca*), witch hazel (*Hamamelis virginiana*), needle palm (*Rhapidophyllum hystrix*), blue-stem palmetto (*Sabal minor*), coral honeysuckle (*Lonicera sempervirens*), sweetgum (*Liquidambar styraciflua*), magnolia and sweetbay (*Magnolia grandiflora* and *M. virginiana*), red maple (*Acer rubrum*), eastern gamagrass (*Tripsacum dactyloides*), climbing aster (*Symphyotrichum carolinianum*).

DISADVANTAGES

Shallow root system may prevent understory plantings.

ALLERGENIC AND TOXIC PROPERTIES

Oils in plants of this genus may rarely cause dermatitis, including rash and blisters. The pollen is allergenic and causes hay fever in some people.

SIMILAR AND RELATED SPECIES

Several members of the elm family occur in Florida, many of which are used in landscaping.

Most closely related are the American elm (*U. americana*) and cedar elm (*U. crassifolia*). However, the family previously also included the closely related sugarberries and hackberries (*Celtis laevigata, C. iguanaea, C. pallida,* and *C. tenuifolia*), the planertree (*Planera aquatica*), and the tremas or nettletrees (*Trema lamarkianum, T. micranthum*).

Ulmus americana

UL-mus uh-me-ri-KAY-nuh

American Elm

Family: Ulmaceae
Large tree
Height: 60 to 80 feet
Spread: 20 to 40 feet

LANDSCAPE USE

An excellent specimen or shade tree for parks, college and school campuses, and large suburban landscapes. Also used in street and highway beautification. Underused as a landscape tree.

FORM

A tall, stately, graceful, deciduous tree with thin, ascending to arching branches that form low on the tree and produce an attractive vase-shaped crown.

NATIVE RANGE

Floodplains and other mixed hardwood forests. Native to much of eastern North America from Canada southward to central peninsular Florida, and west to Texas.

CHARACTERISTICS

Flowers: Small, mostly inconspicuous, greenish red. February to March.

Leaves: Alternate, simple, shiny green above, mostly ovate, 3–6 inches long, 1–3 inches wide, conspicuously asymmetrical on either side of the midrib, especially at the base, margins toothed.

Fruit: A flattened, ½-inch-long samara, greenish with a reddish margin, somewhat inconspicuous. Late spring and early summer.

Bark: Dark gray; scaly, deeply fissured with broad ridges.

CULTURE

Soil: Prefers moist, fertile soils, but tolerates a wide array of soil conditions.

Exposure: Full sun to part shade.

Water: Prefers moist conditions, but may be planted in dry to seasonally wet areas.

Hardiness Zones: 3 to 10.

Life Span: Somewhat fast growing; matures at about 150 years.

BEST FEATURES

Large size. Moderately fast to fast growth rate. Ornamental shape. Excellent for shade.

COMPANION PLANTS

Box elder and red maple (*Acer negundo* and *A. rubrum*), water and pignut hickories (*Carya aquatica* and *C. glabra*), sweetgum (*Liquidambar styraciflua*), sweetbay (*Magnolia virginiana*), loblolly pine (*Pinus taeda*), laurel oak (*Quercus laurifolia*), winged elm (*Ulmus alata*), blue beech (*Carpinus caroliniana*), swamp dogwood (*Cornus foemina*), Walter's viburnum (*Viburnum obovatum*), snowbell (*Styrax americanus*), needle palm (*Rhapidophyllum hystrix*).

DISADVANTAGES

In some parts of the United States, mostly north of Florida, the elms are subject to a variety of pests, some of which are devastating. Florida's plants do not seem to be as vulnerable to these problems.

CULTIVARS

Numerous cultivars and selections have been made to mitigate the damaging effects of Dutch elm and other diseases. These selections are generally not needed in Florida if landscapers restrict their plantings to Florida stock. Plants grown from Florida stock are offered in the trade as *U. americana* 'Florida population.'

ALLERGENIC AND TOXIC PROPERTIES

Airborne pollen may produce allergic reactions.

SIMILAR AND RELATED SPECIES

Florida elm (*U. americana* 'Florida population') is sometimes considered a variety (*U. americana* var. *floridana*) of American elm. Three other elms are native to Florida.

Ulmus crassifolia

UL-mus kra-si-FO-lee-uh

Cedar Elm

Family: Ulmaceae
Large tree
Height: 40 to 80 feet
Spread: 20 to 40 feet

LANDSCAPE USE
Appropriate for most of the same uses as described for American elm, but somewhat smaller in size.

FORM
An erect, deciduous, stately elm with a rounded canopy, somewhat drooping lower branches, scaly, reddish brown bark, and small, doubly toothed, shiny green leaves.

NATIVE RANGE
Across much of the southeastern United States, from the Carolinas southward to northern peninsular Florida and west to Texas. Though confined in Florida mostly to the drainage of the Suwannee River, this tree can be more widely used in the state.

CHARACTERISTICS
Flowers: Tiny, inconspicuous, borne in small clusters in the fall.

Leaves: Alternate, elliptic to ovate, mostly 1–2 inches long, doubly toothed along the margins, and asymmetrical on either side of the midrib at the base.

Fruit: A flattened, papery, winged, mostly circular, one-seeded samara.

Bark: Reddish brown; scaly, with furrows and ridges.

CULTURE
Soil: Prefers moist, alkaline soils, but adapts to most soil types, from wet to dry.

Exposure: Full sun to part shade.

Water: Occurs naturally in floodplain woodlands, but adaptable to well-drained situations.

Hardiness Zones: 7 to 9.

Life Span: Likely to live at least 100 years.

BEST FEATURES
Scaly bark. Erect habit. Shade. Adaptable to a variety of soil and moisture regimes.

COMPANION PLANTS
Pignut hickory (*Carya glabra*), sweetgum (*Liquidambar styraciflua*), basswood (*Tilia americana*), winged and American elms (*Ulmus alata* and *U. americana*), redbud (*Cercis canadensis*), red mulberry (*Morus rubra*), flowering dogwood (*Cornus florida*), American hophornbeam (*Ostrya virginiana*).

ALLERGENIC AND TOXIC PROPERTIES
Airborne pollen may produce allergic reactions.

SIMILAR AND RELATED SPECIES
Four species of elm are native to Florida. Cedar elm is most similar to winged elm (*U. alata*) due to its small leaves, scaly bark, and the corky outgrowths along its branches. However, cedar elm flowers in the fall, and its bark is more reddish brown than that of the winged elm.

Uniola paniculata

yew-NEE-o-luh puh-ni-kew-LAY-tuh (or yew-nee-O-luh)

Sea Oats

Family: Poaceae or Gramineae
Tall grass
Height: 3 to 6 feet
Spread: Spreading as allowed by underground stems

J.C. Putnam H.

LANDSCAPE USE

The most important plant for dune restoration projects. Excellent for dune stabilization and for lessening damage to dunes brought by tropical and winter storms and hurricanes.

FORM

A deep-rooted, spreading perennial grass with dark green leaves and large, showy panicles of tan flowering spikes.

NATIVE RANGE

Beaches and dunes. Coastal Virginia, south to and nearly throughout the Florida coast, and west along the Gulf coast to Texas.

CHARACTERISTICS

Flowers: Tiny, but borne in large, conspicuous, showy panicles of flattened, tan spikelets. Spring to fall.

Leaves: Narrow, pointed, pale green, and rolled inward along the margins.

Fruit: A tiny grain borne in conspicuous spikelets. Summer to fall.

CULTURE

Soil: Dry, well-drained, sandy, mostly neutral soils of beaches and dunes. Very tolerant of salt spray and saline conditions.

Exposure: Full sun.

Water: Irrigation not required.

Hardiness Zones: 6 to 10.

Life Span: Perennial.

BEST FEATURES

A required species for dune and beach restoration and stabilization. Very tolerant of wind, salt, and dry, sandy soil.

COMPANION PLANTS

Seashore dropseed (*Sporobolus virginicus*), salt cordgrass (*Spartina patens*), white indigoberry (*Randia aculeata*), necklace pod (*Sophora tomentosa*), Spanish bayonet (*Yucca aloifolia*), beach bean (*Canavalia rosea*), beach panic grass (*Panicum amarum*), beach morning glory and railroad vine (*Ipomoea imperati* and *I. pes-caprae*).

SIMILAR AND RELATED SPECIES

Few grasses have the appearance or share the habitat of sea oats. River oats (*Chasmanthium latifolium*) is somewhat similar, though smaller, and occurs in wet hammocks rather than on beaches.

Vaccinium arboreum

vak-SI-nee-um ar-BO-ree-um

Sparkleberry

Family: Ericaceae
Large shrub or small tree
Height: 6 to 25 feet
Spread: 4 to 15 feet

J.C. Putnam H.

LANDSCAPE USE

Favored as a profusely flowering specimen tree for sunny or semisunny areas. Also works well as a background shrub and in the mixed understory of naturalistic landscapes.

FORM

An erect, deciduous shrub or small tree with glossy green leaves, profuse spring flowers and summer fruit, a sometimes twisted trunk with reddish to mottled, scaly bark, an irregular, open crown of crooked branches, and beautiful red to purple fall leaves.

NATIVE RANGE

Acidic to calcareous woodlands and sandy clearings. Virginia, southward to central peninsular Florida, and west to Texas and Kansas.

CHARACTERISTICS

Flowers: Small, bell shaped, white, about $5/16$ inch long, borne in profusion in showy, elongated clusters. Spring.

Leaves: Alternate, elliptic, shiny above, 1–2 inches long, with the central vein forming a tiny extension at the tip of the blade. Turning reddish in the fall before falling.

Fruit: A rounded black, shiny drupe.

Bark: Reddish to rusty brown; exfoliating in thin strips to expose mottled new bark. Very attractive.

CULTURE

Soil: Prefers moist, acid, sandy soils, but adapts to a much wider range of soil types than do the other members of the genus.

Exposure: Full sun to filtered shade. Perhaps prefers shade under natural conditions, but flowers profusely in sunny locations.

Water: Prefers moist, well-drained conditions.

Hardiness Zones: 7 to 10.

Life Span: Slow growing and moderately long-lived.

BEST FEATURES

Profuse spring flowers. Attractive reddish to mottled bark and twisted trunk. Shiny black fruit is eaten by wildlife. Attractive fall color. Grows well under pines and other partly shady areas.

COMPANION PLANTS

Saw palmetto (*Serenoa repens*), coontie (*Zamia pumila*), red cedars (*Juniperus* spp.), beautyberry (*Callicarpa americana*), yaupon (*Ilex vomitoria*), persimmon (*Diospyros virginiana*), Simpson's stopper (*Myrcianthes fragrans*), wax myrtle (*Myrica cerifera*), myrsine (*Rapanea punctata*), lowbush and highbush blueberries (*Vaccinium* spp.), summer haw (*Crataegus flava*), sand pine (*Pinus clausa*), Chapman, sand live, bluejack, turkey, and myrtle oaks (*Quercus chapmanii, Q. geminata, Q. incana, Q. laevis,* and *Q. myrtifolia*).

SIMILAR AND RELATED SPECIES

Closely related and somewhat similar in size to a few of the other native Florida blueberries, most notably highbush blueberry (*V. corymbosum*) and deer berry (*V. stamineum*). Also closely related to the lowbush blueberries.

Vaccinium spp.

vak-SI-nee-um

Blueberries

Family: Ericaceae
Small to medium-sized shrubs
Height: 1 to 12 feet, depending upon species
Spread: 1 to 10 feet, depending upon species

J. C. Putnam H.

LANDSCAPE USE

Two forms of native blueberries occur in Florida. Lowbush blueberries (*V. darrowii, V. myrsinites*) are typically used as small shrubs in low hedges or borders, in containers on decks and patios, or in naturalistic settings. Highbush blueberries (*V. corymbosum, V. elliottii, V. stamineum*) serve well as background plants or specimen shrubs. The lowbush species are typically more nearly evergreen than are the highbush species.

FORM

Lowbush blueberries are typically low, densely vegetated shrubs with rounded crowns, small, shiny to dull leaves, huge numbers of small, urn-shaped, white flowers, and abundant shiny to glaucous, rounded fruit. Highbush blueberries are erect, multistemmed shrubs, approaching 12 feet in height with irregular, spreading crowns.

NATIVE RANGE

Flatwoods, sandhills, swamps, and hammocks. Coastal Plain, from about Virginia, south throughout Florida, and west to Texas and Arkansas.

CHARACTERISTICS

Flowers: White, typically urn shaped, elongated to mostly rounded (depending upon species), less than $^5/_{16}$ inch long. Spring.

Leaves: Alternate elliptic; those of lowbush blueberries to about 1¼ inches long, those of highbush blueberries to about 3½ inches long, those of deer berry (*V. stamineum*) whitish or grayish below.

Fruit: Blue to shiny black, rounded drupes.

Bark: Reddish brown to brown.

CULTURE

Soil: All species prefer moist, acid soils.

Exposure: Full sun to part shade.

Water: Moist, well-drained conditions ensure best performance.

Hardiness Zones: 5 to 10.

Life Span: Probably less than 50 years.

BEST FEATURES

As a group, the blueberries are attractive evergreen shrubs that produce large numbers of flowers and fruit, the latter of which are eaten by wildlife.

COMPANION PLANTS

Titi (*Cyrilla racemiflora*), garberia (*Garberia heterophylla*), saw palmetto (*Serenoa repens*), coontie (*Zamia pumila*), scrub oaks (*Quercus* spp.), scrub hickory (*Carya floridana*), sand pine (*Pinus clausa*), lopsided Indiangrass (*Sorghastrum secundum*), muhly grass (*Muhlenbergia capillaris*), tarflower (*Bejaria racemosa*), slash pine (*Pinus elliottii*), beautyberry (*Callicarpa americana*), sweetshrub (*Calycanthus floridus*), arrowwood (*Viburnum dentatum*).

CULTIVARS

Numerous blueberry hybrids and selections are reported. None are currently widely available in Florida.

SIMILAR AND RELATED SPECIES

The blueberries are closely related to the wild azaleas (*Rhododendron* spp.), sourwood (*Oxydendrum arboreum*), fetterbushes, staggerbushes, and dog-hobbles (*Lyonia* spp. and *Leucothoe* spp.), and mountain laurel (*Kalmia latifolia*).

Viburnum dentatum

vy-BIR-num den-TAY-tum

Arrowwood

Family: Caprifoliaceae
Shrub
Height: 6 to 15 feet
Spread: 6 to 15 feet

LANDSCAPE USE
Performs best in hedges, massed plantings, shrub borders, or as a large background shrub. May also be used as a specimen shrub.

FORM
A large, spreading, multistemmed, deciduous shrub producing an arching, broadly rounded crown.

NATIVE RANGE
Hammocks and swamps. Throughout the eastern United States, southward to central Florida.

CHARACTERISTICS
Flowers: Creamy white; borne in showy, mostly flat-topped, 5-inch-broad clusters. Spring.

Leaves: Opposite, ovate to nearly rounded in outline, coarsely toothed, with prominent veins; turning golden to reddish in fall.

Fruit: Bluish to blackish drupes, borne in conspicuous, showy clusters following flowering. Mostly summer, but may persist until late fall.

Bark: Gray to grayish brown.

CULTURE
Soil: Performs best in acid, sandy loams.

Exposure: Full sun to shade.

Water: Prefers moist to wet situations.

Hardiness Zones: 3 to 9.

Life Span: Moderately fast growing; perhaps not exceeding 50 years.

BEST FEATURES
Showy flowers and fruit. Coarsely textured opposite leaves. May be pruned to form a hedge. Fruit eaten by wildlife.

COMPANION PLANTS
Buttonbush (*Cephalanthus occidentalis*), needle palm (*Rhapidophyllum hystrix*), highbush blueberry (*Vaccinium corymbosum*), dahoon (*Ilex cassine*), swamp dogwood (*Cornus foemina*), string lily (*Crinum americanum*), native azaleas (*Rhododendron* spp.), beautyberry (*Callicarpa americana*), sweetshrub (*Calycanthus floridus*), Carolina jessamine (*Gelsemium sempervirens*), swamp chestnut oak (*Quercus michauxii*).

CULTIVARS
Numerous cultivars are known that accentuate various features, from summer and fall leaf color to size and fruiting habit. Weeping viburnum (*V. dentatum* 'weeping') is available in Florida.

SIMILAR AND RELATED SPECIES
Five species of *Viburnum* are native to Florida. Arrowwood and Walter's viburnum (*V. obovatum*) are most often used in landscaping.

Viburnum obovatum

vy-BIR-num ah-bo-VAY-tum

Walter's Viburnum

Family: Caprifoliaceae
Shrub or small tree
Height: 6 to 30 feet
Spread: 6 to 12 feet

J. C. Putnam H.

LANDSCAPE USE

Serves well as a large, unpruned, natural screen, but may be sheared to produce a more compact hedge. Very good as a specimen shrub or small shade tree, or when situated in a mixed shrub bed. Excellent for difficult areas such as parking lots, road and powerline rights-of-way, and highway medians.

FORM

A small, neat, semievergreen to deciduous, densely vegetated tree or large shrub with a broad, spreading, densely twiggy crown, small leaves, and a showy flowering period.

NATIVE RANGE

Coastal and calcareous hammocks, floodplain woodlands, and riverbanks. South Carolina, south throughout Florida, and west to Alabama.

CHARACTERISTICS

Flowers: Individually small, but borne in conspicuous, delicately showy, flat-topped clusters. Spring.
Leaves: Opposite, small, to about 1½ inches long, widest near the middle, sometimes with obscure, small, dull-pointed marginal teeth, especially near the apex of the leaf.
Fruit: A flattened, ellipsoid drupe, changing from red to black with maturity. Summer.
Bark: Dark reddish brown, roughened, divided into small plates.

CULTURE

Soil: Prefers moist to wet, sandy, acid, fertile soils.
Exposure: Shade to sun.
Water: Performs best in moist to wet locations.
Hardiness Zones: 6 to 9.
Life Span: Slow growing; probably exceeding 50 years.

BEST FEATURES

Walter's viburnum flowers profusely in early spring. Its dense foliage and summer fruit provide excellent nesting, cover, and food sources for a variety of birds and wildlife. An excellent screening plant for difficult areas, or when planted along the edges of naturalistic landscapes.

COMPANION PLANTS

Red buckeye (*Aesculus pavia*), pipestem (*Agarista populifolia*), strawberry bush (*Euonymus americanus*), Simpson's stopper (*Myrcianthes fragrans*), buttonbush (*Cephalanthus occidentalis*), eastern gamagrass (*Tripsacum dactyloides*), dahoon (*Ilex cassine*), winged elm (*Ulmus alata*), maples (*Acer* spp.), sugarberry (*Celtis laevigata*), Atlantic white cedar (*Chamaecyparis thyoides*), swamp dogwood (*Cornus foemina*), highbush blueberry (*Vaccinium corymbosum*).

CULTIVARS

V. obovatum 'Mrs. Schiller's Delight,' a dwarf selection, is available and sometimes used in Florida.

SIMILAR AND RELATED SPECIES

Five species of *Viburnum* are native to Florida, three of which are used in landscaping. Arrowwood (*V. dentatum*) is a shrub with opposite, relatively large, coarsely toothed leaves, showy clusters of white flowers, and large clusters of purplish fruit. Possum haw (*V. nudum*) is a small wetland tree that also produces showy flowers and fruits.

Woodwardia spp.

wud-WAR-dee-uh

Chain Ferns

Family: Blechnaceae
Ground cover
Height: 1 to 3 feet
Spread: Forming colonies by underground runners

LANDSCAPE USE

Two species of *Woodwardia* occur in Florida. Both make excellent additions to moist fern beds but may also be used in single-species fern beds or along shady, wet edges of swamps, ponds, and artificial seeps.

FORM

Florida's two chain ferns include netted chain fern (*W. areolata*) and Virginia chain fern (*W. virginica*). Both have erect, pinnately divided fronds and underground stems, and die back only in the coldest winters.

NATIVE RANGE

Swamps, wet flatwoods, and wet hammocks. Confined mostly to the southeastern United States from about Tennessee and the Carolinas southward. Virginia chain fern occurs nearly throughout Florida. Netted chain fern occurs at least as far south as northern Miami-Dade and Monroe Counties.

CHARACTERISTICS

Leaves: Erect, pinnately divided (the leaflets of Virginia chain fern again divided). Lower surfaces of fertile fronds with conspicuous clusters of spore cases.

CULTURE

Soil: Prefers rich, acid soils.
Exposure: Part sun to shade.
Water: Prefers continuous very moist to wet conditions. Tolerates standing water.
Hardiness Zones: 8 to 10.
Life Span: Perennial from underground stems.

BEST FEATURES

Colony-forming habit.

COMPANION PLANTS

Swamp dogwood (*Cornus foemina*), shield ferns (*Thelypteris* spp.), cinnamon and royal ferns (*Osmunda cinnamomea* and *O. regalis*), climbing aster (*Symphyotrichum carolinianum*), river birch (*Betula nigra*), red maple (*Acer rubrum*), blue-stem palmetto (*Sabal minor*), sweetbay (*Magnolia virginiana*), Coastal Plain willow (*Salix caroliniana*), pipestem (*Agarista populifolia*), lizard's tail (*Saururus cernuus*).

SIMILAR AND RELATED SPECIES

Sensitive fern (*Onoclea sensibilis*) is very similar to netted chain fern, but its lowermost pinnae are opposite, whereas those of netted chain fern are alternate. Virginia chain fern and cinnamon fern (*Osmunda cinnamomea*) are also similar, but the latter forms clumps while the former does not.

Yucca aloifolia

YU-kuh uh-lo-i-FO-lee-uh

Spanish Bayonet

Family: Agavaceae
Shrub
Height: 5 to 10 feet
Spread: 3 to 6 feet

LANDSCAPE USE

Well received as an accent plant, either individually or in clumps. The sharp tips of its leaves make it a good choice for discouraging foot traffic, and its tall form makes it useful in corners where a strongly vertical accent is needed.

FORM

A stiff, erect, unbranched shrub with sharply tipped, dark green leaves and large, conspicuous, showy clusters of bright white flowers.

NATIVE RANGE

Originally restricted to the coastal strand, edges of brackish marshes, and dunes, but now more widespread due to heavy horticultural use during the mid-1900s. Virginia, south to Florida, and west to Texas; also West Indies and Mexico.

CHARACTERISTICS

Flowers: Bright white, sometimes purplish tinged, to about 4 inches wide, borne in large, showy, multiflowered, 1- to 3-foot-long panicles at the tip of the stem. Spring to fall.
Leaves: Dark green, narrow, 1–2½ feet long, stiff, ascending, sharply pointed at the tip.
Fruit: A conspicuous, greenish, 1½-inch-wide pod.

CULTURE

Soil: Found naturally in well-drained, sandy soils, but adaptable to a variety of soil situations.
Exposure: Full sun to part shade.
Water: Prefers dry conditions.
Hardiness Zones: 8 to 10.
Life Span: At least 50 years.

BEST FEATURES

Stiff, dark green leaves. Showy clusters of large, white flowers. Erect habit.

COMPANION PLANTS

Marsh and seaside elders (*Iva frutescens* and *I. imbricata*), sea oxeye (*Borrichia frutescens*), saltgrass (*Distichlis spicata*), muhly grass (*Muhlenbergia capillaris*), railroad vine (*Ipomoea pes-caprae*), lovegrasses (*Eragrostis* spp.), cordgrasses (*Spartina* spp.), beach panic grass (*Panicum amarum*), seashore paspalum (*Paspalum vaginatum*), blanket flower (*Gaillardia pulchella*), seaside goldenrod (*Solidago sempervirens*).

DISADVANTAGES

This species has very sharp spikes that make it unsuitable for landscapes frequented by children.

CULTIVARS

At least two cultivars are reported but are not generally available in Florida.

SIMILAR AND RELATED SPECIES

Closely related to Adam's needle (*Y. filamentosa*), which has leaves borne in clumps at ground level rather than along an aerial stem. Some authorities doubt that Spanish bayonet is native to Florida.

Yucca filamentosa

YU-kuh fi-luh-men-TO-suh

Adam's Needle, Beargrass

Family: Agavaceae
Ground cover or small shrub
Height: 3 to 12 feet
Spread: 3 to 4 feet

J.C. Putnam H.

LANDSCAPE USE
May be used to edge driveways and walkways or along the edges of naturalistic landscapes. May also be grown in large containers on decks and patios.

FORM
A low, trunkless, evergreen plant with a large, basal clump of gray-green, arching, pointed, grasslike leaves that give rise in spring to a tall, erect stalk topped by a large and showy panicle of white to purplish tinged flowers.

NATIVE RANGE
Sandhills, dry bluffs, and thinly vegetated, xeric woodlands. Virginia, southward to central peninsular Florida, and west to Alabama.

CHARACTERISTICS
Flowers: Creamy white, sometimes tinged with purple at the base, showy, and borne in large panicles atop tall, erect stems that may reach 12 feet in height but normally do not exceed about 7 feet.
Leaves: Narrow, lance shaped, 2–4 feet long, grayish green, sharply pointed at the tip, with threadlike filaments along the margins.
Fruit: Fleshy, conspicuous capsules that dry out and turn black at maturity.

CULTURE
Soil: Well-drained sandy soils with pH 5.0–6.0. Highly adaptable and salt tolerant.
Exposure: Full sun or dappled shade of pinelands.
Water: Thrives best in well-drained, sandy situations. Supplemental irrigation not required.
Hardiness Zones: 4 to 9.
Life Span: Probably less than 50 years.

BEST FEATURES
Low-growing, clump-forming basal leaves are present year-round. The large, conspicuous, flowering panicles are showy.

COMPANION PLANTS
Wild rosemary (*Conradina canescens*), silver bluestem (*Andropogon ternarius*), wiregrass (*Aristida stricta* var. *beyrichiana*), lopsided Indiangrass (*Sorghastrum secundum*), summer haw (*Crataegus flava*), coontie (*Zamia pumila*), yaupon (*Ilex vomitoria*), lowbush blueberries (*Vaccinium darrowii* and *V. myrsinites*), scrub oaks (*Quercus* spp.), wild olive (*Osmanthus americanus*).

SIMILAR AND RELATED SPECIES
Spanish bayonet (*Y. aloifolia*) is an upright plant to about 10 feet tall, with dark green, very sharply pointed leaves all along its trunk. It also produces large, showy panicles of white flowers, but these are on short stems that are partially covered by the uppermost stem leaves.

Zamia pumila

ZAY-mee-uh PEW-mi-luh

Coontie

Family: Zamiaceae
Ground cover or small shrub
Height: 2 to 3 feet
Spread: 2 to 4 feet

LANDSCAPE USE

The compact, low habit of this species makes it an excellent ground cover or foundation plant, especially when planted in a mass. It also serves well as a specimen shrub or as a border along shady driveways and walkways. Adapts well to difficult areas such as parking lots.

FORM

A dwarf, low, compact, fernlike or palmlike, evergreen perennial with a subterranean stem and cluster of ground level, dark green, divided leaves.

NATIVE RANGE

Oak hammocks, shell middens, pinelands, and rocklands. Northern peninsular Florida and southward.

CHARACTERISTICS

Leaves: Dark green, stiff, fernlike, divided like a feather with a central stalk and numerous opposite leaflets.

Fruit: Borne in conspicuous, distinctive, erect, cylindrical, rusty red, 2–7-inch-long cones arising from the center of the leaves.

Male and female cones borne on separate plants. Male cones often in clusters of two or more. Female cones borne in groups of one to five. The fleshy, bright orange, 1-inch-long seeds are exposed as the maturing female cone begins to split open.

CULTURE

Soil: Dry, thin, sandy, well-drained soils with pH 5.5–7.0, but adaptable to various types of well-drained soils from acid to alkaline. Salt tolerant.

Exposure: Full sun to part shade.

Water: Well-drained to dry sandy sites produce the best results.

Hardiness Zones: 8 to 11.

Life Span: Long-lived and very hardy; can recover from almost any type of damage.

BEST FEATURES

Very hardy and easy to care for. Cold and drought tolerant. Will grow well in any part of Florida, even outside its normal range. An exceptional replacement for the closely related, often-used, but non-native sago palm.

COMPANION PLANTS

Broomsedges and bluestems (*Andropogon* spp.), white indigoberry (*Randia aculeata*), saw palmetto (*Serenoa repens*), lopsided Indiangrass (*Sorghastrum secundum*), long-stalked stopper (*Psidium longipes*), gopher apple (*Licania michauxii*), wax myrtle (*Myrica cerifera*), lowbush blueberries (*Vaccinium darrowii* and *V. myrsinites*), Adam's needle (*Yucca filamentosa*), tarflower (*Bejaria racemosa*), silk bay (*Persea borbonia* var. *humilis*), scrub oaks (*Quercus* spp.), fetterbushes, staggerbushes, and dog-hobbles (*Lyonia* spp. and *Leucothoe* spp.), slash, loblolly, and longleaf pines (*Pinus elliottii, P. taeda,* and *P. palustris*), live oak (*Quercus virginiana*).

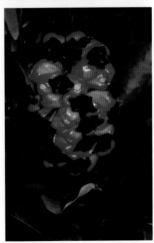

DISADVANTAGES

Red scale is a known pest.

ALLERGENIC AND TOXIC PROPERTIES

Roots have been used as food but have reportedly caused vomiting, abdominal pain, and death when improperly prepared.

SIMILAR AND RELATED SPECIES

Botanists have had a difficult time with the taxonomy of coontie. Various references may list as many as five species of *Zamia* as occurring in Florida. Current opinion holds that there is but a single species.

Zanthoxylum fagara

zan-THAHK-si-lum fuh-GA-ruh

Wild Lime

Family: Rutaceae
Large shrub or small tree
Height: 12 to 25 feet
Spread: 4 to 30 feet

J.C. Putnam H.

LANDSCAPE USE
A good background small tree or large shrub for sunny or partly shady areas and naturalistic landscapes. Thorny branches also make it an effective barrier plant to discourage traffic into delicate gardens or private areas.

FORM
An erect to spreading, typically multistemmed, small, evergreen tree or shrub with irregular, sometimes arching branches, coarse, compound leaves, and slender, gray, zigzag twigs that are often armed with sharp, hooked spines.

NATIVE RANGE
Hammocks. Central and southern peninsular Florida, south throughout the West Indies and tropical America.

CHARACTERISTICS
Flowers: Yellowish green, tiny, borne in clusters at the base of the leaves. Conspicuous when produced in large numbers. Year-round, but mostly spring.

Leaves: Shiny green, compound with a winged midrib, divided into several oval, 1-inch-long leaflets with scalloped margins. Often subtended by sharp, hooked spines.

Fruit: Small, round, rusty brown, splitting at maturity to expose 1 or 2 shiny, black seeds. Typically summer and fall.

Bark: Dark, thin, rough to the touch due to the presence of small scales.

CULTURE
Soil: Prefers thin, neutral to moderately alkaline soils, but adapts to a variety of conditions.

Exposure: Full sun to part shade. Sometimes flowering more profusely in full sun.

Water: Irrigation not required after plant is established.

Hardiness Zones: 9 to 11.

Life Span: Moderate.

BEST FEATURES
Profuse flowering. Tolerance of a variety of growing conditions. Spiny branches make this plant useful in discouraging foot traffic into protected locations. Food source of the caterpillar of the giant swallowtail butterfly.

COMPANION PLANTS
Stoppers (*Eugenia* spp.), red bay (*Persea borbonia*), lancewood (*Ocotea coriacea*), fiddlewood (*Citharexylum spinosum*), lignum vitae (*Guajacum sanctum*), velvetseeds (*Guettarda* spp.), marlberry (*Ardisia escallonioides*), spicewood (*Calyptranthes pallens*), cocoplum (*Chrysobalanus icaco*), Cherokee bean (*Erythrina herbacea*), Simpson's stopper (*Myrcianthes fragrans*), white indigoberry (*Randia aculeata*), coontie (*Zamia pumila*), snowberry (*Chiococca alba*).

DISADVANTAGES
The spiny branches may limit the locations in which this plant may be used.

SIMILAR AND RELATED SPECIES
Four other members of this genus occur in Florida, of which only one, Hercules'-club (*Z. clava-herculis*), is readily available in the native plant trade. Torchwood (*Amyris elemifera*) is closely related but not similar.

Zephyranthes atamasco

ze-fi-RAN-theez a-tuh-MAS-ko

Rain Lily

Family: Amaryllidaceae
Wildflower
Height: 8 to 15 inches
Spread: 1 to 2 feet

LANDSCAPE USE

Most appropriate for shady wildflower gardens in rich soils in conjunction with trilliums (*Trillium* spp.) and native phlox (*Phlox divaricata*).

FORM

An upright, trumpet-shaped wildflower with narrow, grasslike leaves arising from a bulb.

NATIVE RANGE

Mesic woods, rich forests, moist slopes, and shaded limestone outcrops. Virginia, southward to north-central Florida, and west to Mississippi.

CHARACTERISTICS

Flowers: Bright white, sometimes pinkish tinged, trumpet shaped, 3–4 inches long, with 6 bright yellow stamens and 6 lobes, borne at the tip of an elongated scape.
Leaves: Narrow, grasslike, 1–2 feet long, arising in clumps.
Fruit: A 3-parted capsule bearing numerous flat, shiny black seeds.

CULTURE

Soil: Acid to slightly alkaline.
Exposure: Shade to part shade.
Water: Prefers moist conditions. Will tolerate annual flooding.
Hardiness Zones: 7 to 9.
Life Span: Perennial.

BEST FEATURES

Showy, tubular, white flowers. Clumps of narrow leaves.

COMPANION PLANTS

Stokes' aster (*Stokesia laevis*), columbine (*Aquilegia canadensis*), purple coneflower (*Echinacea purpurea*), Indian pink (*Spigelia marilandica*), wild petunia (*Ruellia caroliniensis*).

ALLERGENIC AND TOXIC PROPERTIES

Ingestion in large quantities is reported to cause staggering and death to livestock.

SIMILAR AND RELATED SPECIES

Three species of *Zephyranthes* are native to Florida. Treat's rain lily (*Z. treatiae*) is often seen along moist roadsides in northern Florida. Care should be taken to use these native species rather than the numerous and widely available non-native species.

Zizaniopsis miliacea

zi-zay-nee-AHP-sis mi-lee-AY-see-uh

Giant Cutgrass

Family: Poaceae or Gramineae
Large wetland grass
Height: To about 10 feet
Spread: 5 to 6 feet, but forming colonies along marshy shores

LANDSCAPE USE

Well suited for the edges of marshes, alluvial rivers, retention ponds, and drainage swales.

FORM

A stout, upright, perennial grass with long leaves, underground stems, and a large, conspicuous, paniculate inflorescence.

NATIVE RANGE

Brackish and freshwater marshes, marshy shores, alluvial banks, and wet prairies. Virginia, south throughout Florida, and west to Mississippi.

CHARACTERISTICS

Flowers: Individually inconspicuous but borne in a very conspicuous 1- to 3-foot-long, 6-inch-wide panicle well above the leaves.
Leaves: Narrow, lance shaped to strap shaped, and 5–10 feet long.
Fruit: A tiny achene.

CULTURE

Soil: Hydric, acid soils.
Exposure: Full sun.
Water: Prefers standing water.
Hardiness Zones: 8 to 10.
Life Span: Perennial.

BEST FEATURES

Large size. Tolerance of inundation. Attractive panicles of tiny flowers.

COMPANION PLANTS

Wild rice (*Zizania aquatica*), arrowheads (*Sagittaria* spp.), climbing aster (*Symphyotrichum carolinianum*), smartweeds (*Polygonum* spp.), lizard's tail (*Saururus cernuus*), pickerelweed (*Pontederia cordata*), blue flags (*Iris* spp.), yellow canna (*Canna flaccida*), string lily (*Crinum americanum*), fragrant water lily (*Nymphaea odorata*).

SIMILAR AND RELATED SPECIES

Wild rice (*Zizania aquatica*) is similar and also occurs in standing-water wetlands. Its inflorescence is equally large but the lower panicle branches are spreading while the uppermost panicle branches are strongly ascending.

References

Bowman, Sheryl, Debbie Butts, Betsy Davis, John Marsh, Ann Nord, and Carl Strohmenger. 1997. *The Right Plants for Dry Places: Native Plant Landscaping in Central Florida.* St. Petersburg, Fla.: Great Outdoors Publishing.

Brown, Claud L., and L. Katherine Kirkman. 1990. *Trees of Georgia and Adjacent States.* Portland: Timber Press.

Burns, Russell M., and Barbara H. Honkala. 1990. *Silvics of North America.* Vol. 2, *Hardwoods.* Washington, D.C.: U.S. Department of Agriculture.

Bush, Charles S. 1979. *Flowers, Shrubs, and Trees for Florida Homes.* Bulletin no. 195, 3d ed. Tallahassee: Florida Department of Agriculture and Consumer Services.

Bush, Charles S., and Julia Morton. N.d. *Native Trees and Plants for Florida Landscaping.* Bulletin no. 193. Tallahassee: Florida Department of Agriculture and Consumer Services.

Cerulean, Susan, Celeste Botha, and Donna Legare. 1986. *Planting a Refuge for Wildlife.* Tallahassee: Florida Game and Fresh Water Fish Commission, Nongame Wildlife Program.

Clewell, Andre. 1985. *Guide to the Vascular Plants of the Florida Panhandle.* Gainesville: University Press of Florida.

Collingswood, G. H., and Warren D. Brush. 1974. *Knowing Your Trees.* Washington, D.C.: American Forestry Association.

Dirr, Michael A. 1998. *Manual of Woody Landscape Plants: Their Identification, Ornamental Characteristics, Culture, Propagation, and Uses.* Champaign, Ill.: Stipes Publishing.

Duncan, Wilbur H., and Marion B. Duncan. 1988. *Trees of the Southeastern United States.* Athens: University of Georgia Press.

Florida Department of Agriculture. 1980. *Urban Trees for Florida.* Tallahassee: Florida Department of Agriculture.

Godfrey, Robert K. 1988. *Trees, Shrubs, and Woody Vines of Northern Florida and Adjacent Georgia and Alabama.* Athens: University of Georgia Press.

Godfrey, Robert K., and Jean W. Wooten. 1979. *Aquatic and Wetland Plants of Southeastern United States: Monocotyledons.* Athens: University of Georgia Press.

———. 1981. *Aquatic and Wetland Plants of Southeastern United States: Dicotyledons.* Athens: University of Georgia Press.

Haehle, Robert G., and Joan Brookwell. 1999. *Native Florida Plants.* Houston, Tex.: Gulf Publishing.

Harrar, Ellwood S., and J. George Harrar. 1962. *Guide to Southern Trees.* New York: Dover Publications.

Hitchcock, A. S. 1935. *Manual of the Grasses of the United States.* Washington, D.C.: Government Printing Office.

Huegel, Craig N. 1991. *Butterfly Gardening with Florida's Native Plants.* Spring Hill: Florida Native Plant Society.

———. 1995. *Florida Plants for Wildlife: A Selection Guide to Native Trees and Shrubs.* Orlando: Florida Native Plant Society.

Jameson, Michael, and Richard Moyroud, eds. 1991. *Xeric Landscaping with Florida Native Plants.* San Antonio, Fla.: Association of Florida Native Nurseries.

Kurz, Herman, and Robert K. Godfrey. 1962. *Trees of Northern Florida.* Gainesville: University of Florida Press.

Martin, Alexander C., Herbert S. Zim, and Arnold L. Nelson. 1961. *American Wildlife & Plants: A Guide to Wildlife Food Habits.* New York: Dover Publications.

Minno, Marc C., and Maria Minno. 1999. *Florida Butterfly Gardening: A Complete Guide to Attracting, Identifying, and Enjoying Butterflies of the Lower South.* Gainesville: University Press of Florida.

Nelson, Gil. 1994. *The Trees of Florida: A Reference and Field Guide.* Sarasota: Pineapple Press.

———. 1996. *The Shrubs and Woody Vines of Florida: A Reference and Field Guide.* Sarasota: Pineapple Press.

———. 2000. *The Ferns of Florida: A Reference and Field Guide.* Sarasota: Pineapple Press.

Odenwald, Neil, and James Turner. 1987. *Identification, Selection, and Use of Southern Plants for Landscape Design.* Baton Rouge, La.: Claitor's Publishing.

Osorio, Rufino. 2001. *A Gardener's Guide to Florida's Native Plants.* Gainesville: University Press of Florida.

Perkins, Kent, and Willard W. Payne. 1978. *Guide to the Poisonous and Irritant Plants of Florida.* Circular 441. Gainesville: Cooperative Extension Service.

Radford, Albert E., Harry E. Ahles, and C. Ritchie Bell. 1968. *Manual of the Vascular Flora of the Carolinas.* Chapel Hill: University of North Carolina Press.

Rogers, David J., and Constance Rogers. 1991. *Woody Ornamentals for Deep South Gardens.* Pensacola: University of West Florida Press.

Scurlock, J. Paul. 1987. *Native Trees and Shrubs of the Florida Keys.* Bethel Park, Pa.: Laurel Press.

Stamps, Robert H., and Loretta N. Satterthwaite, eds. 1994. *Common Native Plants of Central Florida.* Orlando: Tarflower Chapter, Florida Native Plant Society.

Stearn, William T. 1996. *Stearn's Dictionary of Plant Names for Gardeners.* London: Cassell Publishers.

Sternberg, Guy, and Jim Wilson. 1995. *Landscaping with Native Trees.* Shelburne, Vt.: Chapters Publishing.

Taylor, Walter Kingsley. 1998. *Florida Wildflowers in Their Natural Communities.* Gainesville: University Press of Florida.

Trass, Pamela F. 1999. *Gardening for Florida's Butterflies.* St. Petersburg: Great Outdoors Publishing.

U.S. Department of Agriculture, Natural Resources Conservation Service. 2002. The PLANTS Database, Version 3.5 (http://plants.usda.gov). National Plant Data Center, Baton Rouge, La. 70874-4490 USA.

U.S. Department of Agriculture, Soil Conservation Service. 1984. *Plants for Coastal Dunes of the Gulf and South Atlantic Coasts and Puerto Rico.* Washington, D.C.: U.S. Department of Agriculture, Soil Conservation Service.

Vines, Robert A. 1977. *Trees of East Texas.* Austin: University of Texas Press.

Ward, Daniel B., and Robert T. Ing. 1997. *Big Trees: The Florida Register.* Spring Hill: Florida Native Plant Society.

Wasowski, Sally, with Andy Wasowski. 1994. *Gardening with Native Plants of the South.* Dallas: Taylor Publishing.

Watkins, John V., and Thomas J. Sheehan. 1975. *Florida Landscape Plants.* Rev. ed. Gainesville: University Press of Florida.

Wunderlin, Richard P. 1982. *Guide to the Vascular Plants of Central Florida.* Gainesville: University Press of Florida.

———. 1998. *Guide to the Vascular Plants of Florida.* Gainesville: University Press of Florida.

Yarlet, Lewis L. 1996. *Common Grasses of Florida and the Southeast.* Spring Hill: Florida Native Plant Society.

Photo Credits

Henry Aldrich: p. 9, bottom; p. 29, top; p. 41, center; p. 51, top; p. 59, top; p. 71, bottom; p. 75, center; p. 101, center two; p. 107, bottom center; p. 115, bottom; p. 119, top; p. 125, bottom; p. 145, center; p. 147, top; p. 155, bottom; p. 159, top center; p. 163; p. 169; p. 205, top; p. 219, top; p. 245, bottom center; p. 261, bottom; p. 271, top center; p. 291, center, bottom; p. 293, center; p. 303, bottom two; p. 305; p. 311, top; p. 321, bottom left; p. 357, bottom center.

Loran C. Anderson: p. 355, bottom right; p. 405, bottom.

Bill Boothe: p. 171, top right, bottom; p. 241, top; p. 378; p. 379, bottom; p. 381, center.

Kathy Burks: p. 331, top; p. 405, top.

Debbie Chayet: p. 35, top; p. 201, bottom; p. 225, center; p. 237, center.

Shirley Denton: p. 39, top; p. 59, bottom two; p. 61, bottom three; p. 65, center; p. 67, center; p. 83, top, bottom left and right; p. 109, top, bottom; p. 113, top two; p. 133, bottom; p. 139, center; p. 165, top; p. 167, center, bottom; p. 185, top; p. 187, top, bottom left and right; p. 227, top, center; p. 239, bottom; p. 247, bottom; p. 265, top; p. 267, top; p. 278; p. 287, top, bottom; p. 289, center two; p. 315, center, bottom; p. 323, top, bottom; p. 326; p. 327, bottom; p. 331, center, bottom left and right; p. 335, top; p. 339, center, bottom; p. 340; p. 341; p. 349, top, bottom; p. 351; p. 355, bottom left; p. 359, bottom three; p. 379, top.

Eleanor Dietrich: p. 17, center, bottom; p. 49; p. 51, center, bottom; p. 55; p. 69, top, bottom; p. 71, center; p. 75, top; p. 127, top; p. 131, top; p. 155, top, center; p. 159, top, bottom center; p. 161, top, center; p. 183; p. 209, top, center; p. 273, top, bottom.

Phil Flood: p. 353.

Chris Griffiths: p. 7; p. 15; p. 23, center, bottom; p. 25, center; p. 43, top, center; p. 45, bottom; p. 47, bottom left and right; p. 53, top; p. 57, top, bottom; p. 77, top two; p. 79; p. 81, center, bottom left; p. 89, center; p. 91, top, center; p. 97, top, bottom left; p. 99, bottom; p. 121; p. 127, center; p. 129, top; p. 133, top, center; p. 135; p. 141, top; p. 151, center; p. 163, top, center; p. 189, center; p. 191, top, center; p. 197, center; p. 217; p. 221, center; p. 224; p. 229, top, center, bottom right; p. 231; p. 235, bottom; p. 253, center, bottom; p. 255, top; p. 261, center; p. 277, top, bottom; p. 295, center; p. 297, center; p. 309; p. 313, center, bottom; p. 319, center, bottom; p. 321, bottom right; p. 323, center; p. 325, top; p. 333, top; p. 337, center, bottom; p. 339, top; p. 345, top two; p. 355, top; p. 361, top, bottom; p. 363, center; p. 370; p. 371; p. 372; p. 373; p. 395, bottom; p. 399; p. 401, top.

Roger Hammer: p. 37; p. 83, center; p. 185, center; p. 197, bottom; p. 335, center; p. 347, top, center.

Walter Judd: p. 381, top, bottom.

Mike Kenton: p. 11, bottom; p. 39, bottom two; p. 47, center; p. 111, bottom; p. 139, bottom; p. 147, bottom; p. 149, bottom; p. 153, top; p. 165, bottom; p. 175, bottom center; p. 185, bottom; p. 215, bottom; p. 245, bottom; p. 257, bottom; p. 263, bottom; p. 267, center; p. 271, bottom; p. 285, top, center; p. 287, top center; p. 369, bottom; p. 385, bottom.

Sharon LaPlante: p. 11, top; p. 17, top; p. 19, top, center; p. 21, bottom; p. 31, bottom; p. 35, center, bottom; p. 41, bottom; p. 63, bottom two; p. 67, top; p. 69, center; p. 71, top; p. 73, top; p. 85, bottom; p. 95, top, center; p. 99, top; p. 103, center; p. 111, center; p. 115, top; p. 125, top; p. 131, bottom; p. 143, bottom left and right; p. 157, center; p. 167, top; p. 175, bottom; p. 179, top; p. 187, center; p. 193, top; p. 197, top; p. 203, top; p. 205, center; p. 207, top; p. 213, top, center; p. 219, bottom; p. 223, bottom; p. 229, bottom left; p. 233, top; p. 243, center, bottom; p. 245, top; p. 256; p. 271, bottom center; p. 279; p. 283, top; p. 293, top; p. 299, top; p. 303, top two; p. 311, bottom; p. 313, top; p. 317, bottom; p. 347, bottom left and right; p. 357, top two, bottom; p. 365; p. 375, center, bottom; p. 385, bottom center; p. 389, top; p. 393, top, center; p. 403, top.

Claudia Larsen: p. 29, center, bottom; p. 75, bottom; p. 95, bottom; p. 107, top center, bottom; p. 115, center; p. 127, bottom; p. 141, bottom; p. 145, top, bottom; p. 147, center; p. 153, center, bottom; p. 161, bottom; p. 325, bottom right; p. 367, center; p. 377, top; p. 402; p. 403, center.

Heidi Moore: p. 151, top, bottom left; p. 157, top; p. 307, bottom; p. 325, center, bottom left; p. 333, center.

Gil Nelson: p. 9, top; p. 19, bottom; p. 21, top; p. 23, top; p. 27, bottom; p. 33, top, center; p. 39, second from top; p. 43, bottom; p. 47, top; p. 53, bottom; p. 61, top; p. 63, top; p. 65, top, bottom; p. 67, bottom; p. 73, center, bottom right and left; p. 81, top; p. 85, top, center; p. 89, top; p. 101, top, bottom; p. 103, bottom; p. 105; p. 109, center two; p. 113, bottom left and right; p. 119, center, bottom; p. 131, center two; p. 139, top; p. 149, top; p. 157, bottom; p. 163, bottom; p. 165, center two; p. 175, top two; p. 177, center; p. 179, bottom; p. 189, top, bottom; p. 201, top three; p. 203, center, bottom; p. 205, bottom; p. 211, bottom; p. 213, bottom; p. 215, top, center; p. 221, top, bottom; p. 223, top, center; p. 233, center; p. 238; p. 239, top, center; p. 241, center, bottom; p. 245, top center; p. 246; p. 247, top; p. 251; p. 255, center, bottom; p. 261, top; p. 263, top, center; p. 265, center, bottom; p. 267, bottom; p. 273, center; p. 275; p. 281; p. 283, center, bottom; p. 285, bottom; p. 291, top; p. 293, bottom; p. 295, top; p. 301, center; p. 317, center; p. 319, top; p. 322; p. 327, top, center; p. 333, bottom; p. 335, bottom; p. 337, top; p. 349, center; p. 352; p. 355, center; p. 359, top; p. 363, top, bottom; p. 367, top, bottom; p. 377, center, bottom; p. 383, top, center; p. 385, top two; p. 387; p. 389, center, bottom; p. 391, top three; p. 393, bottom; p. 394; p. 401, center, bottom.

Jeff Norcini: p. 225, top, bottom.

David Pais: p. 57, center; p. 171, top left; p. 219, center; p. 299, center, bottom; p. 317, top; p. 375, top; p. 397, bottom.

Susan Trammell: p. 13; p. 91, bottom; p. 123; p. 149, center; p. 177, top; p. 191, bottom; p. 211, top, center.

Betty Wargo: p. 27; p. 31, top, center; p. 33, bottom; p. 41, top; p. 45, top, center; p. 97, center, bottom right; p. 99, center; p. 103, top; p. 107, top; p. 111, top; p. 117; p. 137; p. 141, center; p. 143, top, center; p. 177, bottom; p. 179, center; p. 193, center, bottom; p. 199; p. 207, center, bottom; p. 235, top, center; p. 237, top, bottom; p. 243, top; p. 249; p. 253, top; p. 257, top, center; p. 258; p. 259; p. 269; p. 271, top; p. 287, bottom center; p. 289, top, bottom; p. 306; p. 307, top; p. 310; p. 315, top; p. 321, top, center; p. 328; p. 329; p. 342; p. 343; p. 369, top, center; p. 395, top, center; p. 397, top, center; p. 403, bottom.

T. Ann Williams: p. 25, top, bottom; p. 77, bottom two; p. 81, bottom right; p. 87; p. 89, bottom; p. 93; p. 129, center, bottom; p. 151, bottom right; p. 159, bottom; p. 181; p. 195; p. 209, bottom; p. 233, bottom; p. 277, center; p. 295, bottom; p. 297, top, bottom; p. 301, top, bottom; p. 345, bottom two; p. 361, center; p. 383, bottom left and right; p. 391, bottom.

Common Name Index

Gil Nelson is a writer, naturalist, and educator who lives and works in Tallahassee, Florida. He writes and speaks on botany, natural history, ecology, outdoor recreation, and environmental science topics, especially as they relate to Florida and the southeastern United States. His recent books include *Ferns of Florida, Shrubs and Woody Vines of Florida, Trees of Florida, Exploring Wild Northwest Florida,* and *Exploring Wild North Florida.* He is coauthor of the *National Audubon Society Field Guide to Florida,* the *National Audubon Field Guide to the Southeast* and *Florida Wetland Plants: An Identification Manual.*